*For my wife Jenny, my son Mark, daughter Zoe and grandson Zac*

# PLOTS AND GUNPOWDER

A PERSONAL BIOGRAPHY OF THRILLER WRITER GERALD VERNER

## CHRIS VERNER

LEVEL
BEST BOOKS

# PLOTS AND GUNPOWDER

# Praise for Plots and Gunpowder

"In life, as well as in detective fiction, one thing often leads to another. During the course of my work as consultant to the British Library's Crime Classics, I came across the stories of Gerald Verner while working on a prospective anthology. This brought me into contact with Philip Harbottle, the literary agent for the estate, and then with Chris Verner, son of Gerald. It's been a pleasure to re-introduce a number of Verner's short stories to twenty-first century crime fans and I was delighted to learn that Chris was working on a biography of his father.

"I hope that readers of today find this account of the ups and downs of one writer's life as intriguing and insightful as I do." – Martin Edwards

# FAMILY TREE

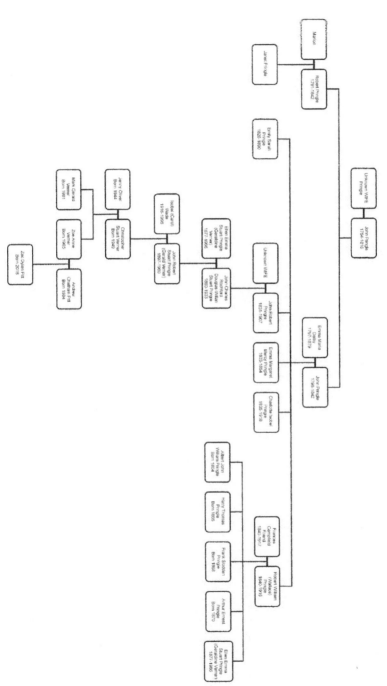

# Foreward

Not long ago, the customary fate of writers of popular fiction was to be forgotten a few years after their careers came to an end. Of course, there were exceptions – the Christies, Chandlers, and Hammetts, and so on, whose work lived on and continued to sell in significant quantities – but the vast majority of less renowned authors were less fortunate. Their work tended to fall out of print and out of favour. Often it was overlooked by all but a few aficionados of the genre, as the attention of publishers, critics, and readers turned to the never-ending flood of younger writers with something different to say.

Things have changed in recent years, and I believe it's very much a change for the better. Crime fans love contemporary fiction, and rightly so, but as older books have been rescued from oblivion, readers have made exciting discoveries, finding new favourites from the past. Many of the books written during the 'Golden Age of Murder' between the wars remain entertaining reads in their own right, and today they offer something extra. They are fascinating social documents. Without – usually – intending to do so, the authors of popular crime novels cast light on their world, giving later generations a perspective that is fascinating and often thought-provoking. As well as being entertained by their work, we are given glimpses of life in the past, and fresh reminders that it is a very, very different country.

One of the writers whose novels more or less vanished from sight for half a century was Gerald Verner. Highly prolific, he published in excess of a hundred thrillers, and his books were successful enough to be translated into more than thirty languages. Among other things, he adapted Agatha Christie's splendid and strangely under-estimated mystery *Towards Zero* for the stage. These are no mean achievements, yet not long ago his reputation languished in obscurity.

In life, as well as in detective fiction, one thing often leads to another. During the course of my work as consultant to the British Library's

Crime Classics, I came across the stories of Gerald Verner while working on a prospective anthology. This brought me into contact with Philip Harbottle, the literary agent for the estate, and then with Chris Verner, son of Gerald. It's been a pleasure to re-introduce a number of Verner's short stories to twenty-first century crime fans and I was delighted to learn that Chris was working on a biography of his father. The heritage of crime fiction is fascinating as well as a precious branch of social history, but much valuable information about the lives and work of writers of the past risks being lost. For this reason, I've been keen to establish and develop the British Crime Writing Archives, currently held at Gladstone's Library in Hawarden, north Wales. It's highly desirable for memories of writers to be placed on record while they remain available in the minds of the living. One of the best ways to achieve this, where possible, is by the publication of books or other material about those writers. When I read Chris's manuscript, I felt that the story of his father's life and work was interesting enough to deserve a wider audience.

The next question was whether an enthusiastic publisher could be found to support this worthwhile project. Thankfully, I was already aware that Level Best Books, a rising star in the publishing firmament, is run by a hard-working and capable team of people whose love of the traditional mystery is second to none. They have already established a significant presence in the niche field of mystery writers' biographies, publishing Sheila Keating's splendid memoir of her husband Harry.

Happily, Level Best shared my enthusiasm for Chris's manuscript, and as a result the book will not only see the light of day, but benefit from expert editorial input and marketing. My congratulations go to everyone concerned. And I hope that readers of today find this account of the ups and downs of one writer's life as intriguing and insightful as I do.

Martin Edwards
www.martinedwardsbooks.com

# Introduction

I was born on 13 December 1949 Christopher Stuart Verner, and I have a birth certificate to prove it! You won't find a birth certificate for my father, with the entry Gerald Verner, because that name was a pseudonym he created.

Who was he?

My father, known for over half his life as Gerald Verner, was born John Robert Stuart Pringle on 31 January 1897 at an address given as 46 Ramsden Road, Balham, in the Registration District of Wandsworth in the Sub-District of Streatham, London. A tendency to disavow his birth name has created nothing but confusion when trying to track down key events in his life and family history and has become as much a mystery as the detective fiction he wrote. He was baptized 18 March 1897 by the curate E. L. Field in the parish of S. Philips, Lambeth, the abode listed as Number 139, Kennington Road, London SE11. His birth date was shown on the baptism certificate as 31 January 1897.

When I first came across a *certified copy* dated 26 June 1947 of John Robert Stuart Pringles' original birth certificate, the first odd thing I noticed was that his parents were both named Pringle. He was the son of John Charles Rochfort Douglas-Willan Stuart Pringle and Ellen Emma Stuart Pringle.

I immediately became involved in a mystery...

Who were they?

Why did my father's parents both have the same surname?

I had never enjoyed any lengthy discussion with my father about his childhood; he always seemed keen to avoid talking about it. Suddenly I was curious, intrigued, and desperate for information that would enlighten me about his family history and early life. Never in my wildest dreams could I have imagined what I would discover.

To solve this mystery, and that of my father's origin, upbringing, and writing career, I began to delve into archives, and to my amazement the clock began to tick rapidly backwards, item after item forcing me back in time until it stopped at the year 1754, and like a huge jigsaw puzzle, the fascinating history of Gerald Verner and his origins as a member of the Pringle family began to emerge.

# Chapter One – Deep Roots

In 1754, John Pringle was born.

John Pringle, cabinet maker and upholsterer, lived and worked in London in an area known as Soho, at 126 Wardour Street. In those days Wardour Street was a location ideally situated for someone involved in the furniture trade. The street was to become famous for antique furniture and curiosities during the nineteenth century. He fathered two sons, Robert, born 1791, and John, born 1798. The two sons were to continue in their father's trade as cabinetmakers and upholsterers of the Regency period 1800-1830.

In *The Cabinet-Maker and Upholsterer's Drawing-Book* by Thomas Sheraton, Cabinet Maker, published in 1793, there is an entry under *list of subscribers*: Pringle, Wardour-Street, Cabinet-maker and upholsterer to the Duke of Clarence. Craftsmen could become extremely wealthy during that time as the demand for furniture as a status symbol increased with the rapidly expanding population of London. By the end of the 19th century, fashions in shopping had changed and the original buildings, small and old fashioned, were no longer suitable for their purpose. They were restricting trade. England was moving swiftly from the artisan/cottage industry firmly into the industrial revolution and the fringes of the Victorian age and the British Empire.

London was evolving towards the modern age at a pace as the population grew at a phenomenal rate. The population of London was one million at the time of the first census in 1801. Half a century later, it had more than doubled to over two million and by 1901 it had exploded to over six and a half million. This rapid increase in population created several pollution problems in relation to the health of those living in London. The air became ever more polluted with the smuts of a coal-fired world. Smoke and fog created a *smog* that became a London trademark. Arrangements for the disposal of the detritus of urban life became more difficult. The sewers and efforts of the *nightsoil* men grew increasingly inadequate to the task of removing the tons of human faeces produced each day. Even the bodies of the dead became a constant problem. The churchyards filled to overflowing, beyond the point where quicklime could speed the process of decay.

John Pringle made his will on 21 October 1815. He died in London aged 62 the following year in Westminster. On 15 August 1816, his sons Robert and John sold the lease of a town residence in the neighbourhood of Grosvenor Square. The house was described as a commodious family house, consisting of two parlours and a large library on the ground floor, a suite of three handsome drawing rooms on the second floor, five bed chambers and roomy attics, extensive servant's offices in the basement, detached kitchen and laundry, together with a large coach house and stabling.

Both brothers were married. Robert to Marion and John to Emma Maria Dalby. They continued the family business which traded as R & J Pringle, cabinet makers, furnishers and estate agents. John Pringle signed a lease for 126 Wardour Street, the same establishment their father had worked from. The lease was probably a renewal and ran for 61 years and 38 days from 26 February 1822. The premises were on the East side of Wardour Street - the second house Southward from Oxford Street, including the corner house. In *Kent's Original London Directory* of 1823, R & J Pringle are listed as upholsterers, located at 126 Wardour Street, their business address, where I assumed the two brothers lived and carried out their work.

In May 1822, with their estate agent hat on, R & J Pringle advertised on a long lease a fashionable town residence in Harley Street as a first-rate house containing four, five and six rooms on a floor, double coach houses and stabling, and every accommodation suitable for a family of distinction. At the same time, they advertised a ten roomed house in the vicinity of the Regents Park, described as elegantly furnished, adapted for a bachelor or small genteel family, to be SOLD, leasehold, subject to a very low rent, or let furnished on reasonable terms, for three years, delightfully situated on the north side of the New Road between Gloucester Place and Baker Street, the back commanding a view of the park. Applications were to 126 Wardour Street.

On 29 June 1824, the brothers, continuing their role as estate agents, are letting another property, 9 Camden Terrace, Camden Town, described as *a very desirable house for a small family, making up four or five beds, folding doors between parlour and drawing rooms, walled garden behind, pleasure ground in front, coach-house and stabling if required uniting all the advantages of town*

2

CHAPTER ONE: DEEP ROOTS

*and country.* Particulars with Messrs Pringle 232 Regent Street. Opposite Hanover Street in St. James.

The brothers had expanded their business.

*Regent Street,* named after George, the Prince Regent, is now one of the world's most prestigious shopping and lifestyle destinations, famous for its flagship stores. I was excited at this discovery. It showed my family were a small part of Regent Street history. I wanted to know more.

Historically, shopkeepers had often been manufacturers, either on or off the premises, but this tradition was to change, particularly in the new, fashionable, shopping streets that developed. Rents were high, space was limited, and emphasis was to be increasingly placed on the display of merchandise that was manufactured elsewhere. The premises were designed to ensure that customers were received, and served, in salubrious surroundings. What was Regent Street like in 1822, when Messrs Pringle and Company traded? To gain further perspective, I went further back to 1807, when John and Roberts' father John was still alive.

Regent Street back then was nothing like it is now. It was an unlit, rambling muddy track, an area of ill repute to be avoided. Londoners after dark stumbled around with lanterns trying to avoid the mud and more unpleasant things. It is hard for us today to imagine London as a city with no pavements and no lighting. That scenario was all set to change of course. The year 1807 saw the first street lighting in Pall Mall, installed by the National Light and Heat Company. Westminster Bridge was first lit by gas in 1813. Much of London was lit by 1816, the year the brothers' father died.

The *New Street Act* was a statute that came into being for the sole purpose of demolishing existing houses for the creation of a new Regent Street. In 1811, the architect John Nash drew up plans for broad, architecturally distinguished thoroughfares and public spaces: Carlton House terrace on The Mall, Piccadilly Circus, Regent Street, and Regent's Park, with its grand terraces. The design was adopted by an Act of Parliament in 1813, and built between 1814, and 1825, taking over fourteen years to complete.

Demolition of run-down areas around Swallow Street meant that many craftsmen and traders found themselves without premises from which to trade. Only the very select were invited to relocate to Regent Street, where the emphasis was on high-end goods to rival nearby Bond Street—which was then considered the most fashionable place to shop. The new Regent Street was to divide Soho, which had become less than

3

respectable, from the fashionable squares and streets of Mayfair to the west.

I came across a flavoursome anecdote concerning John Pringle and his bank. William Marsh, a director of a failing family banking firm *Marsh, Sibbald and Co*, with offices in Berners Street, recorded in his diary his family bank crash of 1824. He listed among the banks many creditors Mr. Pringle of 126 Wardour Street. The story is worthy of one of my father's mysteries, because the bank collapse was due to deliberate malpractice.

The managing partner was *a dastardly chap* called Henry Fauntleroy, who forged cheques for more than a decade before he was found out, causing the bank to collapse with enormous debts. Fauntleroy claimed that he had only forged the signatures of hundreds of clients to keep the bank afloat. However, lurid accounts of his extravagant spending on numerous women filled the papers for weeks after he was found out. One hundred thousand people turned up outside Newgate Prison on 30 November 1824 to see Henry Fauntleroy hanged for forgery and embezzlement. A reworked George III copper penny was refashioned as a macabre souvenir of his hanging. *The Fate of Fauntleroy – To all Insolvent Bilking Bankers & Agents* was

neatly engraved across the centre of one side and around the rim of the other; *Fauntleroy the ROBBER of Widows & Orphans Hanged at Newgate 1824*. There was no mention of how much money John Pringle was owed due to the collapse or swindled out of over several years.

Robert and John took one of the new palatial Nash buildings, trading from 232 Regent Street after 1822. According to the records of The Sun Insurance Company, that's when they started insuring it. They were certainly still trading there by June 1824, giving that address for correspondence and replies to advertisements, including the previously mentioned, 9 Camden Terrace. They occupied the Regent Street premises for a decade until 1835. I was eager to know what trading there was like and what happened to their business when they vacated. A daybook from the business includes an entry *relating to work for Mrs. Bruley, 1821-24*. There is a trade account book containing amongst other things *details of time worked by Pringle employees, 1833-1835*. The dates perfectly fitted the cut -off point in Regent Street.

## CHAPTER ONE: DEEP ROOTS

*Dickins & Jones* was a well-known department store in London, which traded between 1835 and 2007. I traced its origins back to 1790 and discovered that *Dickins and Smith* opened a shop at 54 Oxford Street, at the sign of the Golden Lion. Joseph Stevens joined in 1827 and the shop was renamed *Dickins, Sons and Stevens*. In 1835 they had moved to 232 in the newly constructed Regent Street. In 1869, the store occupied adjoining premises at 234 Regent Street and by 1890 had expanded to include 236 Regent Street and 29-31 Argyll Street. The building was named Hanover House 232-236 Regent Street.

Regent Street was gradually redeveloped between 1895 and 1927, on account of many buildings being structurally suspect and not up to improved building standards, including Hanover House. In 1919, the Dickins & Jones store acquired a new site at 224-244 Regent Street, a short distance from the old one. But this didn't concern me. I wanted to know what had happened to Robert and John who had vacated the premises during 1835 to make way for *Dickins, Sons and Stevens*. Why?

\* \* \*

Against this background of an ever-changing London, John and Emma Maria Pringle raised five children. In 1826 they have their first child, a daughter, Emily Sarah, born in St. James, Piccadilly.

On 1 May 1828, they sign a 21-year lease on a property at 26 Great George Street, St. Margaret and St. John, Westminster, running until 20 August 1843. This was a residence in the heart of Westminster near to Westminster Abbey and the Houses of Parliament. It was a house of good workmanship built under the influence of Robert Adam, and a prestigious house in which to live. To put this into perspective, living at

Number 27, until retirement in 1832, was (Sir) William Garrow, who led a legal revolution championing the rights of prisoners in court. He was also vehemently opposed to the slave trade. *Garrow's Law*, a fictionalised drama series of Garrow's beginnings at the Old Bailey was broadcast by the BBC in 2009. In the early part of the 19th-century improvement schemes ensured that many of these houses were demolished so that only a few of the original houses in this street are now left. Number 26 is not one of them.

By August 1928, the brothers have added 46 & 47 Berners Street to their little empire to service the Regent Street outlet. Furnishing firms occupied much of the east side of Berners Street at that time, congregating no doubt through word of mouth. Property was in demand due to the street's proximity, and ease of access, to Oxford Street and Regent Street.

In February 1929, they insure premises at 19 Chester Terrace, Regents Park. In December 1830, 32 Portland Place is added to the portfolio and in February 1831, 21 Park Crescent, Regents Park, consisting of a house, coach house, stables, and offices—a walk away from Chester terrace.

On 10 April 1831, John and Emma have a son, John Robert born in St. James, Piccadilly.

On 2 March 1832, *John Pringle & William Winkworth, Dealers in Plate Glass*, is added as a separate additional business to operate at their Regent Street premises. Are they expanding or plugging a gap in sales?

In 1833, John and Emma have their third child, a second daughter. Her name is Emma Margaret Mercy. She was born in Hampstead.

The following year, September 1834, Robert & John Pringle extend their presence in Berners Street by adding the leasehold of number 44. In the light of what is to come, this looks like preparation for a transition year in 1835, when they move out of 232 Regent Street so that in November, Thomas Dickens, William Smith and Joseph Stevens (known as Dicken and Co, Linen Drapers), can move in.

And 2 April 1835 sees the birth of John and Emma's third daughter and fourth child, Charlotte Isabel, born in Portland Place. By 18 November Robert & John Pringle have added 4 Hanover Street, Hanover Square, to their plethora of properties adding to a complex and bewildering situation.

\* \* \*

# CHAPTER ONE: DEEP ROOTS

Robert and Marian lead the exodus out of London. By 29 February 1836, they are already living on the outskirts of Margate, west of the harbour, near Westbrook, a tiny hamlet that remained largely undeveloped until after the First World War. They occupied one of a row of cottages, in a cut-off location close to the beach called Buenos Ayres, in the parish of St. John.

Margate is a town on the Isle of Thanet, in the county of Kent, on England's southeast coast. Margate was formerly known by the name of St. John's. Still earlier, as Mer-gate. Gradually, a small fishing town arose at the gate in the cliff called Margate, and this name now applies to the whole town. The town was popular at that time with middle-class tradespeople from London who were growing in strength financially as the population of London increased. Houses were built there around 1802 to be let as lodgings to satisfy the demand for accommodation. The popular method of travel was by steamboat.

The name *Buenos Ayres* provides a clue as to why Robert and Marian might have moved there. The Argentine city of the same name had been captured by the British Invasion in 1806. Bueno Aire means *fine air*. The new lodging houses at *Buenos Ayres* were fully occupied because of a big demand for unpolluted sea air. The Royal Sea Bathing Infirmary was founded in 1791, by John Coakley Lettsom, a Quaker physician who espoused the benefits of treating disease with sunshine, fresh air and sea bathing. With the plans approved, building work began after May 1793 and the hospital was ready by the spring of 1796. The hospital was a charitable institution, funded by subscriptions and donations, intended for people suffering from scrofula and tuberculosis. The crisp unpolluted sea air was thought to cure a variety of chest and tubercular troubles. Looking west, the hospital overlooks the bay towards Westbrook. Out-patients as well as in-patients were treated. Were John and Robert suffering from reduced income through ill health because of growing up and working in polluted London? Was the move to the fresh air of the coast an attempt to rescue their health? The clues are all there and the facts point to this as a likely reason.

Robert appoints his brother John as manager of their joint tenancies in London. John is referred to as an auctioneer and his address is Charlotte Street, St. Marylebone. In that same year 1836, John was called as an expert witness in a well-documented patent case in court, *Jupe v Pratt*, relating to an improved expanding table design. His verbal testimony suddenly brings him momentarily to life:

"I have been a cabinet maker all my life. I know Jupe's expanding table; in my opinion it is quite new. Before he had his patent, I never saw a table that radiated from a common centre. The model of Pratt's which I have seen here today is a combination of Gillow's expired patent, and Jupe's existing patent. Such a table could not be produced without adopting Jupe's patent."

Many of the leased properties in London are likely to have been used for workshops, storage, or sublet, as the Pringle businesses shrink. They can't get out of their original leases. With Robert in Margate someone must administrate all these affairs. An archive from 29 February 1836, confirms an agreement between Robert Pringle, Buenos Ayres, St. John, Margate, Kent, and John Pringle, Charlotte Street, St. Marylebone, auctioneer, about their being tenants in common of certain houses and furniture in London. The agreement appoints John Pringle as manager of this property and agent for Robert Pringle. To add an unnecessary burden to this sorry-state-of-affairs, John and Emma have a fifth child, a second son, Robert William born in Lambeth, on 20 May 1840.

By 24 November 1841, John Pringle has vacated London and is also living in Margate with his wife Emma. He assigns the lease on 26 Great George Street for 2 years, the remainder of its duration, to John Henry Thomas Manners Sutton MP. John and Emma have moved from London to 10 Upper Grosvenor Place, St John Baptist, Margate. Emily is 15, young John Robert is 10, Emma is 8, Charlotte is 6, and Robert William is just 1 year old.

John and Robert were to die in Thanet the following year in 1842. They were 44 years old. I try to imagine the impact of the deaths of John and Robert on their wives Emma and Marian having recently moved to an unfamiliar environment. It must have been catastrophic.

The leases on 21 Park Crescent, 44 Berners Street, St. Marylebone, and coach houses in Wells Mews, were surrendered. There would have been many discussions between them as how to cope with the joint new role thrust upon them as widows and executrixes of John and Robert Pringle respectively. It must have been particularly devastating for Emma with a large family to manage, losing her husband so soon after giving birth to their fifth child, Robert William. Marion doesn't remain in Buenos Ayres. She is no longer the concern of this biography. It is Emma Maria's family that I follow into adulthood.

# CHAPTER ONE: DEEP ROOTS

* * *

Like Doctor Who in the Tardis, I press a button. In a flash, John and Robert cabinet makers and upholsterers of Wardour Street and Regent Street in London have vanished into history. I am in Thanet, in the county of Kent. It is 1861.

The censor finds John's widow Emma Maria still residing in Margate and head of the household. She is 64 years old. The children, all unmarried, are living with her. It is their fifth child who is of interest to me, Robert William, also called Robert Wallace. He is now 21. His occupation is listed as a *Professor of Music*. He will become my father's grandfather and the person who had responsibility and influence on his upbringing.

Two years later in 1862, Robert Wallace now 22, is married to Francis Campfield Friend, born in 1840 at Walmer in Kent. They are the same age. Francis is my father's grandmother.

Remember, in 1831 John and Emma Maria had their first son, John Robert. He is the elder brother of their second son Robert Wallace. Not much is known about him. At 10 years through to 19 years of age, John Robert is living with his family in Margate, but he's no longer with them by the 1861 census. There is a very good reason why. At the age of 29, John Robert fathered a son, John Charles Rochfort Douglas-Willan Stuart Pringle, who was born 1860 in Boulogne-sur-Mer in Northern France. Boulogne was accessible by boat from Folkestone, England from 1843. The birth year is only known because that is the year and place entered on the census forms. No birth record can be found regarding the mother of John Charles. She might have been French.

A covenant (a solemn agreement to engage in or refrain from a specified action) of July 1861, by John Robert Pringle, 59A Beach Street, Deal, Kent, with younger brother Robert William (Wallace) Pringle, 9 Upper Grosvenor Place, Margate, Kent, to produce indenture of appointment of 11 October 1841, relating to a piece of land in Margate, Kent, tells me where John Robert is now residing. What has happened to his son John Charles Pringle, the baby born in Boulogne?

Roll on another ten years, and the 1871 census finds John Charles Pringle, now aged 11, at a small boarding school at Tintern Villa, Portsea, Portsmouth, in the county of Hampshire. The head of the school is Baptist Minister, James Neobard aged 30, with his wife Annie, aged 26. Nine students are boarding.

Moving on yet another ten years, the 1881 census finds a John Charles Pringle boarding with the Senogles family at 1 Spring Gardens, Conchan, Isle of Man, situated in the Irish Sea between Great Britain and Ireland. He is entered as a British Subject born in Boulogne, France. His occupation is Teacher. He is aged 21 and is unmarried.

John Charles Pringle is rather important. He is to become the father of John Robert Stuart Pringle aka Donald Stuart aka Gerald Verner.

Who was my father's mother?

# Chapter Two – Nellie

*T*he *Morning Advertiser* of 12 Oct 1863 published under the heading *Last Notices*: The following licence for music was refused, the application not having been submitted in time: Robert William (Robert Wallace) Pringle, The Dolphin, Church Street, Bethnal Green, London. He is now 23 years of age and married to Francis about a year. The young couple were yet to have any children. How are they getting on?

The Dolphin was a grim looking Public House at 38 Church Street,  with rent out rooms, or maybe a cheap hotel, but certainly no place to bring up a baby. This may explain why their first child, Albert John William Pringle, was born in Walmer, on the Kent coast, a year later in 1864.

I imagine Francis went home to stay with her parents in order to have help with the baby while Robert William stayed in London, evidenced by a small entry in *The Morning Advertiser*, 19 January 1865, announcing the appointment of Robert William Pringle, The Dolphin, 38 Church-street, Bethnal Green, as a new governor of the Licensed Victuallers' Asylum, an institution in Asylum Road, Old Kent Road, London. I thought at first, he was a governor of a place for the mentally ill! Researching further, I was fascinated to learn this was the first free school for deaf children of the poor in the UK. It was founded in 1792 by the Rev. John Townsend and provided hope and support for the forgotten children of London for 176 years.

Why was Robert William listed as a governor with the Dolphin specifically mentioned in the records? He was obviously still lodging there while he taught at the school. For a moment I thought maybe Robert and Francis might have owned the Dolphin establishment, but the Licensee from 1862-66 was Frederick Ritchie.

I noticed that in 1862 some older pupils of the Licensed Victuallers' Asylum moved to temporary accommodation in Margate, where a branch was opened in 1876. West along the coast from Margate is Broadstairs and then Ramsgate—one of the great English seaside towns of the 19th century. In 1883 younger pupils went to Ramsgate, presumably in preparation for the demolition of the old London building in 1886. By 1905 the school had moved in its entirety from London to Margate, so pupils could benefit from the sea air. This connection with the Isle of Thanet, where Robert William (Wallace) grew up, was it a clue?

\* \* \*

In 1866, a second son is born to Robert William (Wallace) and Francis Campfield Friend in Torquay, Devon. He is named Harry Thomas Pringle. By 1868 They have moved to Bridge Street, Newport Pagnell to join Robert's mother Emma. Newport Pagnell was one of the largest towns in the County of Buckinghamshire. She is still head of the household and now 71. Living with her is daughter Charlotte, who is 33. During 1868 at Bridge Street a third son is born. He is named Frank Stuart Slodden Pringle and destined to become a clerk in Holy Orders. A fourth son, Arthur Ernest Pringle, is also born in Bridge Street in 1870, and becomes an actor.

Robert and Francis move to Swansea, where they have their fifth child, a daughter in 1877. Robert's mother Emma Maria remains behind and dies at Newport Pagnell in 1879 aged 82. The daughter is named Ellen Emma Stuart Pringle. She's rather important because without her this biography would not have been written because I wouldn't exist. She will become an actress and my father's mother.

\* \* \*

On Whit Sunday 31 May 1879 there is a special service at Swansea parish church with Mr. Wallace Pringle at the organ. A collection is taken in aid of Swansea Hospital. This snippet in a local newspaper tells me Robert is still living in Swansea and that he is an organist.

At some point between May 1879 and the census in 1881, the Pringle family are split up, for whatever reason. Robert Wallace Pringle, Professor of Music, and his son Harry Thomas Pringle, now 15, who is also to become a musician, are living at 199 St Helens Rd, Swansea, Glamorganshire. There is no mention in the 1881 census of their daughter Ellen Emma Pringle living with them, because she is staying with her mother Francis.

Soon after Ellen was born, Francis took most of the children, her daughter and three sons, to Lowesmoor, Worcester St Martin. Ellen Emma is age 4. John Albert Pringle an actor age 17. Frank Slodden Pringle age 13, and Arthur Ernest Pringle age 11 are both attending school. Francis is now age 42. She is described as a hotel keeper—possibly explaining what she was doing at the Dolphin soon after she was first married. She is a hotel keeper at *Lansdowne Hotel*, Lowesmoor Place, Worcester.

Dominated by the Vinegar Works and other Victorian industrial buildings, Lowesmoor was the centre for industry, trade, and commerce, in the City of Worcester, following the completion of the Worcester and Birmingham Canal in 1815. It is a five-minute walk from Worcester city centre. Francis Pringle had obtained a position in the thriving community of Lowesmoor but her time at the *Lansdowne Hotel* is to be cut short. On 22 July 1882, the hotel is to be sold at auction. The property includes handsomely fitted liquor vaults, a billiard room, newly erected smoking room, 9 Bedrooms, complete domestic accommodation, Brewhouse, and extensive Cellaring. The hotel is available for immediate possession.

Why were the Wallace family split up? A case of *needs must*, perhaps? As an organist, did Robert Wallace bring in insufficient earnings to keep his family of five sheltered, fed, and clothed? Was Francis forced to leave in desperation to find additional income, planning to return when fortunes had improved? These are questions that are unlikely to be answered unless the dead can be made to speak. The sale of *Lansdowne Hotel* must have disrupted any plans they had made. It is easy to forget how tough life could be in those days to earn a living with no inherited wealth or welfare safety net to rescue you. If you were fortunate to have a job it was too valuable to lose and put you at the mercy of the business owner or face starvation.

# PLOTS AND GUNPOWDER

By December 1883 the family are reunited and living in Sandhurst, a town and civil parish in the Bracknell Forest borough in Berkshire and famous for its Royal Military College built in 1812. A successful concert is given in the Sandhurst Schoolroom under the direction of Mr. Wallace Pringle (organist at St. Michaels). A well-trained band gave several excellent instrumental performances during the evening and several performers are involved including Mr. Pringle and Miss Nelly and Master Arthur Pringle, all of whom were well received.

Wallace Pringle is not only playing the organ, but conducting the band and performing, at a musical evening with his son Arthur Ernest Pringle age 13, who is to become an actor, and a Miss Nelly Pringle.

Who is Nelly?

It is at once clear to me who Nelly must be. Looking the name up, I find Nelly, Nela, Nell, and Nellie are female given names, also used as nicknames, which are derived from the names Janelle, Helen, Ellen, Petronella, Chanelle and Cornelia. *Ellen* jumps out at me. Robert Wallace is performing with his daughter Ellen Emma. She is only 6 years old and has the nickname Nelly or Nel. No doubt her father has professionally trained her voice.

A year later, 19 December 1884 to be exact, Robert Wallace has placed an advertisement in *The Stage* newspaper. He is looking for engagements. He gives St. Faith's, Sandhurst, Berkshire, as an address for any replies, confirming this is where they have settled for a while but not for long. Jumping forward to May 1889, I find the family have moved from Sandhurst to 3, Hawley Square, Margate where he is working for Sarah Thorne (1836–1899), actress and manageress of the Theatre Royal Margate between 1867 and 1899.

In 1879 Sarah Thorne lived at 5, Hawley Square and began a successful School of Acting, six years later moving to larger accommodation in 1885. Sarah Thorne is almost certainly why the Wallace family were now based in Margate. Robert Wallace advertises on behalf of the Theatre Royal Margate, in *The Stage* newspaper on 24 May 1889, for musicians, looking to employ a 1st Violin, Flute and Piccolo, for an engagement that commences in June. That Christmas, Robert Wallace has written by request a symphony for the Christmas concert at St. Augustine's College, in the cathedral city of Canterbury, about 16 miles inland from Margate.

Robert Wallace, Professor of Music, and his wife Francis are both 48 years old. Harry Thomas is age 23, and Ellen Emma is age 12. I wonder if

14

their relocation originated with Robert's sister Charlotte Isabel who is 53, and his aunt Emily (Emily Sarah born St. James, Piccadilly, London 1826) who remained behind in Thanet. Charlotte may be looking after Emily who might have been ill at that time because she died there in 1890.

By 3 September 1892, the work at the Theatre Royal has dried up. The family are on the move once more from Margate to Bletchingley, a village in Surrey, where Professor Wallace Pringle is choirmaster of Bletchingley Church. Nellie appears in a concert given on 17 December 1892. She is 15. In a local review that paints a wonderful portrait of the period is corroboration that Nell's father *is* Robert Wallace and that he is training her singing voice and acting abilities:

> "One of the songs of the evening was Miss Nellie Pringle's Scenes *That Are Brightest*, in which the young lady's well trained and eloquently-modulated contralto voice was listened to with rapt attention. The only fault was that the enunciation was not quite clear probably owing to a cold. Her father, Professor Pringle accompanied. Miss Nell Pringle was heard a second time in *True*, and being encored sang *The Stile* very nicely indeed, the enunciation being much better, and we understand she afterwards received a very handsome bouquet of choice flowers with compliments on her singing."

An evening concert on New Year's Day, 1894 was given at the Board School in aid of the Bletchingley Hornets Cricket Club. Miss Nell Pringle's excellent contralto, heard to great advantage in two songs, is singled out for praise, both deservedly encored. Professor Wallace Pringle, as well as giving a pianoforte solo, accompanied the songs. During an evening in January 1895, the Board School is packed again, this time a popular concert under the management of 18-year-old Miss Nellie Pringle:

> "The schoolroom was packed with an enthusiastic audience on Tuesday night on the occasion of a popular concert under the management of Miss Nellie Pringle. That the gathering enjoyed the way in which the well-arranged programme was gone through there can be no doubt; it was certainly the best entertainment of its kind that has been given to the village for some little time. Miss Nell Pringle, a talented vocalist, herself impressed the

audience favourably, and the other performers generally took their parts with credit. These were Miss Helen Butt (contralto), Miss Nellie Simmons (soprano), Mr. J. Charles Pringle (baritone), Mr. C. H. Bishop Reigate (sketch artist), and Professor Wallace Pringle who very efficiently discharged the duties of conductor. A small orchestra was present under the leadership of Mr. Henry Bashford. The programme is appended:

Part One: *Overture*, the Band; song *Tim*, Miss Nell Pringle; song (comic), *The tix gee gee*, Mr. J. C. Pringle; song, The Flight of Ages, Miss Helen Butt; sketch, *The Silver Wedding*, Professor Wallace Pringle; song, *Down Old River*, Miss Nellie Simmons (violin obligato, Mr. Henry Bashford); duet, *The May Bells*, Misses Nell Pringle and Nellie Simmons; character song, *Across the Bridge*, Mr. C. H. Bishop; song (comic), *Just Like the Men*, Miss Nell Pringle; solo and quartet, *The Legend of the Bells* (from *Les Cloches de Corneville*).

Part Two: *Selection*, the Band; song, The Daughter of the Regiment, Miss Nell Pringle; song, *Wait till de sun am hot upon the head*, Mr. J. C. Pringle; song, *To a Rose*, Miss Helen Butt; duet, *With the Tide*, Miss Nell Pringle and Mr. J. C. Pringle; recitation, An Uncommon Patient (from *Three Men in a Boat*), Professor Wallace Pringle; duet and solo, *Mikado*, Misses Nell Pringle and Nellie Simmons; character song, *I'm changed*, Mr. C. H. Bishop; song, *Lazily Drowsily* (from *Little Christopher Columbus*), encored, Miss Nell Pringle; final chorus, *Good-night;* solo, Miss Nell Pringle."

The Pringle family sound a cheerful lot and are successfully contributing to English village life. Here we have Nell Pringle performing a recital with her uncle's son, (Ellen Emma's cousin) John Charles, born in Boulogne and last heard of in 1881 living on the Isle of Man. As I would soon discover, this was a very important and fateful connection, depending upon your point of view.

The next entertainment at the Board School is on a Tuesday evening on 3 May 1895. The report gives great insight into the talents of Professor Wallace Pringle, Miss Nell Pringle and, most importantly, Mr. John Charles Pringle:

"The first part comprised an overture by the band (under the leadership of Mr. Henry Bashford), songs by Miss Helen Butt,

Miss Nell Pringle, Mr. J. C. R. Pringle, a recitation of the murder scene from Shakespeare's *Macbeth*, a coronet solo by Mr. Bashford, concluding with a selection by the Band. For the second part, Professor Wallace Pringle had composed an operetta entitled *Inez, the Dancing Girl*. The scene was laid in an Italian Garden, the characters being Don Georgie Pedrillo, Neapolitan nobleman (Professor Pringle); Andrea Valetta, an amateur brigand chief (Mr. J. C. R. Pringle); Donna Camilla Sylvia, a Neapolitan lady (Miss Nellie Simmons); and Inez Melasquez, the dancing girl (Miss Nellie Pringle).

This must be counted a distinct success. The various parts were well sustained, and the audience were extremely hearty in their applause, especially at the fall of the curtain, when the performers, in response to an undeniable call, bowed their acknowledgments. The entertainment was repeated on Wednesday at popular prices."

Nell and Charles are performing together on a regular basis under the strict leadership of composer, musician, and performer, Professor Wallace. The *Surrey Mirror* reports on another evening in Bletchingley on 13 September 1895 and I learn Professor Wallace is also an author:

"On Tuesday and Wednesday last, Professor Wallace Pringle gave one of his popular entertainments to crowded and delighted audiences. The programme commenced on both nights with Mr. Pringle's very laughable farce, *An Awful Fix*, in which Mr. J. C. R. Pringle admirably sustained the character of Dick Austey. Mr. Cecil Winter playing well a Tom Vyvyan. Lucy Fitzallen charmingly portrayed by Miss Nell Pringle, who is an actress born, and the part of Maud Travers most prettily and daintily played by Miss Nellie Simmons. The character of Mr. Travers, an irascible old widower with two charming daughters, was sustained by Professor Wallace, who is evidently an experienced actor. Not the least noticeable part in the amusing sketch was that of Kitty Travers, the *Objectionable Child*, which was most excellently taken by little Miss Muriel Hulsekopf. The performance altogether was admirable and kept the large audience in roars of laughter. After the farce, Miss Ellen Butt, a very fine contralto vocalist charmed the company by singing Lindsay Lennox's *In The Twilight* and then followed the great feature of the evening's entertainment, the new operetta, *Mimi, or cast up by the Sea* written and composed by Professor Wallace Pringle – a very pretty plot, in which the owner of a yacht cruising round the coast on his honeymoon, discovers in Mimi the supposed daughter of the landlord of The Eagle's Nest, his long-lost sister. Jack, the first-hand on the yacht, falls in love with Mimi, who loves him in return, and the difficulty of social position is cleverly got over by the discovery that *Jack* is really a baronet, and the owner of Dering Towers in Cumberland. The music of the operetta is most charming, and we think even superior to that of *Inez, the Dancing Girl* which gave such pleasure to music lovers some little while ago. Mr. J. C. R. Pringle as Jack, Mr. Cecil Winter as Old Carl Hefler the landlord (a most capital make-up), Professor Pringle as Captain Taffrail, Miss Nell Pringle as *Mimi*, Miss Nellie Simmons as Mrs. Taffrail, all sang and acted well, the difficult and intricate music of the concerted pieces, and the delicate expression in the solos and duets, being most excellently given. The scenery was well painted, and the whole staging, of both farce and operetta, admirable. The performance was repeated last (Thursday) night at Oxted."

A wonderful description is painted of a musical evening out, providing a mine of information on Professor Wallace Pringle as all round entertainer, obviously possessing a great sense of humour, heading a family that enjoys music, songs, and comedy. He has written a farce, *An Awful Fix* and a new operetta, *Mimi, or cast up by the Sea,* with a reference to his previous operetta, *Inez, the Dancing Girl.* Here we also have John Charles again as actor and singer performing with his Uncle, and Miss Nell Pringle enjoying a musical evening, *an actress born,* and taking the lead part of *Mimi* in the operetta. I begin to feel like a sleuth in a real detective yarn, because surely the stage is set for something dramatic to happen - and happen it does!

During early Spring of 1896, John Charles 35, and Ellen Emma 19, conceive a child. That child is my father.

My imagination runs riot as to how this conception might have occurred. A slow passionate burn or a sudden act of wilful lust? I will never know, but it must have caused one hell of a stir at that time!

# CHAPTER TWO: NELLIE

I can confirm Ellen Emma Stuart Pringle (Nellie) married her uncle's son—her cousin—John Charles Rochfort Douglas-Willan Stuart Pringle on 21 July 1896. The wedding took place in Willesden, London. Emma's father's name on the marriage certificate is shown as Robert Wallace Pringle, Professor of Music. John Charles's father's name on the marriage certificate is shown as John Robert Pringle. Their address is given as 5, Callcott Road, which refers to Callcott Road, Brent, London NW6, not far from Willesden Lane.

It is almost certain Emma was married because she became pregnant. A child born out of wedlock was not to be contemplated and required an immediate and effective solution. A fly on the wall would witness some earnest conversations to restore respectability. From their marriage date to my father's birth was a time span of only 28 weeks suggesting Ellen Emma was about 12 weeks pregnant at the time of the marriage. A pregnancy time frame is usually 40 weeks, sometimes as long as 42 weeks, because it is difficult to pin down an exact date of conception, but at a guess, I'd estimate during March 1896. This might explain why it is likely this was a marriage of necessity, not a marriage of love in the true sense, but a *shotgun wedding*.

The child born to Ellen Emma and John Charles is named John Robert Stuart Pringle. He was born on 31 January 1897, at 46, Ramsden Road, Balham, south London.

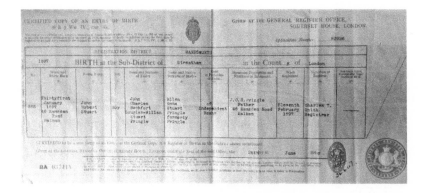

# Chapter Three – Geraldine Verner

I don't believe the marriage between Ellen Emma and John Charles, who was 17 years her senior, was a very loving one, or even amicable. The 1901 Census finds Ellen is living in Edmonton, London, age 24. Though still married to John Charles she is not living with him. John Charles, now aged 41, is living far away in Thanet at The Dingle, North Foreland, Broadstairs, Kent, in the parish of St. Peter Intra. Such a wedding and lack of a parental relationship helps to explain why my father grew up with his grandparents Robert Wallace and Francis.

I seldom heard my father speak of his father (my grandfather) John Charles, except to tell me he had been a schoolmaster, and at one time had taught sports at Stone House School, Lanthorne Road, off North Foreland Road, Broadstairs. I felt goosebumps when I learned of this address. Many years later I would cycle past Stone House every day on my way to school when I was living with my father at North Foreland—a coincidence? Or, does this history partly explain why my father had gone back to his roots at a difficult time. My father presumably didn't speak much of John Charles with any affection because he hadn't received any. As far as I was aware, he had been absent since birth.

*Stone House* was built in 1764 by a wealthy East India Merchant. In 1868, it became the seaside home of Archbishop Tait of Canterbury. From the late 1800s, until its closure in 1972, it was a much-favoured Preparatory School for boys. *Stone House* itself is of Historic importance and is now a Grade 11 listed building split into flats. On the surrounding land, homes have been erected in a Georgian Style.

## CHAPTER THREE: GERALDINE VERNER

Built in 1896, *The Dingle*, North
Foreland, where John Charles
boarded, is one of the founder houses
of the private and prestigious North
Foreland. The house has seen many
changes and owners over the years.
They include the Lord Archbishop of
Canterbury, Archbishop Tait. During
the Second World War, when the

entire North Foreland Estate was evacuated, *The Dingle* served as an
officer's mess for the nearby radar station. In 1963 the house was
substantially damaged by fire and underwent extensive rebuilding.

The 1901 Census, taken in March, indicates *The Dingle* is the main
accommodation for all those teaching and working at Stone House
School. Lodging there are Warton and Elizabeth Flack, who run the
house for the teachers who are boarding. But it is John Pringle (John
Charles) aged 41, born 1860, France, BS, married, who is our main
interest. This confirms he *was* born in France and explains the reason why
I can't unearth details of his mother. He is the only married teacher
boarding, making no attempt to hide his married status. Other archives
show that the Headmaster was Reverend William Henry Churchill in
1908. He would have been headmaster at the time John Charles was there
and no doubt lived at Stone House itself.

Ten years later, the 1911 Census finds John Rochford (John Charles)
now aged 51, still living in Thanet at *The Dingle*. He is the only remaining
lodger of ten years ago. The Flacks have gone. The accommodation is
now run by housekeeper Elizabeth Larcy and her daughter Edith. We do
not know what happened to John Charles after 1911 until his death. The
1921 census, taken in June, would help to establish he was still teaching at
Stone House, but the census was conducted under the 1920 Census Act,
which is still in force and prohibits publication of data. It is unclear when
data will be made available—even under the 100-year rule that was
applied to the 1901 Census and those before. The 1931 Census was
destroyed by fire. The death certificate states simply that John Charles R.
D. W. S. Pringle died in Winchester, Hampshire, between October and
December 1933. He was 73 years old.

* * *

# PLOTS AND GUNPOWDER

The wedding between Ellen Emma and John Charles must have been very intrusive because there was a lot going on in Ellen Emma's stage life at this time. During the first half of 1895, it looks as if the Pringle family were still living in Bletchingley.

*The Era*, 23 May 1896, has an advertisement for vacant dates for *Inez, the Dancing Girl*, apply Elsie Dorron, the Whyte Harte Hotel. *The Era* was a British weekly paper, published from 1838 to 1939, and considered invaluable for reviews, news, and general theatrical information and gossip plus assorted advertisements by and for actors and companies. Robert Wallace had written and composed a new and original comic opera in three acts entitled *Inez, the Dancing Girl*. It was to be produced at the 600-seater Lyceum Theatre, Stafford, by Miss Geraldine Verner's company (it was originally to open at The Theatre Royal, Kidderminster but this got cancelled). Special scenery had been painted for the production. Prior to a tour through the provinces, *Inez, the Dancing Girl* opened at Stafford on Bank Holiday Monday 3 August 1896.

This is the first record I could find of Ellen Emma, or Nell Pringle turning professional at the tender age of nineteen and adopting the stage name Geraldine Verner. Of course, the moment I read that name Geraldine Verner I knew I was looking at the origin of my father's name, but I needed proof. The name raised several questions to which there are only suppositions. Can I be certain Ellen Emma/Nellie Pringle is Geraldine Verner? The answer must be that she is as I know my father's mother was always known as Gerry. But why choose the name Geraldine Verner? To deliberately disassociate herself from the Pringle name.

I can imagine the trauma of Ellen Emma finding herself with child and being forced into a marriage for decency's sake that she didn't want. It is understandable this might have instilled in her a strong desire to become someone else other than a Pringle. But where did the inspiration for this new name originate? I hunted through archives and discovered there was a touring company operating under the name Elaine Verner. Perhaps she chose the name Verner to blend in, so the public might assume she belonged to that family? This seemed a reasonable supposition.

I also have a problem with dates. Ellen Emma must have had a major headache, because my father must have been conceived around March 1896. Emma would have been about 20 weeks pregnant at the time of opening *Inez* at Stafford and she was playing the title role!

## CHAPTER THREE: GERALDINE VERNER

What about showing a bump? It is possible a bump may have naturally not shown. Some women don't show much. If she was conceived later than March, and my father was born premature, it is possible she might have got through the tour without it showing. Had the costume been cut to hide it when performing a clever serpentine dance as *Inez*. She was the boss. Her wedding on 21 July 1896, in Willesden was only a week before opening *Inez* and must have been right in the middle of rehearsals. The wedding covered her in case a bump began to show causing awkward questions. It fixed the situation. My father was legitimate.

I can feel the weight of responsibility on Wallace Pringle's shoulders and Emma's to prove the opera a success.

A review in *The Era*, 8 August 1896, includes:

> "Miss Geraldine Verner, who has acquired the entire provincial rights of the piece, undertakes the title-role. She possesses a pleasing voice, and her histrionic powers seem equal to the part. She appears at the fête in her vocation as the dancing girl and executes a skirt dance with commendable grace and skill."

Following on from the success of *Inez*, and the birth of my father on 31 January 1897, a new production is underway *A Woman Scorned*, a drama in four acts, by Wallace Pringle, opening at the Theatre Royal, Workington in Cumbria on 10 October 1898. Miss Geraldine Verner was 21 at this time and received favourable reviews. 16 January 1900 finds her aged 23 at the Theatre Royal, Cardiff, Wales, in *An American Heiress*. The *South Wales Daily News* reports:

> "Mr. Redford is to be congratulated on securing *An American Heiress* for a week's run at the Theatre Royal, Cardiff. This clever musical comedy, which is by Arthur Branscombe and George D. Day, is just the sort of piece to suit the Cardiff public. Of the ladies, all of whom did well, special mention must be made of Miss Geraldine Verner as Cora Brooklyn and Miss Rita Leslie as Sadie Brooklyn, the American heiress. The piece is certain to have a most successful run in Cardiff."

On 13 March 1900, Ellen Emma, now firmly reborn as Miss Geraldine Verner, is contributing to the fundraising at a Church Bazaar at Southampton according to Devon's *Western Times:*

"...while songs, sketches, etc., were contributed by Miss Geraldine Verner, Mr. Wallace Pringle, Mr. G. Thorne Bicketts, the Beys. G. W. Edwards and G. B. Dade, and many others..."

The *Hampshire Advertiser* 3 October 1900, tells of further activities:

"Some opening verses, composed by Mr. Wallace Pringle, organist at St. Michael's Church, were sung by Miss Geraldine Verner."

These little snippets nicely corroborate the 1901 Census confirming my father's grandfather has moved from Bletchingley. He is living at 163 Shirley Road, Southampton, Hampshire, a county in South East England on the English Channel coast. Robert Wallace, listed as the head of the household, is now 60, still living with his wife Francis, who is 61. His brother John Robert is *a widower* aged 69—John Charles mother (French, or otherwise), has obviously died. Also staying in the house with the two brothers is my father to be, John Robert Stuart Pringle, grandson, now aged 4. John Roberts' father John Charles is living in Thanet, and his actress mother Ellen is boarding at 63, Palace Road, Hornsey, a district of north London in the Borough of Haringey. Ellen joins them when she can.

On 13 December 1902, The *Hampshire Advertiser* reports on *Retribution* adapted from Chas de Bernard's celebrated novel *La Peine du talion* at The Philharmonic Hall:

"...suffice it to say the interest was maintained throughout with the curtain rung down after a very exciting duel, in which the villain is killed. The principal role is taken by Mr. Wallace Pringle, who admirably played his part as the sardonic Count Prinli. Miss Geraldine Verner, as Clarisse de Beaupre was also a great success. Perhaps she was not quite strong enough in demonstrating the violent emotions of her part, but she still acted with a grace and charm which gained her the applause of an interested audience."

The *London Daily News* 16 December 1903 reports that the *Water Babies* will be revived at The Garrick Theatre, London, on Tuesday the 22nd:

"This will be its 101st performance at this theatre. Two days afterwards, Mr. Bourchier has arranged for its production at

Brighton under the management of Mr. Trevor Lowe with a cast including Miss Kate Bis, Miss Marie Lohr, Miss Dorothy Firmin, Miss Geraldine Verner…"

I have found one of those very interesting links that establishes my father's history. Mr. Bourchier is none other than Actor and Theatre Manager, Arthur Bourchier (1863-1927). As a student at Oxford, Bourchier joined the University Drama Society and began his acting career and his life-long interest in staging Shakespeare's plays. In September 1900 he left the Criterion, where he had been in partnership with Charles Wyndham to became lessee of the Garrick Theatre. He managed the Garrick Theatre for six years. He died in Johannesburg, South Africa, on 14 September 1927. My father went to work for Arthur Bourchier when he reached the age of 17, in 1914. Also, in this extract, the name Trevor Lowe leaps out at me from the page. *Trevor Lowe* is the name of the detective that features in many of my father's crime novels.

The following year sees essentially the same production at The Gaiety Theatre, Hastings, a seaside town and borough in East Sussex on the south coast of England. Saturday 13 February 1904, *Hastings and St Leonards Observer* reports:

"By special arrangement with Arthur Bourchier, the beautiful fairy play, Water Babies: an adaptation to the stage of the late Charles Kingley's famous book, is being produced this week at The Gaiety Theatre, Hastings, by Messrs. James Preston and Trevor Lowe and a splendid Company. Perfectly delightful is Miss Dorothy Firmin as Tom, the little chimney sweep who dives into the river and becomes one of the water babies, and no less bewitching is Miss Marie Lohr, a little lady with whom everybody is bound to fall in love as she gracefully portrays the part of Ellie Heartover, Tom's sweetheart in the water world. Even more attractive than these two sweet children, is Miss Geraldine Verner an adult who, as *Queen of the Fairies* acts and sings to perfection…"

November 1905 sees Miss Geraldine Verner as a fine Nellie in a stirring Drama, *The Black Mask*, at King's Theatre, Walthamstow, a large town in east London. And 2 October 1909, finds her appearing in a play

*The Sinner* at The Theatre Royal and Opera House Stockport, a large town in Greater Manchester, where it is noted in *The Era*:

"Vera Ewen is charmingly acted by Miss Geraldine Verner."

Then 18 April 1910, finds Miss Geraldine Verner again in *The Sinner*, now presented in London for the first time at The Elephant & Castle Theatre. *The Era* reports:

"The ladies of the cast are particularly to be praised. Miss Muriel Dean was a prepossessing Honor Thornhill acting throughout with rare refinement and grace. Miss Geraldine Verner played in equally agreeable fashion the role of Vera Ewin, wearing some stylish dresses very becomingly."

*The Stage* newspaper 26 May 1910 and 19 October 1911 prints a crucial corroboration that Ellen Emma Pringle and Miss Geraldine Verner are the same person. It is an advertisement in the form of a professional card telling readers she is disengaged; no doubt having finished in her tour of *The Sinner*. She is looking for work. The address she gives for replies is 308, Stanstead Road, Catford, London. That is precisely the address where the 1911 Census puts the Pringle family.

\* \* \*

On 10 June 1854 Queen Victoria opened the rebuilt Crystal Palace at Sydenham Hill, straddling the borders of the London Boroughs of Southwark and Lewisham, and which soon established itself as the most important single location for public music-making in the country. Orchestral concerts and choral festivals provided weekly performances which offered plenty of scope. The Crystal Palace must have been a magnet to Wallace Pringle, who was always looking for work.

My father told me his grandfather was a conductor there. This employment must have occurred between 1902 (when he was still in

Southampton) and 1911 when the Census finds Robert, Professor of Music, 70, and his wife, Frances, 71, at 308, Stanstead Road, London S.E.6, between Catford and Forest Hill, in the district of Lewisham, situated conveniently for commuting to The Crystal Palace. My father, now a 14-year-old student, John Robert Stuart Pringle is living with them. His father, John Charles, remains in Thanet, and his mother, Miss Geraldine Verner, now 34, is looking for work.

This fits in perfectly with what my father told me. He used to go with his grandfather regularly to the Crystal Palace as a child. It must have been a wondrous experience to visit one of the largest amusement halls in the world, famous for its roof with 25 acres of glass. The whole building was enormous - 1,848 feet long and 408 feet wide, including two huge towers, and many fountains with over 11,000 jets rising into the air. This was the world's first *theme park*. It consisted of a prehistoric swamp complete with life-sized models of dinosaurs. In 1902, an amusement park with water rides and a looping rollercoaster called the Topsy-Turvy was added. There were performances and exhibitions going on all the time.

In the summer months, on Thursday evenings, there were magnificent firework displays. I know they both dazzled and obsessed my father, as he would often describe them to me emotionally, reliving the awe and enthusiasm he felt at the time. He formed a life-long fascination with fireworks, as he watched them delivered to the Crystal Palace grounds, loaded on a procession of horse and carts, by the famous firm of Brock's. The glass palace became the famous trademark that Brock's were to adopt: *Brock's Crystal Palace Fireworks*.

Brocks began life in the early 1700's as the creation of John Brock, with its first factory located in Islington, London. The company became world famous for presenting *Brock's Benefits*, displays for the enjoyment of the common public. The first of these was fired on 10 July 1826. From 1865 onwards, they became a regular attraction at the site of the fabulous Crystal Palace. The displays were fired to live music and the fountains danced in tune to it. Rockets were fired in flights of five thousand at a time!

Imagine that!

BROCK'S BENEFIT CRYSTAL PALACE SEP 24. "ONE SHILLING DAY."

Brock's displays continued regularly, with a decade-long break between 1910 and 1920, until the Palace was completely devastated by fire in 1936. Brock's moved to Hemel Hempstead, Hertfordshire in 1910 and remained in operation until 1971.

My father's interest and considerable knowledge about all things pyrotechnic was to hold him in good stead much later in life when, because of a marriage breakup, he couldn't write, cancelled several contracts he was working on, and was forced to fall back to his knowledge of pyrotechnics to work for Brock's at their factory at Hemel Hempstead.

\* \* \*

When my father spoke of his grandfather, Robert Wallace, it was always with great affection. It was clear his grandfather had taken the place of his real father and contributed a great deal to his education. He described how his grandfather would have a cold bath outside every morning before going off to work, in the winter often cracking the ice that had formed on the surface of the water with his walking stick!

Miss Geraldine Verner still based at 308, Stanstead Road, Catford, takes the title role in *The Girl from Nowhere* at The Grand Theatre Nottingham, 30 March 1911. I can find no further trace of her activities until April 8 1913 which finds her at The Queens Theatre, Leeds, Yorkshire:

> "Mormonism is the subject expounded at The Queens Theatre, Leeds this week, and, *At the Mercy of the Mormons*, which is the title of the piece, contains a great number of *thrills*. California is the scene of all the exciting episodes. A great amount of work rests upon the shoulders of Mr. Pat Sullivan and Miss Geraldine Verner, and they acquit themselves in a workmanlike manner."

Then 25 March 1914 sees Miss Geraldine Verner appearing in *Another Man's Wife* at New Prince's Theatre, Portsmouth. From her

## CHAPTER THREE: GERALDINE VERNER

nickname Nell to professional stage name Miss Geraldine Verner, Ellen Emma has embarked on a successful provincial acting career, as evidenced by these newspaper reports. She is appearing regularly in many productions around the country, too numerous to mention.

# Chapter Four – WW1

At the outbreak of WW1, on 28 July 1914, males aged 18 to 40 were called up. Conscription lasted until mid-1919. I moved forward in time to an interview with my father, in the Surrey Comet, 5 September 1936, which reports him telling them that he was born of an old stage family, but he took an early interest in crime at the age of 16. When he was introduced to some high Scotland Yard officials, he seized the opportunity of chatting with them about notorious cases. He took to joining policeman on their beats—an occupation that taught him a lot about crime and procedure.

At 17, he entered the theatre business as a stage manager for Arthur Bourchier. He played all sorts of parts. While his company was on tour and war broke out, he tried to join the army in 26 towns but was rejected each time. There must have been a reason he was rejected by the army, but my father has always insisted he never knew why. He appeared to me to be a very fit man. He seldom saw a doctor during his life. As one historian pointed out; *a farm lad aged 19 might have escaped call-up in one part of the country whereas a 40-year old, brickie from another part may have been drafted.* Perhaps random selection explains the mystery.

It would be wrong to assume that my father worked for Bourchier until the actor's death. He talks about his early, stage days as a teenager saying that he had *adventures on tour* and was picked to play three parts in *East Lynne.*

Throughout the war, his mother keeps acting. The 3rd of August 1914 sees her appearing in the drama, *The Better Land,* at Holloway Empire. According to *The Era:*

> "Mr. Fred Granville's Company opened here on Monday to a large and appreciative audience with an excellent Bank Holiday attraction, *The Better Land.* Mr. Robert Rosmole enacts the part of Philip Radcliffe earnestly and sincerely, and Miss Geraldine Verner wins all hearts by her clever impersonation of Doris, his wife."

# CHAPTER FOUR: WWI

Robert Wallace, Professor of Music, dies at the age of 75 in 1915 in the borough of Lambeth. His wife Francis was to die two years later in 1917.

My father looked up to his grandfather as a role model. He was someone he wanted to emulate despite the rollercoaster ride that can be the life of a showman, of an entertainer... My father was something of a showman himself. I have no doubt life with his grandfather was where his entrepreneurship originated.

The death of Robert Wallace must have been a bitter blow to the family. They were very close, had travelled all over Southern England, living and performing in different situations together, during which time they must have endured frequent hardship and disappointment interspersed with exciting and happy moments. My father is 18 years old and the sad news will have hit him very hard.

The *Newcastle Journal* of 27 November 1915, finds Miss Geraldine Verner at The Palace Theatre, Newcastle, the university city in northeast England:

> "A sterling drama dealing with our brave Russian allies, entitled *A Gentleman in Khaki* will be presented at The Palace Theatre twice nightly by Messrs Wilson Benge and Fred Bulmer's company. Miss Geraldine Verner takes the part of Countess von Steinmetz, and Mr. Clavering Craig fulfils the title role while there is a strong company to support."

The *Girl from Ciro's,* a farce adapted by J.G. Levy from a farce by Pierre Veber, described by some *as beyond the bounds of propriety*, opened at the Garrick Theatre, London 4 September 1916. A provincial tour followed. On 4 February 1918, *The Girl from Ciro's* was to be found on the south coast of Wales at Swansea Grand Theatre. From 22 May it moved to East Yorkshire and was performed at Hull Grand. The *Hull Daily Mail* review includes the following tantalising snippet:

> "...Stuart Pringle as M. Davigny (the husband of Cecile) *carried on* in a spirited way."

This is the first published indication I could find confirming Stuart Pringle, my father, had entered the theatre business. The Farce was also performed at The New Palace Theatre, Westcliff, 15 July 1918, and no doubt other tour dates.

The First World War came to its end on 11 November 1918, leaving England a very different place from when war began.

*The Purse Strings,* presented by Mrs. Brandon Thomas, produced by Charles Hawtrey, opened at The Garrick Theatre 28 January 1919. Charles Hawtrey was an actor/ manager, who in between successes went bankrupt several times. Following on in 1920 is a provincial tour. My father's life as Stage Manager, or Acting Manager, continues at the New Theatre, Corn Exchange, Boston, a port and market town in Lincolnshire, on the east coast of England, as evidenced by a snippet from Public Notices in the Lincolnshire Standard and Boston Guardian, 1 May 1920:

> "*The Purse Strings*, a comedy in four Acts, by Bernard Parry. The play is produced by Charles Hawtrey. Acting Manager, Stuart Pringle. Stage Manager, Fred Emery."

*The Girl from Ciro's* crops up again at The Brixton Theatre, London, as reported in *The Era* newspaper on 22 Oct 1919:

> "Other parts are effectively rendered by Miss Mona Kinsman, Mr. James Mason, Mr. Stuart Pringle and Miss Geraldine Verner."

This valuable snippet provides further evidence of my father's involvement in stage productions and there is an addition to the company providing a vital connection between my father, Mr. Stuart Pringle age 22, and his mother Miss Geraldine Verner, now age 42. Both are appearing in the same production.

The *Stage* newspaper of 2 Dec 1920 finds my father and his mother working together again in *The Girl from Ciro's,* this time in Kennington, London.

> "…Madame Charcot, who keeps the queer hotel for wives separated from their husbands' and Madame Bru, are made the most of by Miss Geraldine Verner and Miss Enid Dare. Mabel Ray, Sybil Hammersley, Mr. Stuart Pringle, and Mr. E. Montbeau, help materially as three servants and a gendarme."

# CHAPTER FOUR: WWI

*The Stage* newspaper on 13 January 1921 reviews Leslie Kyle's production of *The Girl from Ciro's* playing at Crewe in the county of Cheshire:

> "...Renée is charmingly portrayed by Mabel Ray, as was also the Madame Charcot of Geraldine Verner. Antoine is played by Stuart Pringle, the Acting Manager for the company. The play is well mounted. There is one performance nightly, and a matinee is announced."

When I read these reports, I realise Geraldine Verner now 44, must have bewitched many that watched her since she first trod the boards at 6 years old, accompanied by her father. She had obviously bewitched John Charles! I can't help wondering if any other romance touched her life. With a young son to bring up mostly in secret, it probably didn't. I feel sad that an indiscretion so young in life might have denied her the real pleasure and happiness of a long-lasting marriage with someone she really loved. I will never know. She must have slipped out the stage door one last time never to return. I can find no other mention of stage appearances for Geraldine Verner or her son Stuart Pringle in the newspaper archives after 1921. There was a bond between them that made them inseparable and throughout my fathers' life, his mother was never very far away. It wouldn't have done her career in the theatre any good to have a son, Stuart Pringle became her brother. This subterfuge continued throughout my father's life. My mother was never told the truth, and neither was I. As I grew up, I always believed Aunty Gerry was my father's sister.

Her stage name put to bed, Aunty Gerry/Ellen Pringle became a seamstress and learned to make lampshades out of wonderful heavy brocade silk, and very good at it she was too. As a boy, I remember her legs pumping away working her Singer sewing machine in a treadle stand in the living room of her self-contained flat consisting of a bedroom, kitchen, and bathroom, on the first floor at 15 Marlborough Road, Richmond, where I grew up.

When dark days were upon us and my father and I were forced to leave Richmond, Aunty Gerry was forced to pack up her lampshade business. She sold her sewing machine. This upheaval led to a stroke and she went into hospital and then a nursing home. After disappearing out of my life for nearly a year she joined us at Broadstairs in Kent. Her illness had taken its toll. She had suddenly become a very old and sad old woman who I would see sitting on a balcony at the Dutch Tea House staring vacantly at the sea as the hours went slowly by.

My father's mother, Aunty Gerry/Ellen Pringle, died on 2 December 1966, at Hill House hospital, Minster, Kent. On the death certificate, it states she was 92: Widow of John Charles Stuart-Pringle, a Schoolmaster.

# Chapter Five – Donald Stuart

I have no idea why my father's career as an acting stage manager terminated so abruptly during 1921. London was a tough place between the two world wars. Britain's economic fortunes were in relative decline. Over the next three years, my father frequently found himself homeless, down-and-out in London, collecting dog-ends from the gutters, opening them up, and cramming the tobacco into a clay pipe. He was a serious smoker all his life, unable to resist the compulsion to smoke. I can testify six pipes and forty cigarettes a day was not unusual.

During this down-and-out period in London, he obtained lodgings in a house of crooks, including a fence and a bag snatcher. He describes his life as going from bad to worse during this time. To appease his timid landlady, he sat up all night guarding the body of a dead lodger in his bed. She was terrified the dead lodger would wake up! In return for this gesture, he was absolved from the cost of board and living for the week, which was just as well because he couldn't have paid for it anyway.

He managed to get a job with a firm of ice merchants in Billingsgate. He used to get up at 4 o'clock in the morning and hump ice about until midday. He remarked:

> "I do not say that the pen is mightier than the ice-tweezers, but I found it easier to manipulate."

In the afternoons he designed advertising posters for ice cream for the same firm. He also found work as an artist designing magazine covers and calendars. He was compelled to become a pavement artist and told me he was interviewed and filmed while doing this. He became an accomplished watercolour artist and also worked in oils. I don't have any doubts that if he had chosen to be a full-time professional artist, he would have been a successful one.

* * *

Out of work again, my father was reduced to sleeping in Kings Cross Station, but not for long. The pre-war explosion in nightclub popularity arrived. Helped by an actor friend, he turned to producing cabarets in London's leading nightclubs. During this nightclub boom, earning up to £200 a week, he encountered some very shady people including the Sabini race gang.

Charles 'Darby' Sabini (born Ottavio Handley 1888–1950) was a criminal born in London of mixed Italian and English parentage and leader of the Sabinis. He was king of the racecourse gangs that dominated the London underworld with racecourse protection rackets operated against bookmakers and racecourses throughout the south of England for much of the early twentieth century. His gang was also involved in a range of criminal activities including extortion, theft, as well as operating several nightclubs. Sicilian gunmen were imported in addition to local criminals. Vicious brawls spread throughout London as a gang called the Elephant Boys fought the Sabini gang for a slice of the action. These cockney Capones ran organized crime in London between the wars. The members were also notorious for razor attacks.

At his peak, Sabini had extensive police and political connections, including judges, politicians, and police officials. In 1926 Sabini was declared bankrupt and moved to Brighton using his mother's maiden name, calling himself Fred Handley. He established a similar racket there until his arrest at the Greyhound Stadium at Hove in April 1940. He was interned as an enemy alien on the Isle of Man. He was immortalized as the gangster Colleoni in Graham Greene's novel *Brighton Rock* and appears as Darby Sabini in the epic television series *Peaky Blinders*.

This colourful background must have helped fuel the inspiration for my father's thrillers to come. He witnessed a gang razor fight. Gang women, when drunk, sparred with broken champagne glasses! He helped disguise a man who was marked for death after splitting against his gang. He was introduced to the king of cocaine traffickers. He once shook hands and said *goodnight* to a man who was knifed in the back half-an-hour later by rival gangsters! The nightclub boom eventually died. A revue flopped. He was broke, homeless on the streets once more.

\* \* \*

During the nightclub boom, which operated in the St. Giles area, my father met his first wife, Patricia Sayles. I have no idea how my father met

Patricia or why he left his theatre career. The marriage records show that between April and June 1923 John Robert Stuart Pringle now 26 married Patricia Sayles, born 28 February 1900, in the district of St. Giles, London.

I believe Pat, as he referred to her, was a *house model* for the famous House of Worth, who pioneered fashion shows, employing in-house mannequins. She must have been very beautiful as a young woman, because when I met her many years later in her seventies, she was still beautiful, tall and willowy, still with a good figure, a delicate face, and a sparkling sense of humour.

The role of the *house model* began to be clearly defined in the mid-19th century when Charles Frederick Worth (1825-1895) gained a reputation for showing his designs to prospective clients upon live models. Haute Couture, long dominated by the French, owes its inception to Charles Frederick Worth, who created the concept with his *House of Worth* he founded in the 1850s and grew into a huge global organization. He was the first person to use live models instead of mannequins and was the pioneer of the *fashion show*. When Worth died in 1895, his two French-born sons took over the business. By the 1920s, it was standard practice for fashion houses to employ in-house mannequins though house models remained anonymous and poorly paid until the late 1950s. Such a profession was considered normal enough to be the job of the heroine of the 1927 Alfred Hitchcock film *The Lodger*.

Where they lived as a married couple, what happened when the nightclub boom died, and how he ended up broke back on the street, I don't know. My father was very secretive about these things and avoided discussing them. I assume his wife went to live with her parents for a while, or maybe there was a temporary breakup. Whatever the reason, nights sleeping rough on the embankment inspired him to write *The Clue of the Second Tooth* in pencil on scraps of paper.

My father took his scrappy manuscript to George Heber Hamilton Teed, now recognised as probably the greatest of all pre-war Blake authors. Teed took it to the editor, Leonard Pratt. Pratt bought the story straight away, demanding it be typewritten, and gave my father £20 on account of £70 for it. That was worth quite a bit

37

in those days. My father said it made him feel like a millionaire! He told the editor to deduct the cost of typing the manuscript from his fee. When he received £70, less his advance and the cost of typing, he said he had never recaptured the thrill of that moment. It seemed that he had learned to transfer his own bitter experiences of *life in the raw* to an enthralled audience hungry for detective fiction.

The story appeared in the *Sexton Blake Library* No 105, on 31 August 1927. No author's name is credited as was the norm. The story was published by The Amalgamated Press price 4d. The Illustrator was Arthur Jones. Here is a vivid description of Sexton Blake from the story:

> "Sexton Blake's keen, grey eyes, that never missed the slightest detail, swept the place in a swift, comprehensive glance. The habitual, slightly bored, expression which he usually possessed, had given place to one of intense virility. His well-chiselled nostrils quivered, like a hound on the scent, and his whole personality radiated an atmosphere of intense alertness. Those people who only knew the dreamer of Baker Street would have witnessed a revelation if they could have seen Sexton Blake at work."

Sexton Blake is one of the most written about characters in the English language. He first appeared in 1893 in The Halfpenny Marvel, conveniently filling the gap that followed the death of Mr. Sherlock Holmes when Arthur Conan Doyle killed him off at the Reichenbach Falls in the December 1893 issue of The Strand magazine. Wasting no time, the Halfpenny Marvel published a story called *The Missing Millionaire* written by a jobbing writer, Harry Blyth, under the pen-name Hal Meredeth that same year. The story introduced a character that came to be disparaged as *the office-boy's Sherlock Holmes* or *the poor man's Sherlock Holmes*. Despite these disparagements, Sexton Blake was often thought to be more like Sherlock Holmes than Holmes. Sexton Blake soon outgrew his influences and is said to have had even more admirers than Sherlock Holmes. It was no coincidence that Sexton Blake also lived on Baker Street in London. The golden age of the story papers coincided with Blake's golden age. He became far more action-oriented than Holmes and duelled with a variety of memorable enemies, opium smugglers, bandit chiefs and the Kaiser! For the greater part of the 20th Century, Blake was a household name and a publishing phenomenon, starring in nearly five thousand stories written by over two hundred authors circulating 600,000 copies a month. Today, in the age of the internet, many websites are devoted to preserving the magazine collections and they are regularly traded.

In the 1920s and 1930s, Blake took on near legend proportions in England and in some parts of what was then the Empire. The stories were published by Amalgamated Press, a newspaper and magazine publishing company founded by journalist and entrepreneur Alfred Harmsworth in 1901, gathering his many publishing ventures together under one banner. Alfred Harmsworth, 1st Viscount Northcliffe (1865-1922), was a British newspaper and publishing magnate and pioneer of tabloid journalism. In May 1896 he began publishing the *Daily Mail* in London and in 1903 the *Daily Mirror*. In 1905 he rescued *The Observer* newspaper. In 1908 he rescued *The Times* and acquired *The Sunday Times*. He was a man of great influence, so much so, that during the First World War, Germany sent a warship to shell his Kent home in an attempt to assassinate him for anti-German propaganda.

Amalgamated Press set out to eradicate what was then seen as the corrupting influence of the Dime Novel or Penny Dreadful—a cheaper alternative to mainstream fictional part-works, such as those by Charles Dickens for working-class adults (which cost twelve pennies). 'Penny Dreadfuls' were stories usually filled with violent adventure or crime and issued in installments.

Amalgamated Press published enormously successful magazines like *The Thriller, Union Jack, Detective Weekly, and Sexton Blake Weekly*, for the price of one half-penny, to provide higher quality stories. These publications would not have been possible if it were not for the vastly increased mechanisation of printing and distribution but depended on one other vital necessity; *more people could read.* The lower classes were becoming more literate due to improved education during the Victorian period and provided a mass readership. Here was a new ready and waiting market that demanded entertainment, and lots of it.

G.K. Chesterton famously said:

"My taste is for the sensational novel, the detective story, the story about death, robbery and secret societies; a taste which I share in common with the bulk at least of the male population of this world. There was a time in my own melodramatic boyhood when I became quite fastidious in this respect. I would look at the first chapter of any new novel as a final test of its merits. If there was a murdered man under the sofa in the first chapter, I read the story."

The key persons involved at Amalgamated Press across thirty years from 1904–1934 were three editors: W.H. Back, Leonard Pratt, and Harold Twyman. The 200 or so writers feeding various magazines included: Edgar Wallace, Leslie Charteris, Sax Rohmer, Margery Allingham, John Creasy, Peter Cheyney, Gwyn Evans, G.H. Teed, Rex Hardinge, Anthony Skene, Anthony Parsons, Robert Murray, Pierre Quiroule, Gordon Shaw, Edwy Searles Brooks, William Murray Graydon... and of course John Robert Stuart Pringle writing as Donald Stuart and *not just writing as Donald Stuart*; he became Donald Stuart. He opened a bank account in the name of Donald Stuart and brought the shutters down on his old life. His birth name was kept hidden and only used for legal reasons.

He rented a flat in Piccadilly. I have no idea if his wife Pat returned from exile to join him, or what name she called him. John? Don? Did she become Patricia Stuart or remain Patricia Pringle? Annoyingly, I have not discovered any means of answering these questions. Pat seems to flit in and out of my father's life like a will-o'-the-wisp. He eventually moved to 7 Brunswick Square, London WC with Pat, for certain, as I have a letter written on her personal headed paper.

Donald Stuart began writing regularly for The Sexton Blake Library, hungry to capitalise on the new career opportunity that had opened for him after writing *The Clue of the Second Tooth*. He wrote four titles in 1928, all attributed to an anonymous author, as Amalgamated Press did not credit authors until June 1930:

The Box of Doom (125 January 1928) by Anon.
The Riddle of the Phantom Plague (143 May 1928) by Anon.
The Mystery of Sherwood Towers (152 July 1928) by Anon.
The Mystery of the Phantom Blackmailer (157 September 1928) by Anon.

# CHAPTER FIVE: DONALD STUART

From 1912 Amalgamated Press was based in Fleetway House in Farringdon Street in London. In 1959 the name of the company was changed from Amalgamated Press to Fleetway Publications when the Mirror group acquired it. The Sexton Blake library eventually closed in 1964, but Blake lived on through radio and television. Many adventures were illustrated by Eric Parker.

It was Sexton Blake who was important as far as Amalgamated Press were concerned, not the authors. Many contemporaries, like my father's friend Leslie Charteris, realised they would never achieve individuality and fame unless they created their own characters and eventually stopped writing Blakes for that reason. Charteris created *The Saint* and cleaned up.

During 1929 and 1930, Donald Stuart continues to write Sexton Blake yarns for The Amalgamated press with the following titles:

The Vanishing Death (180 February 1929) anon.
The Silent Slayer (195 June 1929) by Anon.
The Fatal Manuscript (198 July 1929) by Anon.
The Black Skull (217 December 1929) by Anon.
The Secret of the Vault (227 February 1930) by Anon.
The Crime of Four (237 May 1930) by Anon.
The Death Card (255 September 1930) by Donald Stuart.
The Fence's Victim (266 Dec 1930) by Donald Stuart.

He took a short break during 1928 from writing Sexton Blake stories to write his first stage play, no doubt harking back to his theatrical roots. It was called *The Shadow* and was a comedy thriller, produced by Mr. Nicholas Hannen at the Embassy Theatre in London. It featured distinguished comedian Bert Coote and his company.

The inhabitants of the Police Commissioner's eerie mansion in London are being killed one by one by a hooded shadowy blackmailer, dressed in black, who seems to have no substance, darting through the numerous secret passages to appear like a shadow. It is up to Scotland Yard to stop the killings and expose the identity of the elusive killer. Bert Coote plays a writer of crook stories, who wishes to track down the elusive murderer with the aid of a pipe and a violin. This amateur detective, and the Commissioner's daughter, unmask the culprit. The press reviews were unanimously good.

"There is much that is reminiscent of *The Terror* in this new thriller only Mr. Stuart has been more successful in guarding the identity of his master crook than Mr. Wallace was. Viewed from every angle "The Shadow" is a very ingenious play, and, strangely enough the audience derives far more thrill from the play itself than all the accessories, dead bodies, pistol shots, and the like."

*The Evening News* stated:

"*The Shadow* by Donald Stuart, produced at the Embassy Theatre last night was gold entertainment, and it provides a wonderful part for Bert Coote, who stutters, stammers, and muddles his way along in his own delightful, comical way. He is better than ever."

*The Evening Standard* enthused:

"*The Shadow* is a successful thriller. It genuinely rivets the whole attention of a whole audience for a whole evening. This is entertainment… Mr. Donald Stuart wrote his play with a clear head and a distinct sense of the stage. The play lacks the shoddy horrors and fantastic unrealities of many would be thrillers."

*The Shadow* was made into a film in 1933. It was published as a novel by Wright & Brown in 1934 and rewritten as *Danger at Westways* for the Sexton Blake Library, number 645, in November 1938.

I once accused my father of writing stories that were superficial and lacked depth of character depriving them of literary value. He replied that his stories were thrillers, each chapter with a suspenseful ending enticing the reader to press on. There wasn't time for pages of character description. That sort of detail would slow up the pace. My father didn't want his readers to stop and think about his characters too much. He was far more interested in the puzzle of an impossible murder, or the identity of a master criminal, and didn't want character studies to hold up the action. This resulted in characters that by necessity appeared two-dimensional. Sinister figures lurked everywhere. Despite gruesome murders and diabolic situations, the stories are somewhat innocent in nature by today's standards. Like Wallace, he worked out a bare-bones plot, decided which of his characters would take the lead, and forged

## CHAPTER FIVE: DONALD STUART

ahead, letting the story take on a life of its own plunging his characters into seemingly impossible situations he then revelled in getting them out of. He was revealing the story to himself as well as his reader.

# Chapter Six – Sexton Blake

The Great Depression of 1929-32 broke out at a time when the United Kingdom was still recovering from the effects of the First World War. It had its origins in the global Great Depression triggered by the October 1929 Stock Market Crash in New York. A slow economic recovery led to a fall in unemployment from 1933 onwards. Though the effects of this recession were uneven, spending money on entertainment was out of the question for most people. The year 1930 was a tough time to carry on business and called for imaginative and inexpensive forms of entertainment. During that year, Donald Stuart was not only writing for the Amalgamated Press but turning his attention back to the Theatre which was in his blood. He was as much a showman as a writer which, as I have mentioned, was a legacy from his grandfather Robert Wallace. This showmanship manifested itself not only in theatre productions but later in his designs and execution of firework displays as a pastime.

No doubt full of confidence in his own infallibility, he began preparations for a second stage production that capitalized on his experience writing for the Amalgamated Press, and the success of *The Shadow*. It was titled *Sexton Blake* and was a bold detective melodrama with elaborate and expensive stage effects. He ambitiously formed his own production company *Donald Stuart Productions Limited* to produce it. This newly formed syndicate was a private company registered on 5 June 1930 with an office at 27 Shaftsbury Avenue, in London's West End. The Directors were D. Stuart of 7 Brunswick Square WC, and W. R. De La Cour Beamish of 3 More's Garden, Cheyne Walk, London SW3.

The Prince Edward Theatre, Old Compton Street, London W1, an area to be known as the Latin Quarter, and then simply Soho, was named after the Prince of Wales. The theatre opened on 3 April 1930, with a popular show in Broadway, a musical called *Rio Rita* by Harry Tierney and presented by Siegfried. The musical closed after only 59 performances. This disaster was followed by *Sexton Blake*.

# CHAPTER SIX: SEXTON BLAKE

The Prince Edward Theatre, doomed to failure, didn't make money. In 1935, the business consortium that ran the French Casino in New York saw an opportunity to open a London branch and bought the venue for £25,000. They immediately began renovations to turn the venue into a magnificent state-of-the-art restaurant-cabaret. The building reopened on 2 April 1936 as The London Casino and was a great success.

*Sexton Blake* opened on Thursday, 18 September 1930. It was hoped the production would inaugurate a policy of drama at the Prince Edward Theatre, but this was not to be. *Sexton Blake* did not produce a successful run. The play was imaginative but far from inexpensive and would lead to my father's financial ruin. An announcement in *The Stage* newspaper 25 September 1930 stated:

> "A debenture dated 13 September 1930 was taken out to secure £1000, charged on the company's property, present and future, including uncalled capital. Holder: Irene Margolionth, 6, Carlton Mansions, York Buildings, Adelphi, W.C.2."

Sexton Blake was portrayed by the British actor Arthur Wontner opposite Eva Gray the leading lady, a beautiful and distressed heroine, with John Roderick as Tinker. Pedro the Bloodhound posed a casting problem. London was searched in vain for a suitable canine actor. Bloodhounds are not only rare but very nervous except with people they know. Pedro was eventually found in Brighton, but proved to suffer from stage fright, running into the orchestra pit twice in one week.

The action of the play was continuous. There were 4 acts and 14 scenes.

Act One begins outside the murder victim's house, 18a Lowndes Square. After some scene setting, the curtains whisk shut, the 'exterior' is carried off by the stagehands, and the curtains slide apart to reveal Sir John Raeburn's bedroom with the body of Sir John stretched out on the bed, a knife sticking out of his back!

An investigation begins by Detective Inspector Coutts played by David Hawthorne. There is a butler called Creek and Paul Cairns the victim's secretary, played by Wilfred Babbage, who is evasive and becomes a prime suspect. A young reporter is thrown into the mix called Leslie Waring, played by Arthur Macrae. The act finished outside 18a Lowndes Square again.

DONALD STUART
*The Author*

Act Two begins in Sexton Blake's consulting room, Baker Street W1. Mr Midnight is setting a deadly booby trap while the detective, in turn, lays out bait for the master criminal. Even though the drama is increasing, there's still room for Mrs. Bardell, played by Dora Gregory, to give a cameo performance. Her malapropisms must have been fun for the actress who played her: *There's a young lady, Sir, what wants to insult you proficiently!* Tension builds with the audience knowing that Blake is in great danger while he remains oblivious to the fact. The curtain came down just as Blake trips the booby trap, and a bomb explodes. The audience leapt out of their seats as Sexton Blake's consulting room is blown to bits in front of their eyes. Remember, my father's upbringing included watching Brock's Crystal Palace firework displays. It was obviously paying off. He loved explosions!

*The Daily Telegraph*, 19 September 1930, commented:

> "It is all very exciting. There is not a scene in which some deed of violence is not committed; and one of these—the 'dynamite' explosion in Blake's consulting room—is as 'realistic' an effect as we can remember. The whole theatre seems to shake with the detonation and the crash of walls and furniture is terrific."

Act Three begins in the cellar of an empty house. The Midnight gang has gathered. Their leader, his face hidden by a cloak, hat, and scarf, arrives dragging the tied and gagged heroine behind him. Tinker also gets captured. Blake, disguised as one of Midnight's henchmen, comes to the rescue.

With the gang broken up and in custody, Act Four, the final act,

46

again set in Blake's consulting room, brings the two main protagonists together for a last duel. Blake unknowingly swallows poison and the villain makes his getaway while the detective lies writhing on the floor. He's saved by Tinker. They set off in pursuit of Midnight, who escapes in a racing car. These events lead up to a classical climax of melodrama. Midnight tries to evade capture by driving his racing car through Sunningvale level crossing and meets a nasty end as his car smashes into a train!

The production required elaborate and expensive stage effects, including the bomb explosion, and the car smashing into the train at the level crossing. The production also featured an abduction in a real taxicab driving down Baker Street followed by a real motorcycle. There were three dress rehearsals to get all this technically *right on the night*. Taxi drivers were invited to the first dress rehearsal. Detectives from Scotland Yard were invited to the second.

The reviews were not bad, despite a member of the cast missing. One very important actor failed to appear on the first night. Pedro the bloodhound was absent.

The *Daily Herald* commented:

> "Mr. Donald Stuart, the author, explained that Pedro was only a young bloodhound unused to the ways of the stage and that every time he was brought on to the boards, he promptly jumped into the orchestra pit!"

The *Daily Mail* commented:

> "*Mr. Midnight*, the super-criminal of the story, is nothing if not a hard worker. Before one has had time to look around, he has blackmailed and murdered a baronet, abducted the baronet's daughter, poisoned Sexton Blake's coffee, and blown a hole in his consulting room - all this and a deal more before he gets himself blown to smithereens in a crash at the Sunningvale level crossing."

The production was all very exciting but, as ever, the critics try to compare popular entertainment with highbrow culture. This is not Jane Austen or Shakespeare and never intended to be. Snide comments, like those from the *Daily Express*, are to be expected, but miss the point:

"Poison, murder, cellars, and even an unintentional explosion behind the scenes were all there. It seems a pity to put this play on at the end rather than at the beginning of the school holidays."

The evening was supposed to be exciting and fun. Not without humour. It was envisaged as an entertaining escape from the reality of the depression. Judging from the many positive comments it was exactly that. The Times thought the *stunning crash of the bomb* was the plays great moment and the train disaster an anti-climax.

*The Times* covers itself stuffily by saying:

"Those whom it fails to thrill may be amused at it."

Most reviews are at best unsure how to deal with the production, but most concede the play is good unpretentious fun. That is exactly what it was intended to be. Unpretentious fun is what *The Thriller* and *Detective Weekly* were intended to be. They teased the reader, until they were desperate to read what happens next, usually in a frenzy of anticipation. This of course is the purpose of thrillers and pulp fiction.

Arch criminals needed to be presented properly. We had to fear them. In those days to fear them they were portrayed as sinister, hunchbacked, wearing a long coat of black oilskin, a slouched hat, their faces hidden, their eyes glittering...

In an interview, Donald Stuart provides an answer to why he left the theatre or, more precisely, the theatre left him. He said that he read the earlier Sexton Blake stories when he was a boy and when his failure to become a successful actor led him hungry to the Embankment his mind went back to Sexton Blake, his daring and his skill. He has been writing them at a furious rate ever since.

Arthur Wontner also resembled the fictitious Sherlock Holmes. He portrayed Holmes in five films from 1931 to 1937. He came to the filmmakers' attention because he was seen playing Blake at The Prince Edward Theatre.

The play later appeared in novel form as *Mr. Midnight* - in *The Story of the Play* in the *Union Jack* 1422, 17 January 1931, with a photograph of Arthur Wontner on the cover. The story was rehashed as *The Midnight Men* by Nigel Vane 1936 and *The Shadow Men* by Gerald Verner 1961. A hardback book of the same *Union Jack* title was published as *Mr. Midnight* by Wright & Brown in 1953 but bears no relation to the play.

A 78rpm record (HMV C2044) was released of *Murder on the Portsmouth Road*, an eight-minute adventure written by Donald Stuart with Arthur Wontner reprising his role as Blake. The record valiantly attempted to create the right atmosphere in the short time allowed with an unusual *thunder* sound effect!

My father's foray into theatrical production was likely a financial disaster on account of the unusually high production cost of building and operating the elaborate special effects. These would have required a long run to recoup, coupled with the absence of the vast Sexton Blake readership, which could have packed the theatre for a long run, but simply couldn't afford to go there. A facetious press didn't help. The audience was probably too sophisticated for a sensational action play of this nature, which unlike a film with fast cuts from one scene to another, was slowed down by long elaborate scene changes. I suspect the audience wanted to see an unfolding and clever detection of a puzzling mystery in the Sherlock Holmes tradition, not a production in the spirit of pulp fiction and a foretaste of James Bond.

Attempting to recoup some of the costs the production went on tour opening 24 November 1930, at the Lyceum, Sheffield in the county of South Yorkshire. It was well received, but probably went little way in reducing the mountain of debt that had accumulated.

It was to be a painful lesson learned. *Sexton Blake* did not recoup its costs. A receiving order is an order of the court in England or Wales placing the person's assets under the control of the official receiver, pending formal bankruptcy proceedings. On 1 December 1930, such an order was made against Donald Stuart (who had presumably personally guaranteed some of the costs of the production) on a petition filed 8 October 1930. The name on the order was John Robert Stuart Pringle, known and described in the Receiving Order as Donald Stuart. The address given was 7, Brunswick Square, London W.C.1.

I have no idea what arrangements were made for paying off this bankruptcy order. It stalked him for 26 years. He was not discharged from the bankruptcy until 11 Aug 1956.

At the time of this financial disaster, my father picked himself up off the stage and, as Donald Stuart, continued writing Sexton Blake yarns for Amalgamated Press at a pace in an attempt to pay off some of the debt.

The Hooded Raider (278 March 1931)
The Next Victim (286 May 1931)
The Terror of Lonely Tor (302 September 1931)
The Garden City Crime (314 December 1931)
Dead Man's Secret (322 February 1932)
The Squealer's Secret (334 May 1932)
The Embankment Crime (341 July 1932)
The Case of the Missing Estate Agent (350 September 1932)
The Secret of Seven (363 December 1932)

Donald Stuart was also established writing for *Union Jack* which early in 1933 changed into *Detective Weekly*.

The Green Jester (1379 March 1930)
Mister Midnight (1422 January 1931)
The Witches Moon (1488 April 1932)
The Crimson Smile (1523 December 1932)

On 26 March 1932, the editor announced a competition and set out an end of story situation six of their top authors were invited to lead up to:

A heart failure victim Alfred Mowbray Proud, and Sexton Blake are unconscious on top of an empty tramcar in a North London tram depot. Clues are a broken window; a rolled-up banner on the floor; and a fireman's helmet!

The authors were required to come up with their explanation of what had happened. The one who came up with the best solution leading to the ending of the tale would win the competition. They were Gwyn Evans, Donald Stuart, Gilbert Chester (H. H. Clifford Gibbons), Anthony Skene (George N. Philips), G.H. Teed and Robert Murray (Robert Murray Graydon) who had to drop out due to illness. He was replaced by Edwy Searles Brooks, who went on to write the best solution to this now famous *Proud tram* series called *The Mystery of Blind Luke*. The prize was a Pedigree Bloodhound or ten pounds in cash!

My father's contribution, the fourth *Proud tram* story, appeared on 23 April 1932, Issue 1,488. In my father's story Alfred Proud is a jewel robber, the brains behind a two-man partnership that goes well until the arrival of Sexton Blake. The magazine announced my father's contribution on 16 April 1932:

> "Next week, the author of such well-remembered successes as *The Green Jester*, and *Mr. Midnight*, is going to offer an entirely different explanation, of how Alfred Mowbray Proud and Sexton Blake came to be aboard that tram at Wood End. His yarn begins with a B.B.C, broadcast, an SOS for a missing man who vanishes while going to post a letter—and progresses from one sinister and mysterious situation to another, until—presto!—the inexplicable events fall into shape, and hurry to the swift climax you've been expecting and looking for all along, but which seemed to get more and more unlikely all the time. Donald can weave a good plot and clothe it in the words of the right thrill and suspense so that there's nothing else on earth that matters while you're reading them. This series, containing six of the finest stories of six of the most popular authors, is one that gets your interest without fail. See that your newsagent has your order, then, ready for next week, when Donald Stuart tells us the story of that derelict, abandoned ruin of an inn, known as *The Witches Moon.*"

*The Witches Moon* was revised and published as a novel by Wright & Brown in 1938, featuring my father's fat detective Mr. Budd and his sidekick the lugubrious Sergeant Leek. This revised version also *begins with a B.B.C, broadcast, an SOS for a missing man*, Mr. Dench, who has left his house on a wet September night to post a letter and vanishes. A fortnight later his dead body is found in a tunnel a few miles away. He has been brutally murdered. Called in to investigate, Superintendent Robert Budd soon realized that Dench hadn't planned to disappear—dressed as he had been, he wouldn't have got far without attracting attention. But it was not until he had found the secret of the fireman's helmet, the poetic pickpocket, and the Witches' Moon that he discovered why Mr. Dench— and several other people—had been murdered...

# PLOTS AND GUNPOWDER

\* \* \*

The death of Edgar Wallace from diabetes in February 1932 must have been a sad moment for my father and a large proportion of the country's population. The following year my father dedicated his novel *Phantom Hollow* to *Mrs. Edgar Wallace*. Edgar Wallace's second wife Violet, surviving him eighteen months, died April 1933 at the age of 33.

*The Sunday Mail* of June 1932 reported:

> "There is still much heated discussion as to who is likely to fill Edgar Wallace's shoes as the most prolific writer of the moment. Personally, I am inclined to vote for Mr. Donald Stuart, playwright and author, whose ingenious crime stories, together with the startling rapidity with which they are turned out has already attracted considerable notice. Recently he was asked by a Hollywood concern to write a full-length producer's scenario for a mystery film. The usual time allowed for a task of this nature is six weeks or over; Mr. Stuart took just four days. A record, that, I think!"

*The Star* revealed on 29 August 1932:

> "Two of Edgar Wallace's books, *The Man from Morocco* and *King by Night*, have been dramatized by Mr. Donald Stuart, one of our younger playwrights, and negotiations are proceeding for a theatre. Mr. Stuart never met Edgar Wallace. "But," he explained to The Star, "Wallace was always a hero of mine, and I was a great admirer of his work." Mrs. Wallace left the work entirely to Mr. Stuart and offered no suggestions. "It was not easy," said Mr. Stuart, "for both books were very long, with involved plots. But I have taken all the meat out of them, and have stuck closely to the stories, though I have had to put in a good deal not in the books."

What happened to these plays? Edgar Wallace had amassed massive debts, many to racing bookies. Although the large royalties from his greatly popular works allowed the estate to be settled within two years, the death of his wife, who left a share of the Wallace estate to her daughter Penelope (1923–1997) must have resulted in complex probate

52

procedures that may have scuppered any preproduction of the plays. Obviously, the plays were never produced, or there would be a public record. The article in The Star implies they were written and completed. The receiving order following *Sexton Blake* is likely to have tarnished my father's reputation, rendering him untouchable to investors and no doubt reducing any appetite he may have had to venture on stage again for a while. I have never seen any Wallace manuscripts or heard him mention them. They have vanished without a trace.

* * *

It was in 1932, that Donald Stuart, retaining his home in London at 7, Brunswick-square, acquired a second home at Thames Ditton with a garden that went down to the river complete with a mooring. The address was *Carisholme*, River Bank, Thames Ditton, Surrey, with a rather quaint telephone number. I can almost hear him answering the telephone: "Emberbrook 1506." *Emberbrook* was named after the River Ember, which flows close to *River Bank* into the River Thames, upriver from Molesey Lock.

By Christmas he decided to throw a party. It was to be no ordinary party! He decided to host this party in an old haunted country manor house that was originally built by Charles II, for Nell Gwyn. This sounds like the perfect opening for one of his thriller novels, and indeed, during the event, a murder *was* committed!

He arranged for about twenty guests to attend a three-day bash during which they had to track down the murderer who would turn out to be one of *them*, by following carefully prepared clues in the form of gruesome bloodstains, finger-prints, *queer* happenings, plus a ghost—that will be seen flitting along the panelled corridors at midnight on Christmas Eve—at the exact moment of the murder!

At some point, after moving to *Carisholme* my father bought a river cruiser which he moored at the bottom of his garden. He preferred Thames Ditton to London. It was a tranquil place where he could write his stories in peace and quiet, spending his spare time motor boating on the River Thames. He also had a dog called Rex, to whom he dedicated his 1936 novel *The Ghost Man: To the memory of Rex who used to lie beside my chair while I worked.* His love of the river resonates in a supernatural short story he wrote, called *The Weir*, and the full-length thriller *The River Men* published by Wright & Brown in 1936. He would deliver manuscripts by taking his boat downriver to London, moor up at Lambeth Pier, and hand over a manuscript to a representative from the publisher.

By 1933, my father was also writing at full pelt for *Detective Weekly* and *The Thriller* whilst keeping up a good stable of yarns for *The Sexton Blake Library*. Stories were emerging thick and fast. Everything was sinister, grim, or queer! Mood and atmosphere were everything. Every story was crammed with thrills and surprises, and they moved at a pace, rollicking along like a rollercoaster.

Donald Stuart wrote two Sexton Blake Christmas stories for *Detective Weekly;* the first was *The Clue of the Crimson Snow* in 1933. The following year he wrote *The Christmas Card Crime*. This story opened with Blake, Tinker, and a group waiting for a train on Bodmin Station to take them to St. Merryan, a little Cornish Village nestling in the moors. It is snowing heavily, and the platform beyond the shelter is covered with a thick layer of snow which is gradually growing deeper. They board the train, but after a while, a heavy fall of snow from the walls of the cutting ahead, blocks the line. The party get off the train and they set off on a midnight hike down the snow-covered track back to Moorland Halt, the last station the train stopped at a mile or so back. A dramatic event occurs while all this is going on involving a girl, a rope, and a bridge. Later, cutting 2300 words of the opening scene describing the train and railway track, he revised the story to become *The Chained Man* published as part of an anthology published by Faber and Faber in 1936, *My Most Exciting Story*.

Donald Stuart's output was prodigious. I get a sense of strong financial pressure behind this incredible output. I suspect, a large amount of monies received went to the official receiver.

This may well be one of the reasons why, though Donald Stuart was to continue writing for *The Sexton Blake Library*, he sought an outlet for his stories in hardback form, and possibly a way to channel some money away from the receiver's clutches. This outlet came in the form of a new publishing outfit called Wright & Brown and another change of name.

# CHAPTER SIX: SEXTON BLAKE

He wrote six novels for Wright & Brown as Donald Stuart, *The White Friar* in 1934, followed by *The Man Outside*, and *The Shadow*, all published in the same year. *The Man in The Dark*, *The Valley of Terror*, and *Midnight Murder* followed in 1935.

My father's mother took the stage name Geraldine Verner, perhaps to escape from the aftermath of her relationship with her cousin and the (unwanted) birth of my father. I can't help assuming that my father was also escaping—from the aftermath of Donald Stuart Productions, trying to forget the way *Sexton Blake*, the stage production, had started out so exciting an adventure, but ended up so disappointing, leaving him with a mass of baggage around his neck. He clearly adapted his new name Gerald Verner from his mother's stage name, already familiar to him. I think this change of name was an attempt to bury misfortune and start over.

Whatever the true explanation for his change of name, Donald Stuart was relegated to waiting in the wings, while Gerald Verner took centre stage. When my father changed his name to Gerald Verner his wife followed suit calling herself Patricia Verner and remained so for the rest of her life. That is the name on her death certificate of 1988, which also confirms that she was born Patricia Sayles 28 February 1900. I can find no other record of her birth in England.

# Chapter Seven – Gerald Verner

The Great Depression that ran from 1930 to 1935 began an amazingly prolific period for my father, as his bibliography testifies, lasting right up until the outbreak of WW2.

As Donald Stuart, he was writing for *Union Jack*, *The Thriller*, and *Detective Weekly*. As Gerald Verner, he was writing in parallel for *The Thriller*, *Detective Weekly*, *Thriller Library*, *Thrilling Detective*, and *The Boy's Friend-Bulls Eye Library*. He was about to start writing hardbacks for Wright & Brown, most of which began life as stories for *The Sexton Blake Library*.

His first book for Wright & Brown, *The Embankment Murder* was published in 1933. Originally, it was a *Sexton Blake Library* story by Donald Stuart called *The Clue of the Second Tooth*, number 105 August 1927. It was reprinted as *The Embankment Crime*, number 341 July 1932. This book was swiftly followed by *Alias the Ghost*, *The Black Hunchback*, *Black Skull*, *The Death Play*, *Phantom Hollow*, and *The Next to Die*, all first published from Wright & Brown's 12-14 Red Lion Court, Fleet Street, London E.C.4, address.

His next book *The Squealer* was announced in an advertisement in *The Observer* 15 April 1934, with the Red Lion Court address, as just ready at 7/6d, but in *The Sunday Times* of the same date, the same advertisement is run with a 4 Farringdon Avenue London E.C.4 address, indicating that Wright & Brown were in the process of moving to larger premises. I have not seen a 7/6 true first edition of *The Squealer* and wonder which address it is published under?

My father's output became so prolific that to avoid saturating the market with books under the Gerald Verner banner, he sought a second publisher. There was obviously a limit on just how many books Wright & Brown could accept in one year. That second publisher was to be The Modern Publishing Company for whom he wrote five novels under the pseudonym Derwent Steele and another five under the pseudonym Nigel Vane, while he continued to write as Donald Stuart for Wright & Brown and the Amalgamated Press.

In addition to hardbacks, two paperbacks were printed by Modern Publishing in 1940, *The Man Outside* by Donald Stuart and *Terror Tower* by Gerald Verner, both covers displaying the original G. P. Micklewright

artwork for Wright & Brown. It is interesting to note this link in 1940 between Modern Publishing at 6 Farringdon Avenue, London E.C.4 who occupied premises a stone's throw away from Wright & Brown operating from 4 Farringdon Avenue. Surprisingly little is known about The Modern Publishing Company. It may have been in shared ownership with the newspaper *The News of the World*. The stories were issued in hardback format. The usually red, but sometimes blue, cloth backs of the books bear the boldly impressed black wording *News of the World—For Thrilling Serials by the Best Authors*. Advertisements for various products and services were also carried in the front and rear pages. They had attractive multi-coloured dust jackets and were priced at two shillings. It didn't require much rough handling for the books to fall apart. They were usually then discarded, explaining the rarity of some of the titles today. Overall, the physical quality of the books was poor when compared to the product offered by Wright & Brown, which stood up better to the rough handling they received at the lending libraries. One of the unfortunate circumstances of this programme was the fact that books were literally read to pieces and then destroyed. Many of the libraries had a policy of removing and tossing out the dust jackets of all new arrivals. Good copies of these books with jackets are now very hard to find.

My father wrote a sixth Nigel Vane story, *The Midnight Men,* published in 1936 by a new publisher, Stanley Smith, 59 New Oxford Street London W.C.1. This publisher was very short-lived only publishing books during that year. My father probably tried them out at the suggestion of G. H. Teed, the Amalgamated Press editor and author, who also had a book published by Stanley Smith that year called *Five in Fear.*

*The Midnight Men* was a book based on the Donald Stuart play *Sexton Blake* (September 1930 Prince Edward Theatre) and *Mr. Midnight* the story of the play published in The *Union Jack* 1422 January 1931. In 1961 it was revised as *The Shadow Men* by Gerald Verner.

\* \* \*

1933 saw Donald Stuart's play *The Shadow* (1928 Embassy Theatre) made into a film for United Artists with a screenplay by H. Fowler Mear and Terence Egan.

## CHAPTER SEVEN: GERALD VERNER

A group of people in an old dark house are terrorized by a mysterious hooded figure dressed in black who proceeds to kill them off one by one.

Directed by George Cooper and starring a gifted West End revue artiste Henry Kendall in the role of Reggie Ogden, the film ran for 74mins. This film was described as:

"A typical low budget British quota-quickie comedy thriller, with an unusual amount of entertainment value. Often mistaken for a screen adaptation of the popular American radio series, the British *The Shadow* was actually based on a play by Donald Stuart."

The film is now available through USA outfit *Sinister Cinema* on VHS and DVD format and runs for 1 hour 10 minutes. The film format is Full-Frame (1.33:1) as you would expect. Overall quality is far from perfect, but it is watchable. The Sinister Cinema website lists their transfer as being sourced from a 16mm print. *The Shadow* by Donald Stuart was published in novel form by Wright & Brown in 1934 and in November 1938 was rewritten and published as *Danger at Westways* for Sexton Blake Library, number 645.

Later, in 1933, *The Man Outside* was a screenplay also by H. Fowler Mear from a story by Gerald Verner. It was also directed by George A. Cooper. When bumbling private eye Harry Wainwright investigates a case of stolen jewels, he finds that the police inspector is at the head of the heist. In 1934 this story was published as a novel by Donald Stuart for Wright & Brown and then later in August 1938 rewritten as *The Secret of Moor House* for *Sexton Blake Library*, number 634. In 1964 it was rewritten again as *The Moor House Murders* for Wright & Brown.

Rewriting or rehashing stories was not unusual among Blake writers. They received a one-off fee and took no share in the profits reaped through their work selling in large numbers in England and across the world. They looked to capitalise on their stories as best they could. Pseudonyms were as common as they were confusing.

Republishing *The Thriller* and *Detective Weekly* stories by both Donald Stuart and Gerald Verner as published novels by Wright and Brown was to become the norm, resulting in a complex bibliography, as many of these stories were retitled and locations and the names of the detectives changed. For example, *Guilty but Insane* by Donald Stuart Sexton Blake Lib 385, June 1933 would be *deblaked* to become Trevor Lowe and Arnold White in *The Hangman* 1934,

for which my father *designed and painted* the jacket, one of several he was to invent for Wright & Brown.

\* \* \*

The 22nd of May 1935 saw an announcement in *The Bookseller* that The Prince of Wales has honoured a detective story writer, Gerald Verner by graciously accepting a special Jubilee edition of fifteen of his novels. The set has been printed on special paper and bound in Jubilee blue with gilt lettering on the spine. The *National News Agent* 11 May 1935, wrote:

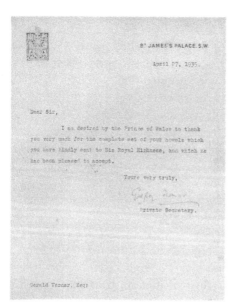

"Gerald Verner is a proud man these days and, if it were not for his natural modesty, his size in hats would have to be increased. Why? The Prince of Wales admires his mystery thrillers and has accepted the presentation of a complete set of them. It is being prepared for him, printed on special paper, bound in Jubilee blue with gilt lettering along the spine. This is the sort of appreciation that not only makes an author walk on air but adds materially to sales-figures. Those have already passed the two-million mark and look like putting even Edgar Wallace's enormous figures in the shade. Messrs. Wright & Brown, in adding Mr. Verner to their long list of first-rate writers, evidently 'knew a thing or two.'"

How did this publicity scoop come about?

My father told me The Prince of Wales was an ardent fan of crime thrillers and he had met him on several occasions, with other like-minded individuals, in a private room at a well-known pub in Fleet Street where stories and events were discussed in convivial surroundings. There followed a letter to His Royal Highness 19 February 1935 from V. A. H. Crawley representing Wright and Brown offering a specially bound set of his novels to The Prince of Wales which achieved a reply from his Private Secretary Geoffrey Thomas on 12 March 1935 which included:

> "I regret that your letter of February 19th, which came to the Equerry in Waiting when the Prince of Wales was abroad, was not acknowledged at the time. I am now desired by His Royal Highness to thank Mr. Verner very much for his kind thought and to say that he will be pleased to accept from the publishers a set of the novels in question."

A special edition, printed on special paper, bound in Jubilee blue with gilt lettering along the spine was duly delivered. Private Secretary Geoffrey Thomas responded:

> "I am desired by the Prince of Wales to thank you very much for the complete set of your novels which you have kindly sent to His Royal Highness, and which he has been pleased to accept."

\* \* \*

Detective Weekly No. 288, 27 August 1938, featured on its front cover Gerald Verner's Grand Competition Serial *The Huntsman* and displayed the following offer which began:

> "You can win 35 autographed novels by Gerald Verner—see inside."

These stories were treated as commodities rather than anything approaching literature, which is why, when they first rolled off the printing presses, the Sexton Blake authors didn't receive a credit. This was pulp fiction and nothing more pretentious than that. They were action stories devised to provide much-needed entertainment before the advent of television. The stories by modern standards are nostalgic, set in a bygone age. That is their charm, and they have been criticised by modern readers as simplistic, lacking in realistic detail. Those critics miss the point. These

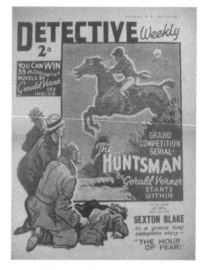

stories weren't meant to be realistic. They were escapist fantasy, often ingenious, as they explored original ideas that have been rehashed on television and film so many times since they were first written, these originals can appear cliché. They belonged to a genre all their own. A modern audience should be mindful that hindsight is a wonderful thing, that there was no forensics, DNA testing, computers for fingerprint correlation, or CCTV in those days. Items were picked up at the scene of a murder without any notion it was contaminating a crime scene. The detectives in those days seem naïve as we look back on them, but not to those thousands who read the stories at the time of publication. They were dependent on melodrama, atmosphere, and deduction, in the classic Sherlock Holmes tradition. They represent a golden age of detective fiction. The techniques have been built upon and extended to create the crime thrillers we enjoy today.

Many authors sold their stories on to Wright & Brown following publication in magazine form to take advantage of the lending libraries. Whereas the United States had the pulp magazines, the market in the United Kingdom was quite different. As there was no television in those days there was huge demand for easily digestible light romances and *whodunits* not just from public libraries but from subscription libraries. The first circulating libraries in the UK were formed during the mid-eighteenth century and allowed books to be borrowed for a specified loan period after payment of a subscription providing an opportunity for those that could not afford to buy them outright. Several libraries were attached to shops, notably W. H. Smith (1860-1961), Mudie's Select Circulating Library (1842-1937), and Harrods. In those days, in seaside towns like Margate, nearly every newsagent in the guest house area had a subscription library. Holiday makers would choose their books to read on the beach.

One of the most prolific chains of lending libraries was Boots.

By 1896, Jessie Boot owned sixty shops in twenty-eight different towns. Jessie's socially conscious wife Florence Boot was the driving force behind the Boots Book Lending service which was established in 1898. By 1903, when there were 300 Boots stores across the country, 143 had a *Boots' Book-Lovers Library* which charged borrowers for membership costing from 10/6 (ten shillings and sixpence) a year for one volume up to 42/- (forty-two shillings) for six. Alternatively, a borrower could take a book for half a crown (2/6) returnable deposit and a penny or two pence a week. The photo shows many features of the typical Boots library—it was usually on the first floor and was fitted with wooden bookshelves, chairs, tables and even notepaper and fresh flowers. By 1920 there were 500,000 subscribers and by 1938 books were being exchanged at the rate of 35

million each year reaching a peak during the Second World War when books were borrowed to be read in shelters during air raids. When the books got too tatty, they were sold off. By the middle of the 1960's television and the low cost of paperbacks contributed to the downfall of the high street libraries and they faded away. The lending libraries demise was assisted by the Public Libraries and Museums Act of 1964 which required councils to provide free public libraries and the cultural explosion that was the *Swinging Sixties*. Boots Booklovers Library Service gradually decreased in size, before closing fully in 1966.

During their popularity, the lending library world was hungry for product and provided Wright & Brown a secure client base. Their advance sales to these libraries allowed them to judge their print run accordingly. The Directors were H. Wright and J.H.G. Brown. They operated from 12-14 Red Lion Court, Fleet Street, London E.C.4. They were so successful they were soon forced to find larger premises, moving in 1934 to 4 Farringdon Avenue, London E.C.4. In less than five years their output increased to many millions of books, including Westerns and Romances; but it is the Mystery novels that have stood the test of time.

One of the unfortunate circumstances of this lending library program was the fact that books were literally read to pieces and then destroyed. Many of the libraries had a policy of removing and tossing out the dust jackets of all new arrivals. Good copies of these books with jackets are now very hard to find and highly collectible. Original vintage cover art is becoming one of the hottest areas for collecting as are dustjackets, often deciding the asking price for a book irrespective of the contents. It is the jackets, such as those by G. P. Micklewright, that contribute to the high prices these books are now fetching in good original condition.

* * *

The son and grandson of blacksmiths who worked as coach-makers, George Peace Micklewright was born to Richard Henry and Elizabeth Micklewright in West Bromwich, Staffordshire in 1894. Staffordshire is a landlocked county in the West Midlands of England not far from the great West Midlands industrial metropolis of Birmingham. Micklewright lived at 16, Hill Top. Before the outbreak of the Great War, he chose a different career from his forebears, attending the Ryland Memorial School of Art and Crafts in West Bromwich. Afterward he studied art in Paris.

With the arrival of WW1 in 1914, Micklewright, like other unfortunate young British men, was subjected to conscription. A Quaker, he was exempted from combat service under the conscience clause in the 1916 Conscription Act. The Pierce register of WW1 confirms Micklewright was a *Conscientious Objector*—1 of 18,000 other English pacifists over the course of the conflict

He was drafted into a combatant unit in Staffordshire and was sentenced to 84 days with hard labour for refusing to obey the order of a superior officer (This sentence was commuted to 56 days without hard labour). Dartmoor Prison was closed as a criminal prison and converted into a Home Office Work Centre where Conscientious Objectors, many intelligent and talented men, were put to work on mostly meaningless tasks. Some produced postcards amongst other artworks. It would appear Micklewright was one of these talented men, because he designed a series of cards portraying the experience of the beleaguered conscientious objector in visual form on paper, in his *The C.O. in Prison* series.

The Armistice ended fighting on the Western Front on 11 November 1918. Soon after he was released, he must have gone back to West Bromwich. Micklewright was 25 years old. He was married there in 1919.

He adopted a style all his own, representative of the period, and became an accomplished book jacket artist, providing over 2000 vivid jackets, mainly for Wright & Brown's mysteries and westerns, some for The Modern Publishing Company, and Methuen. He was brilliant at depicting animals and in this regard, he is best known for his wonderful illustrations to Anna Sewell's *Black Beauty*. The jackets of *The Mastermind of Mars* and *Tarzan The Magnificent* both by Edgar Rice Burroughs, illustrate his consummate skill in creating a moment of action.

He died in 1951 in Surrey.

The early 4 colour Wright & Brown jackets were originally printed by Ebenezer Bayliss, The Trinity Press, based in Worcester and London and dating back to 1858. Much later they merged with John Goodman and Sons of Birmingham to form Goodman Bayliss. The Trinity House print works closed in 2008 when the company went into administration with the loss of about 115 jobs. I had a vision of a small attic-type room somewhere with discarded piles of book jackets. I then discovered the old building had been recently demolished to make way for a new Waitrose. I have always wondered what became of the original Micklewright artwork.

Wright & Brown jackets were also printed by Charles Mitchell Limited, originating in the 1850's—run by Mitch Mitchell. They operated from premises at 4 West Harding

Street, Fetter Lane EC4, until the printing works were destroyed during the Blitz. Any original Micklewright artwork would likely have perished also. But surely some survived somewhere? I began some research and came across an original signed gouache painting of a *half-timbered mansion with figures in 17th-century dress*. Amazingly, it was for sale and I bought it immediately. I have no idea if it was ever commissioned for a book.

Wright & Brown 1st editions were sold at 7/6p and usually (but not always) had Red boards. The same printing was bound in Orange Boards to be sold later at 3/6p. Some editions were never released in the 7/6 format and went straight into print at 3/6p. They produced a sturdy, though plain product, that held up to multiple readings for the rental libraries.

* * *

Gerald and Patricia Verner lived at 9, Albert Bridge Road, London SW11 but my father had a bolt hole at *Carisholme,* a three-bedroom, two-bathroom, two reception, detached house in Thames Ditton.

*Gerald Verner* became the flagship my father operated under. He dedicates his book *White Wig* to her: *To Pat with Love.* The book was first published in 1935. This might help solve the *Riddle of the Nieces,* not another detective story title but a real-life riddle. A succession of further dedications to cousins, which must have belonged to Patricia's family (that I know nothing about) because almost certainly my father had no brothers or sisters.

In 1935 *The Crooked Circle* was published by Wright & Brown. It is inscribed: *To my Niece Shirley Pamela who may live to read this book when she grows up.* I have no idea who this was, and it intrigues me. My father was an Uncle? I am assuming Shirley Pamela must be the daughter of either the sister or brother of wife Patricia.

*The Token* published in 1937 is dedicated: *To my Niece Patricia with love and sincere wishes for a long and happy life.* Another niece!

Then, finally, in 1938, *The River House Mystery* is dedicated: *To my Niece*

## CHAPTER SEVEN: GERALD VERNER

*Ivy with love and sincere good wishes.* Three nieces to consider: Shirley Pamela, Patricia and Ivy? From what stock did these nieces originate? I apologise there are more questions than answers.

\* \* \*

By 1936 at the age of 40, my father was one of the most successful crime writers in the country having sold some one and a half million copies of his stories and having written 23 novels in five years as well as nearly 100 short stories, serials and plays. He also used to edit the quarterly magazine *Crime*. His favourite authors were Charles Dickens (particularly *Bleak House*) and Wilkie Collins (*The Woman in White* and *The Moonstone*) followed by John Dickson Carr/Carter Dickson, Edgar Wallace, Dorothy L. Sayers, Ngaio Marsh, Mary Roberts Rinehart, Philip MacDonald, Peter Cheyney and Agatha Christie.

An article, *I Know What You Read*, in the *Manchester Evening News* of 20 January 1936 began:

> "'I want another book by that Verner man," said the charming old lady with the gentle and cultured voice. "Something with plenty of murders in it, please.'"

And she was true to type.

Like Edgar Wallace, my father used to dictate his novels into a Dictaphone, which was a wax cylinder dictation machine. Alastair Sim, playing the part of a writer dictating a thriller for a magazine, uses one in the first of the Ealing comedies, *Hue and Cry*. The name *Dictaphone* was trademarked by the *Columbia Graphophone Company* in 1907 (later to become

EMI Records), which soon became the leading manufacturer of such devices. This perpetuated the use of wax cylinders for voice recording up until the end of World War II. *The Lending Library*, August 1934 featured a photograph of a shop window display by Dictaphone Company of a dummy of Gerald Verner dictating into a Dictaphone machine with copies of his books piled up all around him. Underneath was the caption:

"Gerald Verner looks like proving a speed merchant in literature. Wright & Brown, his publishers, are so appreciative of the continuity with which he can produce new "thrillers" that recently they gave him a three-year contract for the publication of one book a month. This author dictates all his work to his "silent secretary"—the Dictaphone."

My father could dictate several books at once, without losing track of the plots boasting that if pushed could dictate a book in a day, which then of course had to be typed up as a manuscript. He didn't work alone. *The Black Hunchback* (1933) is dedicated: *To Ernest my friend and secretary.* This mass production, pride, and obsession with speed of writing, followed in the footsteps of Edgar Wallace, whom he never met but greatly admired. He emulated Wallace in more ways than one, particularly when it came to chain-smoking, cups of tea, and reeled off stories at speed to keep debtors at bay. While *one book a month* may sound impressive it was detrimental to quality, putting the author under an incredible pressure that was not likely to result in great literary merit, though the potential was there, evidenced by these opening paragraphs from *The River Men*:

"The morning was cold and raw, with a thin mist that hung over the Thames partly obscuring the silent wharves and deserted warehouses that line the banks of the river in Greenwich Reach, softening their ugly lines and lending to them a dignity that was lacking in the revealing light of day. Somewhere in the east, the sun was rising, but as yet no hint of the coming dawn was visible in the dark sky. The river slept, though in less than an hour it would be waking to the clamour of another day of toil. Already, farther up towards the Pool, splashes of light marked the places where the big cargo boats had been loading and unloading for the greater part of the night. Here the squeak and rattle of derricks, the muffled voices of men shouting orders and the bumping and scraping of heavy cargo broke the stillness which farther down-stream in the Reach was only disturbed by the

lapping water as it swirled round the rotting piles of the wharves and rippled against the blunt noses of the barges as they strained at their creaking moorings. Presently Billingsgate Market would splutter to life under the cold glare of many arcs, and along the mist-shrouded banks other lights would be springing up to remain twinkling blearingly until the daylight came to rob them of their usefulness."

In 1935 he dedicated *The Cleverness of Mr. Budd*: *To Edgar Wallace who still lives in the memory of his friends*. Like Edgar Wallace, my father never possessed money for long and, though he earned a lot of it, money quickly slipped through his fingers. He was always tearing off a story desperate for money, frantic to pay off some pressing bill, or to meet a deadline for a monthly publication. Perhaps these pressures account for his obsession with his speed of writing. While his stories started off well, they often felt rushed towards the end. This dialogue from the opening of *The Clue of the Green Candle* could almost be autobiographical:

"What about the instalment of that serial for *Fiction Weekly?*" she said, rising to her feet and brushing the creases from her neat tweed skirt. "We promised they should have it by four o'clock to-morrow."

Tempest made a wry grimace.

"Did we?" he muttered. "Well, we'd better do it in the morning then. Darn these people! They *always* seem to be wanting an instalment! How much more of *Red Fingers* have we got to do?"

She wrinkled her forehead and made a rapid calculation.

"Forty-thousand words, roughly," she answered.

"As much as that, eh?" he said frowning. "We've got to deliver that on Saturday morning, and to-day's Wednesday. Oh, well, we'll do it somehow."

\* \* \*

From 1932 to the outbreak of the Second World War were my father's golden years of writing detective fiction. He was very popular. His books sold in hundreds of thousands in Great Britain, Australia, New Zealand, Canada, and in the USA published by Macaulay Company, New York. They were translated into Polish, Hungarian, Norwegian, French, Dutch, and in Germany by Eden-Verlag, Berlin. Stories were serialised across the world, like *The Silver Horseshoe* in The Australian

70

Women's Weekly. He was reportedly earning £200 a week, a fortune in those days.

A report on a speech given by Gerald Verner to the London Writer Circle in August 1935 offers practical advice for the writer of thrillers:

> "Rigid specialisation in the study and practice of this type of work is essential if substantial reward is to be earned. He himself reads nothing but thrillers. Aspirants frequently attempt the magazine and serial markets before settling down to a full-length story. It is often better to start with a book, as any reputation thus achieved will render other markets easier of access. Everything should be done to make a murder story seem credible. The characters should be the ordinary folk one meets every day. The villain, even, should be normal in little things, and never wholly bad. The murder should be committed in some simple, obvious manner, not by the employment, for example, of mysterious death rays or other extraordinary means. A story too exactly planned may check the creative impulse. The writer should not be afraid to allow a plot to work itself out. Mr. Verner confessed that his stories were often well advanced before a solution of the mystery lay in his mind."

A favourite detective, featured in fourteen books, was Trevor Lowe - backed up by his assistant Arnold White. Did my father arrive at the name consciously or subconsciously remembering the co-producer of *Water Babies* back in 1904? The first of these stories for Wright & Brown was published in 1933 and titled *Phantom Hollow* and was dedicated to Mrs. Edgar Wallace. Trevor Lowe is described thus at the beginning of Chapter Three:

> "He was a man of middle height, dark, with greying hair at the temples and clean-shaven. His face, without in any way being handsome, was very pleasant, and when he smiled—as he did very readily—his smile was truly delightful. Despite his success he had never acquired that air of conscious superiority that marks—and mars—so many men of his profession, but at the same time no one who came in contact with him could fail to realise that this was no ordinary man. He seemed in some indefinable way to exhale a tremendous sense of latent power.

His chief asset may be described in one word—charm—a rare and subtle thing, but a thing which Trevor Lowe possessed in abundance."

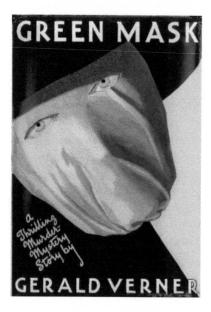

*Green Mask* (1934) introduces Mr. Robert Budd, a fictional Superintendent of the C.I.D. Scotland Yard. Many of Gerald Verner's stories featured Mr. Robert Budd who was a Londoner, with his own house at Streatham, where he enjoyed growing roses. He acquired the nickname 'The Rose-bud'. This seemingly sleepy-eyed, ponderous detective had portly, rather obese features. Despite his bulk he could move surprisingly quickly when he needed to and was very shrewd. He could think well and resolved his cases as well as any slick private detective. His rough and ready speech gave him a down-to-earth aspect. He smoked evil-smelling thin black cigars whenever the opportunity arose. His abode at Scotland Yard was a small cheerless room, and his aide was the melancholy Sergeant Leek, a somewhat slow-witted man who bore the brunt of Mr. Budd's caustic criticisms, suffusing this unsettled relationship with humour.

Mr. Budd and Sergeant Leek first appeared in *Detective Weekly* or *The Thriller Library* in stories published 1934 – 1940 and these novellas were brought together to form many Wright& Brown collections, each book

usually containing three separate stories involving the detective that first appeared in one or another of the magazines, including *The Cleverness of Mr. Budd* (1935). *The Valley of Terror* was cut down to create *The Devil's Footprint* by Gerald Verner for *Detective Weekly* May 1937, and rewritten as *The Devil's Footprint*, Book 3 of *The Return of Mr. Budd* by Gerald Verner for Wright & Brown in 1938 and published in the USA as *Case Book of Mr. Budd* by Macaulay Company, New York. *Mr. Budd Again* followed in 1939. *Mr. Budd Investigates* continues the trend in 1940 containing three stories originally published in *The Thriller Library* beginning with *The House of the Goat* in December 1939. *The House of the Goat* was followed in January 1940 by *The Seven Sleeping Men* and in February 1940 by *The Seal of Solomon*. They were written as the storm clouds of war were gathering and lives were to change forever.

An illustration by Eric Robert Parker, a prolific British illustrator and comics artist born in 1898. He became a staff artist when the Amalgamated Press formed in 1922 and worked for them until his death in 1974. He was best known for illustrating the adventures of Sexton Blake in various periodicals.

"They're coming!" whispered Sergeant Leek mournfully. Mr. Budd hid as much of his bulk as he could behind a tree and fired twice at the oncoming boat. He had to stem the invasion somehow.

# Chapter Eight – The War Years

**M**y father's lifelong friendship with Noel Lee began with a fan letter forwarded to him from his publishers (I knew him as Noel so I shall refer to him by his Christian name. These letters are *one way*, from my father to Noel. Noel's letters to my father have been lost. These letters were left to me in Noel's will together with a collection of my father's books). In the letter, Noel is complimentary about his thrillers and obviously has questions. An excerpt from my father's reply, written from Carisholme, 15 March 1939, explains writing as both Gerald Verner and Donald Stuart:

> "I write under both names, but mostly under my own—Gerald Verner. In my early days I used to write entirely under the name of Donald Stuart. *The Valley of Terror* was written several years ago and cut down recently to a long-complete story featuring Mr. Budd, because the editor was in a hurry, and there was no time to write a new story. The first book I ever wrote is *The Embankment Murder*, and it may interest you to know that this was written on the Thames Embankment on odd scraps of paper—and the locality was not one of choice!"

The letter is an additional corroboration of my father's *down and out* period and an indication of the pressure editors of the pulps put upon authors to meet deadlines. Noel sends the opening chapters of a book he has written and asks if my father will read them and express an opinion. 4 April 1939 my father's reply includes:

> "I like the beginning of your story, and if you finish as well as you have started it, I think I can arrange for its publication in book form. Don't run away with the idea that this means a fortune, though. You will get £25 down on account of a 10% royalty. This is the largest amount that a publisher is currently

willing to pay a new author. It is quite likely that is all you will get out of your first book, because it is very doubtful if it will earn more than this advance. Most publishers lose money on the first three books by a new author, but they are willing to do this if there is a chance of the author becoming popular. I tell you this not to discourage you, but so that you shall not have any false ideas. The public did not become aware of my existence until my seventh book had been published. Writing is not an easy way of earning a living, but if you are moderately successful it is a very pleasant way."

Britain declared war on Germany on 3 September 1939. The war was to engulf most of the world's countries before it ended 2 Sep 1945. During April 1939, conscription began, the Peacetime call up for Military training of men of 20. In a letter of 6 September 1939 my father writes to Noel encouragingly:

"I think you will be well-advised to continue with the book. There may be a little delay in getting publication, but the war will make very little difference to the publishing trade in general. In fact, from past experience, books usually have something of a boom in wartime. I apologise for the delay in replying to your letter, but my secretary has already been called up and I have not yet found another."

As things were to turn out this letter is extremely optimistic. At the beginning, to many of those living in London, the war was remote, going on elsewhere. They had the unshaken belief the British Armed Forces would sort it out. In a letter dated 3 October 1939, my father writes to Noel from 9 Albert Bridge Road:

"I regret I did not answer your letter before, but I have been extremely busy. I am at present engaged on propaganda work for the Government, as well as my own, and there is very little time for anything. As you will see from the above address, I am staying at my London house. This saves a certain amount of time in journeys. There is a shortage of paper at the moment, so I expect you will have to wait for some time before publication."

In the same letter he also refers to the shortage of paper which is holding up many publications. Several thriller writers at that time also participated in writing propaganda for the government, including my father's friend Ernest Dudley, to whom he dedicated his 1939 book, *Mr. Budd Again*. Dudley was established as a writer for BBC radio, his most successful character being *Mr. Walker,* a cockney rag and bone man who dispensed worldly advice on dilemmas and crises facing ordinary people. So popular was the character that in January 1939 Dudley was syndicated to write *Mr. Walker* posers for the *Sunday Chronicle*. Interviewed in 1997, he recalled:

> "I was the first bloke to put Sexton Blake on the radio, in early 1939. By that time, I'd been a journalist and a writer for quite a time, and I got to know the chap who ran Amalgamated Press— Monty Hayden. Because of the success of *Mr. Walker Wants To Know* he thought I knew something about radio writing and he got me to write this serial about Sexton Blake and that was the first time that Sexton Blake was ever done by the BBC."

Dudley's script for *Enter Sexton Blake* was adapted from *The Frightened Man* by Berkeley Gray (E.S. Brooks) that had appeared the previous year in *The* Sexton *Blake Library* No 641. Brooks returned the compliment by adapting the radio play as a Berkeley Gray text serial that ran concurrently in *Detective Weekly* through to April 1939. The radio serial ran for 12 instalments as part of the magazine programme *Lucky Dip*, with George Curzon playing Blake.

Hayden commissioned Dudley to write two Blake novelettes for *Detective Weekly* starring Mr. Walker, *Mr. Walker Wants to Know* and *What Would you Do?* in March 1939. Following advice from his friend Gerald Verner, Dudley then *de-Blaked* and expanded the stories into the book *Mr. Walker Wants to Know*, which was submitted to Wright and Brown, who published it in 1940, launching Dudley's career as a novelist.

By 9 November 1939 the war is beginning to bite. My father has now received Noel's completed manuscript. The original title of this manuscript is never mentioned. He writes back to Noel:

> "I daresay you will have to wait for some time before I can let you know the publisher's decision. There is a paper shortage at the moment which is holding up the publication of several

books, my own included, and this may cause some delay. I will, however, do my best to hurry things up as much as possible. I have glanced through the story and I think for a first novel it is excellent."

One can only imagine the effect these words had on fledgling author Noel Lee who unbeknown to my father is desperate for the advance of £25.00. He will have faced any delay with dismay, though my father's endorsement and the fact the book was awaiting Wright & Brown's decision was a pretty good result by anyone's standards. My father was very busy currently and when Noel presses for a progress report from his wife, Patricia writes back to him on 12 Dec 1939, from 9 Albert Bridge Road:

"How nice of you to write me. I can't tell you how sorry I am you have to leave home, it's beastly for you. Please don't worry about your manuscript, you'll find Gerald extremely slow in starting anything, but he always manages to get things done in time and at the right moment. I appreciate your anxiety, but these things are rather like a birth, aren't they? One can't hurry them. I haven't read your manuscript, but Gerald is most enthusiastic about it. You say he is kind; yes, he is, and most loyal, and he'll see that it is fixed. You know I expect it's quite a thrill for an older man to find a protégé in the same profession. Of course, you'll come back and write reams, all good, I hope. You're a very lucky young man to know exactly what you want and to go after it. I wish I had your gift. Excuse my writing block but my usual notepaper isn't in yet if I ever get it again. It's beastly cold down here. I wish it were always Spring and Summer. Thanks again for your letter and please accept my sincere wishes for Christmas."

The letter is signed Patricia Verner. It provides proof she was still living in London during Christmas 1939. These letters are pieces of a jigsaw that represents the early years of the war but doesn't provide a complete picture. I have no idea what happened between my father and his first wife before and during the war. Perhaps there was some sort of amicable separation.

January 1940 heralded the start of food rationing in England. It was the coldest month in Britain since 1895 heralding a harsh winter. By 17

January the river Thames froze over for the first time since 1880. At the end of the month, a great snow and ice storm occurred, historically as one of the most dramatic weather events recorded. Practically all warlike activity ceased. This was a time of discomfort, anti-climax, inaction and stalemate, defining the *Phoney War* on the Western Front in Europe before the Nazi invasion of France.

Boots were buying books at the rate of 1,250,000 a year. The number of subscribers increased from 500,000 to a million, which gave the company considerable influence in a publishing world that was running out of paper. Germany invaded Norway 8 April 1940. The supply of pulp for paper slowed dramatically. Canadian Timber was also at risk from submarine warfare in the Atlantic. Many magazines were sacrificed to allow scarce paper for use in major newspapers like *The Times*, considered to be essential for propaganda purposes.

The effects of the War were beginning to bite.

Between the New Year and the beginning of May 1940 the Verner's are no longer living at 7 Brunswick Square. Pat goes into hospital with chest trouble—perhaps caused by the unusually bitter winter. My father continues to live in Thames Ditton, but no longer at *Carisholme*.

Tremendous upheavals.

What happened to them both?

\* \* \*

By May 1940, my father had moved a short hop from *Carisholme* to a little cottage called Lazyland, Albany Reach, still in Thames Ditton. He is living with his mother Geraldine (always referring to her as his sister). Albany Reach offers stunning views over the Thames to Hampton Court Palace, which are among the best in Greater London. After a communication gap of nearly six months, on 7 May 1940, my father writes a letter to his friend Noel Lee from Lazyland:

> "Thank you for your letter. I am sorry you have had so much bother in finding me, but you will see from the above address that I have moved. The paper rationing has, I regret to say, hit me rather badly. In fact, it has hit all authors and publishers, and I have been compelled to cut down expenses drastically. Is there any chance you may come to London before you go abroad? If so, let me know, and I would meet you somewhere for a cup of tea and a chat."

## CHAPTER EIGHT: THE WAR YEARS

Another letter to Noel from Lazyland, 19 June 1940, illustrates the desperation the war has created:

> "Owing to the paper rationing and the closing of the serial monthlies I am in a very desperate situation until my royalties come in at the end of next month—"

Books went out of print fast and there was insufficient paper to reprint them. A letter to Noel Lee, 1 July 1940, nine days before the commencement of *The Battle of Britain*, explains:

> "The result of the paper rationing has been to create chaos among those people who, like myself, earn their living by writing. In one week, the Amalgamated Press sacked 1,100 of their employees. In two hours one of my editor friends had £1,500 a year wiped off his income and what is so terrible about it is that the majority of these people, among whom I numbered a great many friends, will not be able to find another job. I am sorry I cannot give you a telephone number at the moment. My wife has had to go into hospital with chest trouble and I am living with my sister at this little cottage. Things are very bad, but we live in hope that they will improve. I don't know how it can be arranged but I should very much like to meet you and have a chat. There is a possibility that I may be able to arrange something regarding your story in the very near future and I should like to have a word with you about that."

This letter is the last evidence of Pat's existence until 1972 when she visited my father at Broadstairs out of the blue and I was to meet her for the first time. The letter also represents the last communication from *Lazyland* to Noel Lee. My father doesn't write to Noel Lee again until after the war, October 1945 when I discover what had happened to his manuscript.

\* \* \*

From 1938 and throughout the war Sexton Blake Library reprints began, old stories from the past. Many of the writers had died or joined the Forces. Four issues a month is dropped to two and the page count drastically reduced. Perhaps due to a shortage of authors, ready cash, and paper, the war-stricken Amalgamated Press developed a deplorable policy of reprinting abridged Sexton Blake stories from living and dead authors during 1939 and 1940 creating puzzling anomalies for fans. For example, *The Sign in the Sky or The Secret of the Tong* by Alfred Edgar SBL 254 1922 popped up as *The Secret of the Tong* by Hylton Gregory (H. Egbert Hill) SBL 520 1936. *The Red Heart of the Incas* by Jack Lewis SBL 86 July 1919, was republished as *The Secret of the Sacred Ruby* by Hylton Gregory SBL 704 January 1940.

Gwyn Evans died in 1938 just 39 years old. His yarn *The Case of the Jack of Clubs* SBL 164 October 1928 reappeared as *The Case of the Jack of Clubs* by W. J. Bayfield SBL 728 1940. *Dead Man's Bay* by Mark Osborn (John W Bobin) SBL 358 1932 is rewritten as *The Riddle of Dead Man's Bay* by Australian-born author J. G. Brandon, real name John Gordon Joyce (1879-1941) SBL 734 1940. Andrew Murray was the pseudonym of Captain Malcolm Arnold. He died aged 49 in 1928 after suffering a severe mental illness that caused almost complete paralysis. He wrote his last Sexton Blake story in 1924. Two of his stories were rewritten, abridged, and republished as by Donald Stuart: *The Secret of the Hulk*, SBL 708 Febuary1940, from *The Secret of the Hulk; or, The Stricken Town* 1st series No 63 1918, by Andrew Murray and *The Burmese Dagger* SBL 675 June 1939, from *The Case of the Burmese Dagger* by Andrew Murray 1st series No 102 November 1919.

There are many more examples. No doubt these *shenanigans*, for want of a better word, shifted copies and appeased shareholders. What readers made of these archaic yarns I can't imagine, betrayal springs to mind.

My father dedicated his 1939 novel *The Football Pool Murders* to a friend W. W. Sayer with the words: *To W. W. Sayer Author and Innkeeper whose beer and books are both excellent.* This refers to Sayer's public house at Winkfield near Windsor. Sayer was a Wright & Brown author, but also wrote Sexton Blake stories for The Amalgamated Press as Pierre Quiroule. Sayer developed two very popular characters in his stories, Granite Grant, and Mademoiselle Julie. In 1930 he left writing for Amalgamated Press to join The London General Press, a feature agency. Fans were crying out for more stories with Grant and Julie and another Blake author, Warwick Jardine (Francis Alister Warwick), stepped in to take them over. He wrote two, *The Crime In Park Lane* SBL 403 October 1933 and *The Man from Tokio* SBL 409 December 1933. Jardine's style of writing and the stories didn't work, deeply disappointing fans and forcing

Amalgamated Press to reprint old originals starting with *Dead Man's Diary* SBL 416 January 1934, which was originally *The Secret of the Frozen North* which appeared in SBL 163 1921. The same story was also reprinted in Detective Weekly issue 263, as *The Secret of the Last Survivor* in 1938, illustrating just how complex stories histories could become.

*The Third Victim* 653 January 1939 was originally *The Next Victim* by Donald Stuart Sexton Blake Library 286 May 1931 then rewritten as the novel *The Next to Die* by Gerald Verner published by Wright and Brown in 1934. *The Mystery of Sherwood Towers* 714 April 1940 by Donald Stuart was a reprint of his own 2nd series No 152 1928 and there is another Blake of his with mysterious origins called *Twenty Years of Hate* 732 August 1940.

*Dene of The Secret Service* by Gerald Verner was published by Wright and Brown in hardback form in 1941. One astute reader realised he had read the story before as SBL 409 December 1933, *The Man from Tokio* by Warwick Jardine. De-Blaked, Sexton Blake and Tinker had become Trevor Lowe and Arnold White, Granite Grant became Michael Dene, and Mademoiselle Julie remained unaltered. Unfortunately, this process doesn't show much respect for fans who rush out to buy these titles only to find they have already read them under a different name.

In a letter to a friend, May 1939, my father wrote:

> "In reply to your question regarding *The Phantom Pearler* my friend Rex Harding was in a hurry for a story and I sold him *Midnight Murder* for use in Detective Weekly."

The story was published in May 1939 as written by Rex Harding, as my father's letter states—but the story was originally *Midnight Murder* by Donald Stuart, published by Wright & Brown in 1935. It was not unusual for writers to help each other out in a fix, because the editors had deadlines that had to be met come hell or high water. Sadly, no one is alive today to account accurately for these activities, so rumours abound!

*The Hidden Menace:* or, *The Case of the Secret Slaves* was a Sexton Blake story originally anon. but written by John W. Bobin 1st series No 71 March 1919. The subject matter is opium addiction. It was then supposedly rewritten by Donald Stuart and published in the Sexton Blake Library in October 1939 number 690 using the original title *The Hidden Menace*. If you're going to pinch someone else's story would you use the same title with the same publishers? The same story was reprinted by The

Amalgamated Press as *The Mystery of the Dope Den* by John Andrews in The Boy's Friend Library 2nd series issue 691 5 October 1939. My father's title *The Hidden Menace* was nothing to do with any of this but rewritten from his 1935 Wright and Brown book *The Q Squad*.

In 1939, G. H. Teed dies at age 53, the man to whom my father took his first manuscript *The Clue of the Second Tooth* back in 1927. *Detective Weekly* dies too, 25 May 1940, after 379 issues, mainly due to paper rationing.

\* \* \*

Where did Patricia Verner go after her hospital visit? It's a real-life mystery. I think it unlikely she went to Thames Ditton. Following her illness, perhaps she went to convalesce with relatives outside London.

From letters to Noel and events during the war, I try to reconstruct what misfortune might have befallen my father in the first few months of 1940. Royalties were not due until the end of July. His own words: *I have been compelled to cut down expenses drastically*, suggest to me strongly his income had dried up forcing him to leave both rented properties, 7 Brunswick Square and *Carisholme*.

My father told me his river boat was commandeered for *Operation Dynamo*, the evacuation of over three hundred thousand allied soldiers from the beaches and harbour of Dunkirk, by a hastily assembled fleet of over eight hundred boats between 27 May and 4 June 1940. He never saw the boat again.

As Editor of the quarterly magazine *Crime*, my father was sent boxes of new crime novels to review on a regular basis, enabling him to read *nothing but thrillers*. These review copies, together with books he had collected himself, accumulated in number until he owned one of the finest libraries of crime fiction in the country.

Disaster struck in the form of a German parachute landmine.

According to my father, the parachute landmine didn't go off immediately. The parachute had got caught up in the branches of a tree. The mine was spotted hanging from these branches a few feet off the ground. Wardens immediately evacuated nearby roads.

The clockwork fuse in the mine was ticking…

The mine blew up half an hour later causing extensive damage. All my father's papers, library of crime books and other belongings went up with it.

## CHAPTER EIGHT: THE WAR YEARS

In a letter to Noel Lee, 15 July 1961, my father elucidates further:

> "Actually, it was a delayed action landmine that destroyed all my stuff in Thames Ditton. It came down by parachute and hung in a tree in the garden until the morning. It exploded half an hour after we were evacuated from the house."

My father provides no specific date for when this disaster occurred, but it must have been while he was living at *Lazyland* after he had vacated *Carisholme* because Parachute *Mines* were *first* used against land targets on 16 September 1940 in the *early* stages of the Blitz.

German air raids killed and injured many people in the Elmbridge area, as well as destroying many family homes and local businesses. I have done my best to reconstruct what I think happened, but it is mainly conjecture.

Compiled by the Ministry of Home Security the *Aggregate Night Time Bomb Census* attempts to provide an overall picture of where bombs fell across the UK for the period 7 October 1940 to 6 June 1941. The census records that at some point during this period a mine fell at Thames Ditton near Aragon Avenue, Long Ditton, Elmbridge. No specific date is given. Was this the mine my father remembers? They were probably after Hawker's Kingston factory and the parachute mine had caught the wind and been blown off course.

The official British designation for these weapons on land was *Parachute Landmines*, but they became known to the British populace as *Landmines*. The first intentional use of magnetic mines against land targets was on the night of 16 September 1940, when the mines' explosions caused considerable blast damage in built-up areas. The mines were released from Heinkel III bombers and drifted to ground level by parachute. They were so heavy that if not slowed down, they would bury themselves so far underground on impact that the explosion would be muted. They detonated either by contact or by a clockwork mechanism. When the parachute became entangled in buildings they often failed to explode, leaving those who had to face defusing them with the uncertainty that there might also be a clockwork timer operating.

These mines, weighing 4,000 lbs, were designed to act as blast bombs. Greater blast damage was the result of the mine exploding at ground level and producing a shock wave that spread straight outwards, rather than burrowing a hole before detonating which creates a crater and funnels much of the blast upwards. The intention was to take out whole streets, wiping out residential or industrial buildings. The blast from parachute mines exploding above ground therefore caused extensive damage, demolishing houses in the vicinity and breaking windows as far as a mile away.

I have no more evidence of what happened to my father following on from this disaster but assume that during the summer of 1941, or earlier, he moves to Richmond-upon-Thames and surfaces at 207 Litchfield Court.

\* \* \*

From 24 August 1940 Britain's cities endured a long and terrible campaign of bombing that destroyed large parts of the country, killed thousands and left hundreds of thousands homeless, but the appearance of German bombers in the skies over London during the afternoon of 7 September 1940, heralded a tactical shift in Hitler's attempt to subdue Great Britain into surrender.

At around 4:00 PM, 348 German bombers escorted by 617 fighters blasted London until 6:00 PM. Two hours later, guided by the fires set by the first assault, a second group of raiders commenced another attack that lasted until 4:30AM the following morning. This was the beginning of the Blitz, a period of intense bombing of London and other cities that continued until the following May 1941. London suffered 57 consecutive nights of heavy bombing (by an average of 150 bombers) from 7 September onwards, and during November had just one night's respite, when bad weather prevented the Luftwaffe from coming. During October 1940, London suffered its 200th air raid. In London, attacks were concentrated on the City and the East End, the River Thames providing a shiny silver path for the bombers to follow to the docks.

Before the war, historic Paternoster Row EC4 had been the centre of the publishing trade in England since the sixteenth century. My father's book *The Silver Horseshoe*, published in 1938, is dedicated to *The Paternosters*, a club where writers met situated in the narrow street that was Paternoster Row. This club was destroyed in the Blitz on a terrible night of bombing on the evening of Sunday 29 December 1940, when during a period of twelve hours, more than 24,000 high explosive bombs and 100,000 incendiary missiles were dropped, causing fifteen million books to go up in flames, creating a rain of charred and burned paper that fell for miles around. Twenty-seven publishing firms were destroyed, including Longmans, who had been there since 1724. Paternoster Row has now largely been replaced by the bleak Paternoster Square, the home of the London Stock Exchange.

The 10th of May 1941 saw the heaviest and last major air raid on London. Fourteen hundred civilians were killed. Wright & Brown's headquarters at 4, Farringdon Avenue, London, E.C.4 was hit, and the company thrown into disarray. At 6, Farringdon Avenue, The Modern Publishing Company was also hit on the same night. Many books in print and manuscripts were destroyed. Wright & Brown were forced to move to temporary accommodation at 1, Crane Court, Fleet Street, London EC4. In the autumn of 1941, they produced a 28-page list of new books with the following announcement attached to the first page:

> "As a result of enemy action, a considerable amount of stock was destroyed on May 10th last. All these titles have been deleted from the present list and owing to paper shortage cannot be reprinted at present. Also, owing to labour shortage, some curtailment of supplies is being experienced. It would therefore be advisable to order your requirements as early as possible to avoid disappointment."

This Wright & Brown book list of Autumn 1941, from their new temporary address of 1, Crane Court, shows as already published, and with a price increase from 3/6d to 4/-, *The Poisoner*, *The Vampire Man*, and *Dene of the Secret Service*. The first editions are all from 4, Farringdon Avenue, *not* Crane Court.

The original jacket for *Dene of the Secret Service* is an original Micklewright; a man holding a gun with a smiling face. The subsequent reprint editions have a jacket that has been hastily re-worked by a different illustrator to show essentially the same man but with a grim face. There is a lack of detail. It is not a Micklewright but follows closely the style of his original.

# PLOTS AND GUNPOWDER

On the heels of the Wright & Brown list of Autumn 1941 arrives Spring 1942, another much shorter list of only four pages. The only book listed by Gerald Verner at 4/6d is *The Nightmare Murders* which has the 4 Farringdon Avenue address on the book like the others. *The Nightmare Murders* is a strange hybrid book, which may well have its genesis as a stage play. There are large tracts of dialogue, and the continuities read like stage directions. It starts off in a new style and finishes up in an old one, with a clever ending that is as amazing as it is unexpected, but rather nonsensical. The back pages of *The Nightmare Murders* show a list of W&B Autumn 1940 new 7/6d novels. Confusingly, one of them is *The Nightmare Murders,* suggesting it was supposed to be in process of being printed in spring or summer 1940 ready for an autumn release. The other listing was *The Secret Weapon* which was never printed as a novel under that title—the story originated from *Secret Weapon* Detective Weekly No 377 May 1940. It was eventually published by Wright & Brown as *The Heel of Achilles* in 1945.

These examples reflect the chaos into which Wright & Brown were plunged as they attempted to get back on their feet, running parallel to my father's personal upheavals. I think it fair to say, Wright & Brown never fully recovered from the war. While they kept going, the writing was truly on the wall. The times were changing. My father's style was not moving with the times being entrenched in the 1930's. Reading his stories now is nostalgic, set in a bygone age, some say *a golden age*. At the time of publication or broadcast these stories had to be cutting edge. The war drew a line under this *golden age* and many authors were forced to turn to radio and then to television for work.

In 1943, the Ministry of Supply mounted a drive to collect and pulp unwanted books; paper was in such short supply. No books by my father were published from 1942 to 1944, but after the war he was busy writing again.

\* \* \*

At some point during the war after July 1940 (presumably following the date of the landmine exploding) my father moved out of London and Thames Ditton to Richmond-upon-Thames, in Surrey. He lived at 207 Litchfield Court, which consisted of two art deco blocks of flats, completed in 1935, 23 Sheen Road, situated opposite the Ritz Cinema where my father obtained a job as manager. He continued to write when

he could, hampered due to paper restrictions and the number of publications allowed per author.

The Ritz opened on 19 May 1938. Designed by Samuel Beverley, working in association with Leslie H. Kemp, it was a luxury cinema building befitting the affluent district of Richmond. The façade was designed in a Neo-Georgian style, the auditorium refined Art Deco. The cinema boasted a cafe-restaurant for the convenience of patrons and the public and a 2150 seat

auditorium. It was re-named ABC in 1961, closed ten years later and was demolished.

While managing the cinema my father met Carol, probably around 1942, who was to become his second wife, and my mother. He always called my mother Carol because that was how he'd been introduced to her, but her father, Norman Wade, called her by her birth name, Isobel. He was my other grandfather, but never felt like one, as I had little to do with him. He always struck me as a very dry, unemotional, Yorkshireman. This might have been an unfair assessment. I learned recently from a newspaper cutting that he had received an OBE in recognition of his bravery for clawing at rubble for three hours with his bare hands at a blitzed house in Barnes to rescue a woman who had been buried alive. He moved to a basement flat in Cardigan Road off Richmond Hill in 1949, the year I was born.

My mother was a war widow, with two sons, my half-brothers, Anthony, and James Jack Ronald. Isobel Wade was first married in Hammersmith, London, between April and June 1937, to Richard J Ronald. Her husband, known as Jack Ronald, had been killed at El Alamein in 1942. He was the adopted son of an English writer James Ronald (1905-1972) who wrote 25 crime novels between 1932 and 1953 and wrote for *The Thriller*. He wrote seven novels under the pseudonym Michael Crombie and one under Kirk Wales. *This Way Out* (1940) was turned into the Film Noir *The Suspect* (1944) starring *Charles Laughton* and directed by Richard Siodmak. His most notable success was *Old Soldiers Never Die* also known as *Medal For The General* published in 1942, and made into the film in 1944 directed by Maurice Elvey. Unsurprisingly, on the odd occasion he came to visit, my father and James Ronald got on extremely well.

My mother was a hairdresser by profession and worked at Maison Simmons in Richmond, run by a dubious individual with a bow tie. I used to wait at the salon after school, for what seemed an eternity, for my mother to finish work and take me home. I still hate the smell of ammonia, an ingredient used in hair products for tinting and colouring hair. When she first went to work there, they mistakenly called her Carol instead of Isobel and the name stuck.

My father's connections with Italia Conti of the famous stage school led to both sons attending and adopting the name Verner, eventually cemented by deed poll, and creating the somewhat ludicrous situation that no one in the family was living under their true identity! They both went on to have extensive careers in the theatre profession, acting, directing, and producing.

Between 9 September 1940, when high explosives bombs fell on Mount Ararat Road, and March 1945, when one of the last V2 rockets exploded in Richmond Park, the town suffered over 450 separate bombing incidents, most of them in the winter of 1940/41.

In June 1944 the first flying bombs fell on London; they were usually called 'buzz-bombs' or 'doodle-bugs.' During the *doodlebugging* of Richmond and Kingston, my father, mother, and her two boys, Anthony and James, who I called Tony and Jimmy, would run to shelter in the cellar at the home of Claude Perkis, a lifelong friend of my fathers who owned an antique shop and later a popular and affordable Knightsbridge restaurant called *Fiddlers Three* in Beauchamp Place.

The restaurant was very well thought of and specialised in East European cuisine like goulash, boiled silverside and dumplings, whole small pigeon, stuffed baby marrows, prune and orange jelly, home-made soups, kedgeree with cheese sauce, and home-made cream cheese. It was one of the first London restaurants to display the blue and red circle of the *Relais Routiers*. Claude Perkis was eventually to sell the restaurant and retire to the Isle of Wight but always managed to meet my father for lunch every two or three years for a chat.

* * *

## CHAPTER EIGHT: THE WAR YEARS

A young German Jewish émigré David Gottlieb launched the twin publishing imprints of John Westhouse and Peter Lunn, based at 49 Chancery Lane, London WC2. The venture was an ambitious but short-lived one. Between 1943 and 1948 Gottlieb published some 70 John Westhouse books for adults and 120 Peter Lunn books for children before he went bust.

The book my father sent to John Westhouse was titled *Thirsty Evil* for which a first payment of £50 was sent to him on 20 October 1944. On 8 November he received £105 from the same publisher in respect of all rights to a *witchcraft anthology* to be published as *Come not, Lucifer!* The book was published in 1945. My father was not credited. In the Publisher's note he writes:

> "The Romantic writers (that is to say, in this context, writers whose work is of the romantic type) were men perpetually afraid, perpetually disgusted, yet perpetually fascinated. This is true of such divergent personalities as Charles Dickens and Auguste comte de *Villiers de L'Isle Adam: it is particularly true of these magnificent great figures – Herman Melville and Edgar Allen Poe (strange that the two largest exponents of the old 'dark' type of writing should have been nurtured in the newest – and therefore, presumably, the cleanest – of literatures!). It is the paradox of this joint essence of disgust and fascination that makes the Romantics and Decadents what they are. What disgusted yet fascinated them? The answer must vary with the individual, but in the most general sense it was life itself, and all that lay hidden beneath the surface of it – particularly this latter: the other side of the coin – the shadow of the shadow."*

The book is described as a classic anthology of macabre and chilling tales from the inkwells of some of the greatest literary masters of the 19th century with phantasmagoric illustrations. R. A. Brandt's drawings reminded me of the work of Mervyn Peake. They are alive with the feeling of torture and fascination of these twelve stories in which the Romantic mind has found its creative expression:

Edgar Allen Poe - King Pest
Edgar Allen Poe - The Case of M. Valdemar
Edgar Allen Poe - The Black Cat

# PLOTS AND GUNPOWDER

Herman Melville – Bartleby
Charles Dickens - The Signalman
Joseph Sheridan Le Fanu - The Watcher
Honore de Balzac - The Oath
Auguste Villiers de l'Isle Adam - Torture by Hope
Alexander S. Pushkin - The Pistol Shot
Alexander S. Pushkin - The Queen of Spades
Robert Louis Stevenson - Thrawn Janet
Robert Louis Stevenson - A lodging for the Night

December 1944 produced another letter from John Westhouse regarding *Thirsty Evil*, enclosing a cheque for £50 and confirming Gerald Verner had to date received £150 on account of the book with a final payment due of £50 on publication. By February 1945 my father had sent the first 194 pages of the book. A letter from John Westhouse requests when they might expect the rest of it! By March 1945 they have the entire book and write:

> "I liked the book very much indeed and have no doubt in saying that it will be a success. The manuscript is now with the printer."

John Westhouse launched *Thirsty Evil* in October 1945. The story is divided into three parts, *Bubbling Cauldron, Devil's Brew*, and *Dregs*. It is set in a typical English village. Murder then strikes! Suspense and mystery are thrust suddenly and overpoweringly into the life of this small community, incidents building to a thrilling climax. The story was rewritten as *Grim Death* by Gerald Verner for Wright & Brown in 1960.

*Thirsty Evil* was followed by *Prince of Darkness* in June 1946. It was a collection of fact and fiction about Witchcraft. The book is divided up into four sections beginning with *Witchcult*, followed by *Satanism, Sorcery*, and finally *Lycanthropy*. As part of his introduction my father said:

> "Witchcraft is an absorbing subject whether you approach it as a sceptic, a believer, or just one of those people who adopt a well-there-may-be-something-in-it attitude."

The book included verse from *The Witches Moon* he called *The Covens:*

Midnight, and the air is foul
With flying figures rushing fast
Toward the wood. A ghastly band, they howl
And shriek with frenzied glee as they go past
Into the night to meet Asmodeus.
A dreadful chorus, with a wailing croon,
Across the fair face of the Witches' Moon.

When John Westhouse went bust, Rider picked up the book and reprinted it in 1951.

Having read a spate of Dennis Wheatley, the bestselling author of several black magic novels, including *The Devil Rides Out*, considered the best thing of its kind since Bram Stoker's *Dracula*, and a masterpiece that scared the pants off me, *The Haunting of Toby Jugg*, I became fascinated in the subject and wondered if there *was* something in it. Has science explained away witchcraft and sorcery these days so that everything is simple and straightforward? Of course, there is much evidence every day of evil in the world but summoning the devil?

I asked my father about the supernatural. Is Evil real? He was not a religious person but had a healthy respect for anyone with a personal experience of the supernatural. He told me he knew Dennis Wheatley, who had told him he held a puritanical fear of the occult and strongly recommended anyone *not* to get involved in any aspect of it, and that Wheatley regretted his own involvement in writing such books. He prefixed his stories with earnest warnings about its dangers which only added to their allure and I bet he didn't regret the royalties. I was both fascinated and impressed by his answer and immediately delved into as many occult books as I could lay my hands on both fictional and factual. The more deeply religious a person is, brought up to believe in the actual existence of the devil and demons and to fear them, the greater the substance of the Black Mass ritual.

\* \* \*

By April 1944 my father still lived in Richmond but had moved from Lichfield Court to a Victorian house at 15, Marlborough Road, a now sought-after prestigious address on Richmond Hill. My father rented the top floor, known as Flat 4.

A contract arrived from Wright & Brown on 31 January 1945, sent from 1 Crane Court. The contract was for two novels, *The Heal of Achilles* and *The Twelve Apostles,* to be published at 7/6d.

*The Heel of Achilles* (The erroneously listed *The Secret Weapon*), was dedicated to my mother: *For Carol. The Twelve Apostles* followed in 1946. He received an advance of £70 for each of these books against royalties of 10% up to the sale of 2,000 copies; 12.5% up to the sale of 4000 copies; 15% on the books over and above the first 4000 copies. There were further royalties for oversees and cheaper editions.

I have a typewritten sheet of paper dated 3 September 1945 acknowledging the sum of £195 for the absolute copyright of *The Seven Lamps* to Wright & Brown. My understanding of the publishing date for this book is 1947. It must have taken over a year for it to come to print or this deal was postponed to a later date.

To everyone's relief, Germany surrendered unconditionally on all fronts at 2.41pm on 7 May in Rheims, but Japan didn't surrender until 15 August 1945. The surrender documents were finally signed at Tokyo Bay on the deck of the American battleship USS Missouri on 2 September 1945. The war was officially over.

# Chapter Nine – Richmond

I n July 1946, my father married Carol, my mother, Isobel Ronald, in the registration district of North Eastern Surrey. The wedding records have entered both names belonging to my father, both Gerald Verner and John R. S. Pringle. My mother became Isobel Verner, late Ronald, and formerly Wade, born 29 November 1916, at Patrington in Yorkshire. They took a coach trip to Switzerland as a honeymoon.

I have a letter from my grandmother Aunty Gerry (still masquerading as my father's sister) to my mother. Aunty Gerry's address is 10 Granville Road, Sidcup, Kent. It is dated 12 July 1946:

> *"My Dear Isobel, first let me wish you the best of good wishes on your marriage with my brother and may you both be very happy. I have been trying to think of a suitable wedding present for you and I have decided to make over to you the entire copyrights of the play entitled "Mr & Mrs Bluebeard" which I have held for some years now. I feel if you could do something with it one day it would bring you in a nice little nest egg.*
> *Geraldine."*

\* \* \*

I was born Christopher Stuart Verner, by caesarean birth, by an eminent consultant at a private hospital in Twickenham, on 13 December 1949. It was an auspicious beginning that was destined not to last. From this point forward, this biography includes me as an observer and witness to some events, resulting in a more personal, emotive, and perhaps critical viewpoint.

By my arrival my father was renting the rest of 15 Marlborough Road, all three floors, except the basement. He bought most of the furniture from the antique shop owned by his friend Claude Perkis, and very nice pieces they were. I always thought the house a rambling, cold, impersonal place. There was a bathroom on every floor with an Ascot gas water heater. Condensation would collect upon the ceiling swelling to produce cold drips that bombed you while bathing. The ground floor consisted of a large living room/dining room, with a kitchen at the back. The first floor was divided into two areas off a landing. Number 15 no longer exists; it has been amalgamated with the house next door to form one large house converted into expensive apartments. The tall privet hedge and front garden is gone, replaced with a residents parking area.

My father's mother, Aunty Gerry came from Sidcup to join the new family. She occupied the area overlooking the back garden, consisting of a self-contained living room, bedroom, bathroom, and small kitchen. A large round table took up most of the living room beyond which by the window stood her *Singer* sewing machine worked by a treadmill. She made lampshades and there was usually always one in the process of being completed.

My father's mother was known to the Verner family as Aunty Gerry or Geraldine. They never knew her as my father's mother as my father never confided this truth. She was always introduced as his sister, a continuation of her stage days when it would never have done to have been married with a son—hence her stage name Miss Geraldine Verner not Nelly Pringle. I didn't find out the truth until I began researching this biography in 2012.

When my parents went out in the evening it was *Aunty Gerry,* never Granny, who looked after me. Following the ritual of listening to *The Archers,* she often put me to bed. She had a black and white cat called Flook. A strip cartoon series ran in the *Daily Mail* from the year of my birth to 1984, featuring Rufus and his magical animal friend Flook. They were up against the villainous Moses Maggot and his sidekick Bodger. I was very fond of Flook, both the cat and the cartoon series.

Opposite Aunty Gerry's self-contained abode on the first floor, at the front of the house, was a spacious drawing room leading to a cramped study where my father wrote. His study was packed with books, a

compact desk on which stood a typewriter, a desk lamp and, in macabre fashion, a real skull. Artwork of a skull, with his signature across it, was a trademark for his novels:

The top floor was devoted to bedrooms. My spooky bedroom was at the back. It overlooked the garden.

At the bottom of the garden a row of tall poplar trees swayed in the wind casting eerie shadows over my bedroom walls when the moon shone through them. We had Valor paraffin heaters that added flickering patterns on the ceiling and stank when the wicks burned low. There was an old wicker chair in one corner painted gold behind which I was convinced something was lurking. When I went to bed at night, I felt isolated and often scared to death, imagining a real supernatural presence in the room where shadows would coalesce to form a threatening entity. The top floor of this house would have made an ideal setting for one of my father's murder mysteries, more macabre to me than anything he had written. My parents could be faintly heard two floors down. I used to smuggle knives to my bedroom and keep one within easy reach under my pillow as protection. On a stormy night I used to lie in bed petrified as the rain slammed against the windowpanes and shadows leapt alive around the walls enhanced by my imagination. The air had the sulphurous whiff of gunpowder. A narrow archway opened from my bedroom to a *firework* room. With the light turned off this became a menacing place from which a host of ghastly entities threatened to issue forth... Ditto, the underneath of the large mahogany wardrobe. No *Amityville Horror* or *The Conjuring* could hold a candle to the terrors of my bedroom once the lights were out and the shadows began dancing. I often sat on the stairs, comforted by listening to the laughter emanating from two floors below, freezing in pyjamas, my feet bare and turning to blocks of ice, as I waited until someone came up to bed and I knew I would be safe.

The firework room was a small box room packed with bottles of chemicals where my father would spend hours mixing formulae to improve coloured fire for *stars* which he put into shells and other pyrotechnic devices for his firework displays, gradually filling the upstairs rooms with fireworks of every description until the night of the display. These fireworks were not 5 November type stuff in boxes but full-size set-pieces in the style he had witnessed at The Crystal Palace. These displays became a local annual event in the gardens of *The Marlborough* public house in Friars Stile Road. When he'd completed a bout of writing he would come to this room to relax and experiment. He made a Heath-Robinson gadget to grind course powders to fine. This consisted of a Cocoa tin containing glass marbles powered by a wind-up clockwork motor from an old gramophone player.

One day he brought back a glass jar and gleefully showed me the contents, an emerald-green crystalline powder. *This is very poisonous*, he told me solemnly, *and you must never touch it!* I stared with fascination at the toxic green powder, thrilled at how dangerous it was, thinking I could now dispose of any enemies whenever I wanted!

*What's it for?* I asked.

*It makes wonderful blue stars,* he told me. *It's called Paris Green.*

On another occasion he came home with a box of shotgun cartridges which he opened to extract the gunpowder. It was a miracle we weren't burned alive or blown to bits! He taught me all the firework formulas. By the time I was eight years old, I knew a great deal about the chemistry and art of pyrotechnics. I knew how to make fireworks. Never, at that time, did I imagine this knowledge would prove lucrative much later in my life. It opened many doors, rewarding me years of financial stability and a lot of fun.

In the basement lived Mr. & Mrs. Keene, who had use of the back garden. We didn't see much of them. Mr. Keene's face was hidden beneath white bandages. I was told he had been a news vendor and chewed copper pennies. This had given him cancer. Part of his face was eaten away. I was too young to feel sorry for Mr. Keene at the time, his appearance just terrified me. I had nightmares about him slowly unwrapping his bandages to reveal a dreadful countenance. So, whenever he appeared, which was seldom, I scooted into hiding.

\* \* \*

A letter to Noel Lee written from Flat 4, 15 Marlborough Road, 16 October 1945, picks up on what happened to the manuscript sent by Noel to my father back before the war in 1939, which has been published by Wright & Brown in 1940 as *The Poisoner* by Gerald Verner.

"I was surprised and pleased to hear from you. The last news I had of you was a Yorkshire paper containing a column interview referring to *The Poisoner*. I can quite imagine that you have a heap of comments to make about that. My version of it would fill up pages so I can only answer you that it was never my intention that the manuscript should reach publication under my name. I was in the middle of writing *The Poisoner* when it became tremendously urgent to find some money quickly. I sent your manuscript to Wright & Brown at the time with the intention of exchanging it later for the proper one. To my consternation, it was rushed through the printers and I was presented with a proof and a comment that they couldn't see why the story had been called *The Poisoner!* I made a single alteration in the story to account for this and wired you with the intention of explaining. A landmine blew the whole place to smithereens—I'm very lucky to be alive—since then, as you say, quite a lot of things have happened. However, it seems that this unfortunate incident of *The Poisoner* has done what you wanted and turned you into a fully -fledged author in double-quick time. I understand that you are writing for Wright & Brown. In the normal way, with paper restrictions, no new authors, however good, would have stood a hope of getting published. I congratulate you on your marriage and am sorry to hear that things are financially tight. They are tight with me and look like remaining so for some time— particularly with the Labour government in control."

When many years later I personally found out from Noel Lee about this subterfuge I tackled my father about it in disbelief. He reiterated the fact that it had never been his intention for Noel's manuscript to be published and admitted it had been a foolish and thoughtless act of desperation. One can only imagine the disappointment and despair this generated in Noel at that time with his first attempt at writing a thriller vanishing in front of his eyes. My father reiterates his own manuscript was destroyed by the bomb which fell on Thames Ditton and was obviously *really* about a poisoner. To my knowledge, this story has never been reimagined or resurrected. There had been no attempt to plagiarize Noel's story, evidenced by the bemused enquiry from the publishers as to why the story had been called *The Poisoner!* Also, he dedicated the book to *Noel Lee to whom I am indebted for this story.*

In a letter dated 8 November 1945, my father writes with a distinct change of tone revealing an uncharacteristic arrogance as he attempts to salve his conscience.

> "In reply to your letter of the 3rd inst. I have seen Mr. Brown of Messrs. Wright & Brown Limited and I understand that you have drawn £75.15.2 in royalties to date for *The Poisoner*. I cannot, therefor, see any reason for my *making amends* as you call it. Apart from this you have been able to publish a number of new books which you would certainly not have been able to do otherwise. In fact, you have come off extremely well over the whole matter. I cannot, in the circumstances, agree to your proposal that I should supply you with a manuscript of mine to rewrite. This is quite definite and there would be no point in your coming to see me. If you wish to discuss the matter further, I suggest that you arrange for Mr. Brown to act as arbitrator, otherwise there is nothing more I have to say."

Previous letters have seen signed with yours sincerely, this is coldly signed yours faithfully. However unjust my father's actions appear, they did open the door to Wright & Brown for Noel at a time when it would have otherwise been firmly closed and allowed him to publish further books. Following *The Poisoner* in 1940, which has to be recognized as Noel Lee's first book, came *Papers Mean Peril* 1942, and *Danger In Numbers* 1944. From the back of the dust jacket this is part of a brief resume:

> "Unlike the last war, this present conflagration has produced few new writers, but of the few it has produced, none is more fitted to take an honoured place than Noel Lee. Serving himself soon after the outbreak of hostilities, then later discharged from the Army after a series of illnesses, Mr. Lee returned to civilian life and to his pre-war hobby of story-writing to find that of the few newcomers to be recognized, he was one."

The next communication to Noel Lee is not for almost a year. On 20 September 1946 my father writes:

> "I am expecting a cheque very shortly and as soon as it arrives I will at once forward you the £2. Until it reaches me, I'm afraid I'm not in a position to do so. I am very sorry to hear how bad

things are with you, but, although I realise it is little consolation, most people these days are in the same boat."

He is back to signing off, sincerely. The following month he sends a letter enclosing the £2 and hopes Noel Lee's situation will rapidly improve. On 21 October 1946 he writes again:

"I would willingly offer the second serial rights of *The Poisoner* for you if there was any market to offer it to but there isn't. There is no serial market, neither first nor second left in this county except in the women's magazines and weeklies and they require love romances. If you can find a market for thriller serials, I shall be only too pleased to hear about it."

Desperate to raise money Noel Lee asks my father about other opportunities. My father replies 24 October 1946:

"With regard to Mellifont, Cherry Tree, etc., for the cheap rights of your novels, Mr. Brown has always dealt with these for me and perhaps he will do the same for you. I would not, however, bank on any quick money from these sources. They quite often take a long time to push a cheque through. Markets are very difficult just now, but I suggest that you try some short stories 1,500 words to 2,000 with newspapers like *The Evening News*, or any pictorial weekly that publishes short stories."

On 9 November 1946 my father replies to a request from Noel Lee for a copy of *The Poisoner:*

"I have not got a copy of *The Poisoner.* The manuscript was destroyed by the bomb which fell on Thames Ditton. Perhaps Mr. Brown can let you have a copy of the book. I expect he would also offer the cheap rights if you asked him."

There are no more letters until 3 June 1948 when my father is still writing to Noel Lee discussing paper restrictions which are still a major stumbling block to the publishing world getting back on its feet. Noel lived in Malton, Yorkshire. His final book, *Fear Without End*, was published in 1949.

# PLOTS AND GUNPOWDER

In his letter of May 1949, my father writes to Noel Lee, and the problems of *The Poisoner* appear to have been resolved if not forgotten. A genuine friendship is slowly blossoming.

\* \* \*

The research my father carried out for *Prince of Darkness* must have stirred his imagination. I surmise that he had two stories in mind at this time, one was to become a classic macabre tale *They Walk in Darkness* and the other was *Wizard's Window,* which with a change of title, would emerge to become *Sorcerer's House,* a book with a supernatural atmosphere to be published by Hutchinson in 1956. The publication marked a more successful second attempt to move away from Wright & Brown, at least for a while.

*They Walk in Darkness* was originally titled *Witches House.* My father looking for a passport away from Wright & Brown arranged for the manuscript to be sent to Hodder & Stoughton at the end of February 1946. Mr. Hodder Williams replied to my father's agent early March:

> "Mr. Verner can grip, but he has not written the right book for Hodder & Stoughton. We fight shy of the Black Mass—and we shall go on fighting shy of the Black Mass."

Disappointed, my father then re-titled the manuscript *They Walk in Darkness* and sent it to David Gottlieb at John Westhouse who on 21 March 1946 agreed to publish it on the same terms as *Thirsty Evil.* However, suffering financial difficulties, Gottlieb would not pay on account of royalties until publication day and then only £200. I am sure my father read this reply with shock, so nothing further happened. Two attempts at transferring to a new publisher had temporarily been thwarted.

Meanwhile my father sold *Wizard's Window,* as a title only, to Wright & Brown in May 1947, for which he received £195 plus five guineas for the cover design. The book they received for this contract/sum was the other story *They Walk in Darkness* which they published in November 1947.

The story is laid in the Fen country. This sombre background with blank wastes of marshland formed a fitting setting for a powerful and absorbing tale that was macabre in its conception concerned with horrifying events in the village of Fendyke St. Mary. The book was constructed in four parts beginning with *The Eve of All-Hallows*. Part two was *The Black Man,* part three *The Coven,* ending with part four *Absolute Evil.* I think it fair to say this story is his best work. It is packed with atmosphere and foreboding. Reviews emphasised:

"…this was a story of Fenland Satan worship and vile ritual murder, not for the faint hearted, and hardly a bed-time tale!"

\* \* \*

Diversification following the war was essential for survival. Of course, I knew nothing about any of that! In 1948 Gerald Verner wrote *The Royal Flush Murders* for Wright & Brown. He was also busy writing for the Radio:

"A warning voice on the telephone, a shot in the dark, and the mystery criminal is front page news."

From 5 April–24 May 1948, saw the opening on radio of Gerald Verner's serial thriller in eight episodes *The Tipster* with James McKechnie, Belle Chrystall and Laidman Browne. The serial was produced by David H Godfrey. My father was paid the exact sum of £31.10.0 per episode. The Radio Times reported:

**8.0**    **James McKechnie and Belle Chrystall in**
**'THE TIPSTER'**
Serial thriller for broadcasting by Gerald Verner
Produced by David H. Godfrey
1—'Information from the Tipster'

| | |
|---|---|
| Gordon Cross | James McKechnie |
| Vicky Cross | Belle Chrystall |
| Superintendent Budd | Clifford Buckton |
| Colonel Blair | Laidman Browne |
| Iris Latimer | Betty Linton |
| Masters | Ian Sadler |
| David Kenwood | Lewis Stringer |
| Maurice Swayne | Oliver Burt |
| John Tully | Sidney Monckton |
| Detective-Sergeant Leek | Alan Reid |
| George Dowling | Rodney Lovick |
| Lord Latimer | William Trent |

(BBC recording)

"For many years Gerald Verner has wanted to try his hand at radio drama, but a contract with his publishers calling for seven full-length novels a year and commissions for a great number of short stories and serials left him with no time to spare for anything else. Now, however, owing to paper restrictions and difficulties in the book binding and printing trades, it is impossible for him to publish more than two books in a year, and he has had time to realise his ambition. The result is The Tipster, opening as an eight-part serial in the Light Programme on Monday. Gerald Verner believes that radio is the ideal medium for the detective, mystery, or thriller story. Why? Because 'it is possible to create an atmosphere of fear, horror, and suspense, with greater realism than can be achieved on the stage or film or with the printed word.'"

And 31 August–19 October 1948, sees a second radio serial in eight parts of 30 minutes called *The Show Must Go On* with Marjorie Westbury, Geoffrey Lewis, John Bentley, and Olaf Olsen. This production featured lyrics by Edward J Mason and music by Basil Hempseed. It was produced by Martyn C Webster and Archie Campbell.

The star of a London musical walks out before curtain-up at The Regency, a supposedly haunted theatre, but the show must go on. Forty years previously the star of Hamlet was

9.30  'THE SHOW MUST GO ON'
A new serial in eight episodes
by Gerald Verner
Lyrics by Edward J. Mason
Music by Basil Hempseed
1—'Overture and Beginners'
Tangye Ward........Marjorie Westbury
Clifford Brett..............Geoffrey Lewis
Keith Gilbert........................John Bentley
Ronald Hays................Cyril Gardiner
'Nutty' Potts..............Charles Lamb
Olivia Winter..........Elizabeth Maude
Philip Defoe......................Olaf Olsen
Madelain Peters...Catherine Campbell
Angus Macdonald................Ian Sadler
Maysie Sheringham...Beverley Wright
Victor Price..............Kenneth Morgan
Pianists:
Peggy Desmond and Bert Whittam
Production by Martyn C. Webster
and Archie Campbell

murdered, and more are dying to keep a dark secret. In the first instalment a theatrical company is rehearsing a new revue in the theatre rented by an ex-army batman who has won £70,000 on the pools. Then the fun begins....

Collie Knox of the *Daily Mail* wrote:

"Gerald Verner shares his success not only with an excellent cast but with producers Martyn C Webster and Archie Campbell. Technically this production was vastly complicated. The work done at the control panel and the gramophone turntables by Frederick Bell and his staff in these multi-microphone shows is vital. Mr. Bell has no superior in his own line. With effects miracles achieved, from the gurgle of a strangulated heroine to an echo in a valley."

The contract, between the BBC Light Programme and Gerald Verner, dated 17 June 1948 paid a fee of £36.15.0. per instalment, with one instalment in advance and the remaining seven as accepted. A further contract was issued on 4 October 1948 after the initial broadcast on 31

August 1948, for £196.0.0. for the BBC to have the right to make recordings and to broadcast them in any part of the world for up to three years. It was signed by Gerald Verner on 7 October 1948.

A BBC production aired from 9.30 to 10.00 pm on 2YA Auckland, New Zealand, on 29 June 1949. It was cited in the Bay of Plenty Times as "a musical thriller by Gerald Verner, telling of the adventures of a theatrical company at rehearsal in a haunted house." The serial also aired on the following dates on these radio channels: (possibly repeats) 13 July 1949 - 2YA Wellington; 25 October 1949 - 3YA Christchurch; 27 November 1949 - 3YA Christchurch.

Currently, to my knowledge, no recording of this serial survives. By 1939, 78 rpm acetate disk recording technology was available to the BBC but resulted in sound quality that made it obvious one was listening to a recording and was not up to the quality of a live broadcast. Tape was also in use but in its infancy. The fact that gramophone turntables were used by Frederick Bell and his staff speaks for itself. Many took the view that a recording was not a genuine performance and so recordings were not in favour.

*The Show Must Go On* was turned into a book by Gerald Verner for Wright & Brown in 1950. He also adapted the story into a screenplay for a 70-minute B Movie made in 1952 called *Tread Softly*. Described as a musical with a mystery angle, a chorus girl investigates a series of mysterious happenings at a derelict theatre. The film was made by Albany Films, directed by David Macdonald, and made at Marylebone Studios. The auditorium scenes for the Regency Theatre were filmed at the former Granville Theatre of Varieties on Waltham Green (now Fulham Broadway) demolished in 1971. The outside views of the theatre are of *The Palace Theatre*, Shaftesbury Avenue.

Frances Day played the lead supported by Patricia Dainton, John Bentley (reprising his role from the radio serial, and known for three films based on Francis Durbridge's Paul Temple the amateur detective, John Laurie (known to many for his role in *Dad's Army*) and Betty Baskcomb (her screen debut was in the 1934 film directed by Alfred Hitchcock, *The Man Who Knew Too Much*). It marks the first film appearance of Sir Kenneth MacMillan (uncredited) later to be considered one of the greatest choreographers, who died backstage in the Royal Opera House, Covent Garden, in 1992. The title song is *End of the Day*, music by Basil Hempseed and lyrics by Edward J Mason.

A good rendition of the film is available on DVD (Black & White,

Mono, Aspect Ratio 1.37: 1); *The Renown Vintage Chiller and Thriller Collection*, as one of nine classic British thrillers. There also is an interview with Patricia Dainton on her 86th birthday recalling how she wanted to be a ballerina and train in Russia but her mother refused, insisting she go into acting.

My father appeared in a radio programme 3 June 1948, called *Stump the Storytellers*. It was a challenge to famous authors (Gerald Verner, Stewart MacPherson, and permanent fixture in all the programmes L.A.G. Strong). It was introduced by Franklin Engelmann and Produced by Alastair Scott-Johnston. Four objects in a sealed box. Four minutes to tell the tale.

Later that autumn my father appeared on a regular radio programme beginning 26 September 1948: *Answer Next Week* (1948-49). It was described in the *Radio Times* as:

> "A problem programme including posers on crime, chess, codes, law, and bridge set by Gerald Verner, William Winter, H.C.G. Stevens, a lawyer, and Terence Reese."

*Answer Next Week* was introduced by Norman Hackforth and Edited by Ian C. Messiter. Four actors performed short sketches in Gerald Verner's case to deduce a crime problem. The programme ran from 7 November 1948 to 3 April 1949.

\* \* \*

**8.30**   Ivan Samson and
         Joan Matheson in
'NOOSE FOR A LADY'
A serial in eight parts
specially written for radio
by Gerald Verner
I—'Seven Days to Live'
Simon Dale.................Ivan Samson
Jill Hallam.............Joan Matheson
Martin Gale..........Richard Hurndall
Margaret Hallam......Grizelda Hervey
Mrs. Barrett.................Elsa Palmer
The Chaplain...........Hamilton Dyce
The Wardress.............Joan Geary
Superintendent Shelford, C.I.D.
                            Neil Tuson
Other parts played by Anne Firth,
Hugh Manning, Bryan Powley, John
Turnbull, Anthony Jacobs, and
Donald Gray
  Production by David H. Godfrey

My father's fictional detective Simon Gale is first featured in a BBC eight-part Radio Serial Play *Noose for A Lady* which was broadcast 24 July – 11 September 1950, with Ivan Samson and Joan Matheson. It subsequently became a book published by Wright & Brown in 1952. Simon Gale's first appearance takes place in a London restaurant:

"Jill lit a cigarette and looked around her. There was some kind of altercation going on near the entrance, but a pillar obscured her view, and she couldn't see what it was about. Presently a deep, booming voice reached her ears. "No room?" it roared, rising above the chatter and clatter of the place. "Nonsense, my good girl. There is an empty chair at that table over there – where that lady is sitting. I can think of no good reason why I should not occupy it. May I suggest that at the first opportunity you consult an oculist? Warne, of Wimpole Street is an excellent man."

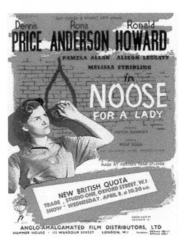

*Noose for A Lady* was made into a 73-minute B Movie in 1952 by Insignia Films Directed by Wolf Rilla (*Village of the Damned* in 1960). It was made at Merton Park, the studio that from 1960 – 64 made many *Edgar Wallace Mysteries* films. In 1992 the BFI initiated a search for some of the best lost British films. As part of this effort, they published a book *Missing Believed Lost* which listed and described 92 of the most sought-after films. *Noose for A Lady* was on that list but fortuitously has recently been found and issued on DVD by Network Distributing as part of its valuable *The British Film* collection. It is a new transfer from the original film elements.

The film features his detective Simon Gale played by Dennis Price, but quite unlike my father's description of the detective. The production unfolds against the clock ticking as Cousin Margaret (played by Pamela Alan) waits to keep a date with the hangman, wrongly convicted of poisoning her husband, unless Simon Gale, home on leave from Uganda, finds the real killer.

*Noose for A Lady* became a Wright & Brown book in 1952.

From the balcony at the *Ritz* cinema at Richmond, it was possible to look down on the booking office and the back of the cashier's head. This vantage point gave my father the idea for *The Whispering Woman*, a Superintendent Robert Budd novel about a beautiful haughty young cinema cashier who is found murdered in her booth shot in the back of the head. The story was published by Wright & Brown in 1949.

## PLOYS AND GUNPOWDER

This book was followed by *The Tipster*, the novel of the April 1948 BBC Radio Serial Play.

# Chapter Ten – Three Stage Plays

I t was as if writing the radio plays had conditioned him to a new format. My father began a spate of adapting and writing stage plays at the rate of almost one per year, beginning with the book *Towards Zero* by Agatha Christie. My father was a great Christie fan. My regular Christmas ritual was to present him with the new Christie from Collins.

Dame Agatha Mary Clarissa Christie, Lady Mallowan, DBE was an English writer known for her sixty-six detective novels and fourteen short story collections, particularly those revolving around fictional detectives Hercule Poirot and Miss Marple. Neither of these characters appeared in *Towards Zero*, published in America in three weekly instalments of *Collier's* magazine from 6 to 20 May 1944 as *Come and Be Hanged* prior to being published in hardback by Dodd, Mead and Company on 12 June 1944.

Unbeknownst to the wider public, three adaptions of *Towards Zero* were penned for the stage, including Agatha Christie's 1944 'outdoor version', L. Arthur Rose's embarrassingly inept 1947 rendition, and my own father's 1956 'indoor version' which is the official and by far best-known, having delighted generations of audiences in numerous countries around the world, and, in the process, boosting the Christie estate's coffers. The fact three different typescripts were commissioned indicates the rocky road travelled between inception and eventual West End debut.

The 'outdoor version' of *Towards Zero* was scripted by Agatha Christie and first produced by the Shubert theatrical dynasty in America in 1945. The legendary Lee Shubert had scored a major hit with *Ten Little Indians*, based on Agatha Christie's 1939 novel *Ten Little Niggers*, which opened at the Broadhurst Theatre on Broadway on 27 June 1944, later transferring to the Plymouth Theatre before closing on 30 June 1945, making it Agatha Christie's first major US success as a playwright. In August 1944, six weeks after *Ten Little Indians* opened on Broadway, Lee Shubert, recognizing Christie's marquee-pulling power, commissioned her to turn her newly published novel *Towards Zero* into her next big theatrical crowd-pleaser.

Agatha Christie later told her English literary agent, Edmund Cork, that *Towards Zero* was an unusual title for the Shubert organisation to commission as a play from her stock of novels. But owing to her precarious financial situation she was not about to turn down the fee of $5,000, half of which was payable on signature and half on delivery, with an author's royalty ranging between five and ten per cent depending on different bands of box office returns.

As I have already described in relation to my father's work, the advent of World War Two shrank the magazine serial market in England owing to paper shortages unlike America where demand for first and second serial rights of her work remained high. The bulk of Christie's income came from the US serial market, but the impact of the war, coupled with the arcane tax laws of the day, saw the American government embargo most of her US income. Christie struggled to keep afloat financially because the English tax authorities were forcing her to pay double taxation on her UK and US income despite the fact the American authorities were not handing over the large sums of money owed to her. Her decision to adapt *Towards Zero* into a play arose from her gratitude to the Shubert dynasty for master-minding her current success with *Ten Little Indians* and a frantic desire to remain financially solvent by generating further income for herself in the hope it would reach her bank accounts.

## CHAPTER TEN: THREE STAGE PLAYS

Agatha Christie's 'outdoor version' of *Towards Zero* was delivered to the Shuberts on 14 December 1944 seven weeks before its official deadline of 1 February 1945. The Shuberts had six months in which to produce the play which premiered with a cast of thirteen at Martha's Vineyard Playhouse for a limited run of six performances from 4 – 8 September 1945. London-based Christie never saw the production because she remained in England for the duration of the war which ended two days before the play opened. The production might have fared better if she had had the opportunity to attend rehearsals and make amendments to the typescript, as she had done with *Ten Little Indians* which was first tried out as *Ten Little Niggers* in the English provinces prior to a successful London West End run before crossing the pond to Broadway. The Shubert brothers cancelled plans to bring *Towards Zero* to Broadway after many of the reviews in the press were negative. Lee Shubert had hired Robert Harris to 'Americanise' the typescript to ensure audiences were able to connect with the play. Where adaptations of Christie's work in the world of entertainment are concerned, the Americanising or doctoring of her work often compromises the quintessential Englishness and integrity of her characters. This leads to a debasing of her currency and audiences are quick to spot a counterfeit. After the ill-fated week-long try-out at Martha's Vineyard, Lee Shubert wrote to Christie on 18 October 1945 asking her to rework the ending: 'We found the climax came too suddenly and the final situation was not plausible to the audience.'

The demands on Christie's time, both personally and professionally, were too great for her to fulfil Lee Shubert's request and the week-long 'outdoor version' of *Towards Zero* slipped from public consciousness. It was forgotten for decades until a copy of the typescript was discovered in 2015 in the Shubert Archives in America, then published in 2017 with the permission of the Christie Estate and marketed by Samuel French as the 'outdoor version' to differentiate it from my father's 1956 'indoor version'.

In November 1947, Christie's literary agent, Edmund Cork, entered into an agreement with the prolific playwright L Arthur Rose (1882-1958) to write a new adaptation of *Towards Zero*. Rose was best known as the co-writer of the book and lyrics for Noel Gay's hit 1937 musical *Me and My Girl*. Rose's version of *Towards Zero* was so dire it was deemed an embarrassment to both Christie and Rose and all plans to produce it were permanently shelved.

# PLOTS AND GUNPOWDER

On 28 February 1950, Christie wrote to Edmund Cork from the Middle East, where she was assisting her husband Max Mallowan on one of his archaeological digs, in response to a request from Robert Benton to dramatize *Towards Zero*:

> "It may be the natural apathy of the Near East, but I don't feel very enthusiastic about the proposed dramatization of *Towards Zero* ... I have become a bit bored with the perennial humorous policeman, but don't really care ... the Whodunit with everyone suspected in turn, and plenty of comic red herrings thrown in, really by now quite sickens me on the stage! And it's not the kind of story that *Towards Zero* is! ... Don't twist the kind of book that hasn't the right atmosphere. You might just as well start with an entirely new story. There is a large class of my books which is not full of thrills and humour, such as, for instance *Towards Zero*, *Sparkling Cyanide*, *Five Little Pigs*, *Sad Cypress*, *The Hollow*, etc. And you can't really turn a class B story into a Class A story – it doesn't lend itself to such treatment, and it doesn't seem fair to encourage Robert Benton who is an intelligent and artistic young man to do so when I probably shan't like the result. Frankly, as you know, I have never seen *Towards Zero* as good material for a play...its point is not suspicion on everybody – but suspicion and everything pointing towards the incrimination of one person – and rescue of that victim at the moment when she seems to be hopelessly doomed. But if fun and thrills are wanted, go to some other of my fifty offspring! I think, really, it might be better to give the whole thing up. What do you think?"

*If* the young Robert Benton mentioned in Christie's letter was Robert Douglas Benton, born on 29 September 1932 in Waxahachie, Texas, USA, the successful American screenwriter and film director who won the Oscars for Best Adapted Screenplay and Best Director for *Kramer vs. Kramer* (1979) and who won a third Oscar for Best Original Screenplay for *Places in the Heart* (1984), at the time of writing a dramatization of *Towards Zero* he would have been eighteen, battling with dyslexia, and may have been looking to write a screenplay, as opposed to a stage version of the play.

Christie's declaration that *Towards Zero* was not a suitable vehicle for the stage, (possibly arising from her disappointment over her own failed version and the debacle of Rose's aborted offering) might suggest that my father was inheriting a poisoned chalice when he accepted the commission of adapting it into a play.

An agreement was made on 2 March 1951, between Agatha Mary Clarissa Mallowan c/o Messrs. Hughes Massie & Co. Ltd of 40 Fleet Street, London WC4 and Gerald Verner of 15 Marlborough Road, Richmond, Surrey, to adapt *Towards Zero* for 50% to the Author and 50% to the adapter.

'The Adapter shall complete a dramatic adaptation of the said work, which shall meet with the approval of the Author within six months from the date of this agreement and shall secure a contract within twelve months from the date of this agreement for a first class production of such adaptation for a run in the regular evening bill of a London West End Theatre and shall obtain a first class production of such adaptation in the West End of London within two years thereafter…'

My father wrote his version of *Towards Zero* within three months of signing the contract. He changed the setting of the play from the garden of Lady Tressilian's home in Christie's 'outdoor version' to the drawing-room and cut the cast from thirteen to a more cost-effective eleven. Christie's approval was forthcoming under the terms of the contract my father had signed with her, indicating she considered it a vast improvement on L Arthur Rose's aborted effort. Even so, the delays in transferring my father's adaptation of *Towards Zero* from the page to the stage were interminable.

As early as 6 June 1951, Cork wrote to Christie:

> "I am afraid Bertie Meyer is going to do *Towards Zero*. He held us to the arrangement that you had told him that if he could get a good version made then he could – because of old associations – do the play. Gerald Verner's version was quite unobjectionable, in fact it is damn good, so this is all in train now, and the Howard and Wyndham people who, as you know, control most of the Number One dates, like the play, and are not only giving Bertie a selection of good dates in the autumn, but are taking a share in the show. The Howard and Wyndham participation is contingent on the parts of Neville and his two wives being played by suitable stars, which is useful reassurance from our point of view!"

This is the same B. A. Meyer who produced *Meet Mr. Callaghan*, adapted by Gerald Verner from Peter Cheyney's *The Urgent Hangman*, which opened at the Garrick Theatre on 28 May 1952. Meyer was a well-known British theatre *producer* and impresario involved with West End theatre productions for over fifty years. Sir Henry Irving had been one of his leading actors. He had been involved with other adaptations of Christie books into plays. *Alibi* a play by Michael Morton based on Agatha Christie's *The Murder of Roger Ackroyd* was presented in 1928 at the Prince of Wales Theatre starring Charles Laughton as Hercule Poirot. Meyer also produced *Ten Little Niggers* at the St. James Theatre in 1943. In 1950 he turned down an adaptation of Christie's novel *The Hollow*, which became the first of her hit plays to be produced by Peter Saunders after a notable absence of the author from the West End for several years. From Christmas 1954, Meyer enjoyed huge success with a stage adaptation of Enid Blyton's *Noddy in Toyland* which ran for six years at the Stoll Theatre in Kingsway, and which I went to see as a young boy. The goblins scared me stiff reminding me of the wardrobe in my bedroom.

'I am sending you a copy of Gerald Verner's version of *Towards Zero*,' Cork wrote to Christie on 6 June 1951, 'which several people think is pretty good. I was talking to Bertie Meyer about it this morning, and he doesn't seem to have got very far with the casting'

Why was Bertie Meyer dragging his feet?

The problem was Peter Saunders, who was busy mounting the original production of Christie's murder mystery play *The Mousetrap* which she had adapted from her radio play *Three Blind Mice*. Directed by Peter Cotes, the play opened in the West End of London on 25 November 1952 at the Ambassadors Theatre before moving across the road to its current home St. Martins Theatre in 1974. Soon afterwards, Peter Saunders also produced *Witness for the Prosecution*, a courtroom thriller adapted by Agatha Christie from her short story, which opened on 28 October 1953 at the Winter Garden Theatre. It was directed by Wallace Douglas and, like its predecessor, was an immediate hit.

Peter Cotes was keen to direct and produce *Towards Zero* (if Bertie Meyer was no longer involved) presumably because he envisaged it being a similar success to *The Mousetrap*. Indeed, Christie herself had presented Peter Cotes with a copy of my father's adaptation of *Towards Zero* as a first night gift for directing *The Mousetrap*—an endorsement of Verner's 'indoor version' if ever there was one! But it was thought by Cork that Peter Saunders ought to have first crack at *Towards Zero* if Meyer faded away.

# CHAPTER TEN: THREE STAGE PLAYS

It was not until August 1953 that Bertie Meyer finally bowed out allowing Peter Saunders to option the play, obviously looking to fit it in when *The Mousetrap* came to the end of its West End run—which of course it didn't! A year later Saunders arranged to extend his licence for *Towards Zero* at six monthly intervals. You can imagine the exasperation my father felt after writing the play to be deprived of any income from it due to these postponements. In April 1954, Edmund Cork (who was also acting as my father's literary agent) wrote to Christie:

'As you know, we have been putting off the production of *Towards Zero* so that it would not clash with your other plays. These postponements have not been entirely and altogether convenient to Gerald Verner, who is not directly interested in the other plays. He would be willing to dispose of his interest in the play for a cash sum, and I wonder if you would have any objection to ... buying out Verner? Actually, Verner's rights under his original contract would expire next September if the play is not produced by that time, but I don't suppose you would mind giving an extension of his rights for say a year, as it was to suit us that the play has not been done.'

On 15 April 1954, a company owned by the Cork family, who formally owned Hughes Massie, bought out my father's rights to *Towards Zero*, as originally outlined in the 1951 agreement, for the sum of £2,000, a not unreasonable sum in those days.

1954 was a career-defining year for Christie because *The Mousetrap* and *Witness for the Prosecution* were still going strong and on 14 September her latest play *Spider's Web* opened at the Savoy Theatre, making her the first and only female playwright in the history of the British Theatre to ever have three plays running simultaneously in the West End. The year ended on a greater celebratory note for her when an American production of *Witness for the Prosecution* premiered at the Henry Miller Theatre in New York on 16 December. How many playwrights can boast one of their plays is appearing in the West End and on Broadway simultaneously?

Due to a change in copyright law, the assigned American rights in *Towards Zero*, including film rights, reverted to me after twenty-five years as my father's heir following his death in 1980. I was pleased to receive my share of American productions of the play plus 25% of any film rights, details of which are covered in the final part of this book *Postmortem*. As it turned out the 1954 *buyout* of my father's rights in the play had not been such a bad business decision on his behalf, after all.

In mid-1956 *Towards Zero* finally went into rehearsal under the direction of Murray Macdonald (who in 1952 directed my brother Jimmy Verner, playing a schoolboy in *Red Letter Day* at the Garrick Theatre). Charles Osborne in his book *The Life and Crimes of Agatha Christie* talks about the author being painfully shy but toughening up as rehearsals progressed. Apparently, when unknown actress Mary Law asked her if she could change a line she was having difficulty with, Christie replied from the stalls: 'Yes, I do mind. I want you to say, "I hate her, I hate her, I hate her".'

Mary Law, who appeared in *The Mousetrap* in 1957 and then again in 1976, elaborated on Christie's reasons for being such a stickler about dialogue in Gwen Robyn's biography *The Mystery of Agatha Christie*.

'Her dialogue does not bear any resemblance to what one says in normal life. She always seems to have a great deal of repetition. You have to say "horrible, horrible, horrible" three times or "he's dead, dead, dead." It's very strange but in fact, she was absolutely right when she refused to let us cut it down to one. It's much better in a funny way when you say it three times. Whether it is because the foreigners in the audience only get it on the third round, I am not sure, but for the actors making these repetitions sound viable it is very difficult. I reckon if you can act in an Agatha Christie play you can play in anything. It's rather like a lesson. I think that everyone at drama school should be made to do an Agatha Christie. If they can make it real and make it sincere then it works 100 per cent, let's face it, but if they can't, it is better to give up. It is a real test for everyone.'

It is interesting to note that at the time of writing this biography, the Wikipedia stage entry for *Towards Zero* inaccurately states: 'In 1956, Christie adapted the book into a play' whereas, in fact, *Towards Zero* was adapted by Gerald Verner in 1951, with no collaboration from Christie, the adaptation being all his own work, as evidenced by terms of the contract and the Cork letters. Was my father's original adaptation edited by Christie? As she sat in the stalls, did Peter Saunders encourage her to alter the typescript so he could legitimately present the play as a co-adaptation?

In a letter to researcher Michael Prichard dated 30 March 1968, Christie stated diplomatically that she 'had a certain amount of collaboration with Gerald Verner in *Towards Zero*' while in an undated letter she penned to her daughter Rosalind in July 1971 she was blunter, writing that Saunders 'urged me into helping with *Towards Zero*' and that she 'never liked it'. This tallies with a remark once made by Christie to the effect that she disliked collaborations because both parties are left feeling as if they have done all the work and only received half the money. This might appear to imply she did a substantial amount of tinkering on my father's typescript whereas, in fact, it must be remembered she went to the far greater effort of writing the novel in the first instance during the deprivations of wartime England.

There is no evidence that Christie made any significant changes to my father's version, although in the absence of any working drafts or indeed any correspondence between the two writers, it is impossible to identify either Verner's original material or the exact extent of her contribution. Intriguingly, the typescripts held in the Christie archive credit neither of the 'collaborators' and even the copy submitted to the Lord Chamberlain's office carries neither of their names, although it is filed under Christie's alone. There are some desultory scribbles from her on what appears to be, to all intents and purposes, a performance-ready typescript, and this already includes a sequence in the opening stage directions for which, from Notebook 17, we know she was responsible. Some jottings relating to her work on this version of the play can be found elsewhere in the notebooks, and at some point, between the undated typescripts a few minor changes regarding the division of the scenes when it morphed from a three-act play into the two-act one with which audiences are familiar today.

Most notably, all available typescripts of the play contain a dramatic plot twist which does not feature in the book but for which there is a prototype in Christie's 1944 'outdoor version.' The killer departs from the stage pursued by the police only to make a surprise return to the stage to finish off the one character who has remained behind. We shall probably never know if my father was asked to include this scene from Christie's 1944 'outdoor version' or if it was added by Christie when she edited his typescript. The scene certainly makes for exciting theatre.

After a try-out in August at the Theatre Royal in Nottingham followed by a short provincial tour, *Towards Zero* opened on 4 September 1956 at the St. James's Theatre, King Street, London SW1. The play starred George Baker, in his first West End starring role, with William Kendall, and Gwen Cherrell. By this time, my father will have spent the money he earned from his various theatrical ventures, including the £2000 pocketed from the *Towards Zero* rights buy out in 1954. The opening must have been a sad occasion for him as by then he had little to do with it.

PLOTS AND GUNPOWDER

On the title page of the programme the play was billed as:

## TOWARDS ZERO
By Agatha Christie
Adapted from Agatha Christie's book. "Towards Zero", by the
authoress and Gerald Verner

ST. JAMES'S THEATRE
KING STREET, S.W.1

Sole Proprietors: S. J. & L. Ltd.
Joint Managing Directors: GILBERT MILLER and PRINCE LITTLER
Licensed by the Lord Chamberlain to PRINCE LITTLER
Under the direction of Sir LAURENCE OLIVIER

PETER SAUNDERS
presents

**TOWARDS ZERO**
by
AGATHA CHRISTIE

Adapted from Agatha Christie's book, " Towards Zero ",
by the authoress and Gerald Verner

Directed by MURRAY MACDONALD

Décor by Michael Weight

First Performance : Tuesday, 4th September, 1956

Is the side-lining of my father's credit as full adapter of the play the reason for a telegram from Peter Saunders to him dated 4 September 1956, the day the play opened? The telegram read:

'I hope that we are still friends. Good luck and best wishes, regards, Peter Saunders.'

*Towards Zero* cost £3,456 to put on. Though only a moderate West End success, sometimes playing to half-empty houses, this 'indoor version' is now accepted as the official dramatization of the novel. Much to Peter Saunders chagrin, one of Christie's most ardent admirers Her Majesty Queen Elizabeth II visited on just such a half-empty house occasion. Some blamed the short run, on Milton Shuman, the acerbic *Evening Standard* theatre critic, who gave away the identity of the killer at the end of his review which led to a torrent of complaints. Kenneth Tynan (who I met on several occasions when I worked for the National Theatre and who terrified theatre directors with his biting criticisms of their work) said the writing was flat. However, the reviews were generally favourable, and the play ran until 6 March 1957 notching up a total 205 performances. Once the play had closed, so too did the theatre which was demolished to make way for an office block. The play under licence to Geoffrey Hastings Ltd immediately went on a tour of the English provinces and following the publication of the Samuel French edition in 1958 has thrived ever since in repertory and amateur productions. For reasons that are not clear, there was no American production of *Towards Zero* until June 1977 at the Olney Theatre in Maryland.

# CHAPTER TEN: THREE STAGE PLAYS

In numerous articles, books and productions over the years, my father's writing credit has frequently been dropped. This has led to a number of confused assumptions: namely that Agatha Christie adapted the 'indoor version' directly for the stage by herself or, Agatha Christie and Gerald Verner were co-collaborators who passed the typescript back and forth between each other as part of a joint consultation process that saw them sharing equal writing honours, *or Towards Zero was* adapted for the stage with the additional help of *Gerald Verner serving as a script-doctor. If* any of these scenarios were true, my father would have been entitled to only 25% instead of the contracted 50%.

Although Agatha Christie's last four plays had been hits, history shows she was not immune to failure and the envy of critics. Her next West End theatrical venture was a huge flop. *Verdict,* an original play written by Christie alone, also produced by Peter Saunders, opened on 22 May 1958 at the Strand Theatre and ran for only 36 performances. Saunders later remarked it received some of the most savage reviews he'd ever known. Christie knew only too well there were no sure-fire guaranteed successes on the stage. Plays were like racehorses that could disappoint or delight. Both *Towards Zero* and *Verdict,* along with the plays Christie wrote by herself, have enjoyed an extraordinarily successful after-life on the professional and amateur theatre circuits throughout the world, as one would expect from a literary goddess who also happens to be the most popular female playwright of all time. *The Mousetrap* continues to run and run in the West End all these decades later up until the present day.

\* \* \*

During the protracted birth of *Towards Zero* as a play, my father turned his attention to Slim Callaghan, a fictional British private detective in the American *hard-boiled* mode. Callaghan was the central character in several popular Peter Cheyney novels including *The Urgent Hangman* and *Dangerous Curves.*

It was revealed in a biography by Michael Harrison, *Peter Cheney - Prince of Hokum,* that Cheyney knew my father in the late 1920s as Donald Stuart. Cheyney was an avid Sexton Blake reader and told my father he was writing a Blake yarn entitled *The Clue of the Yellow Moccasin.* Knowing my father was an established Blake writer he asked him if he would show it to H. W. Twyman, the then Editor of the story paper *Union Jack.* My

GARRICK THEATRE CHARING CROSS RD., LONDON, W.C.2.
LESSES : Parrem Scault Studios Ltd. Licensed by the Lord Chamberlain to GILBERT BROWN.
Direction : JACK BUCHANAN

By arrangement with JACK BUCHANAN
B.A. Meyer and Concanen
present

Peter Cheyney's
"Meet Mr. Callaghan"
Terence de Marney

SPECIAL MATINEE: FRIDAY, SEPTEMBER 19th, 1952
in aid of
LYNMOUTH DISASTER FUND
NORTH DEVON & WEST SOMERSET RELIEF APPEAL

father did so and Twyman turned it down flat! Not to be put off by this rebuff, Cheyney suggested he write a regular feature for *Union Jack* called *Tinker's Notebook*. Sexton Blake's young assistant Tinker would supposedly relate modern police and detective methods, discuss famous criminal cases, and recall some of his *Guv'nors* own cases and adventures. The feature was quite successful but ended after about eighteen months. In addition to his literary skills, Cheyney was a fencer of repute, a golfer, a crack pistol-shot, and a jiu-jitsu expert. He lived much like his characters, working too hard, living the fast and careless life with a breath-taking abandon that eventually caught up with him. After having fallen into a coma, he died aged 55.

An agreement was made on 6 February 1952, almost a year after the *Towards Zero* agreement of 1951, between the estate of the late Peter Cheyney, Justin Judge Esq. of 25, East Street, Bromley and W.A.R Collins, Esq., of 14, St. James's Place, London SW1, and Gerald Verner to adapt Peter Cheyney's novel *The Urgent Hangman* for 50% to the Author and 50% to the adapter. The resulting stage play was to be titled *Meet Mr. Callaghan,* the first-ever adaptation of a Peter Cheyney novel.

*Meet Mr. Callaghan* was produced by B. A. Meyer and Concanen, the company formed by brothers Terence and Derrick de Marney. It was directed by Derrick de Marney and the title character of the detective was played by his brother Terence.

Prior to opening in London, the play had a try-out tour opening at The King's Theatre, Southsea on 25 February 1952, followed by Prince of Wales Theatre, Cardiff; Theatre Royal, Nottingham; Golders Green Hippodrome; The Streatham Hill Theatre; King's Theatre, Hammersmith; Dolphin Theatre, Brighton; and finishing on 29 April at Bournemouth Pavilion. *Meet Mr Callaghan* was a well-oiled machine when it opened a month later on 28 May 1952 at the Garrick Theatre, London, and ran for an impressive 340 performances.

## CHAPTER TEN: THREE STAGE PLAYS

The production brought in money for our family and must have been a welcome relief following the austerity of the war years. My father and mother often dined out at the *Savoy*. The band at the Savoy would play the *Callaghan* theme tune when he arrived, a haunting melody composed by Eric Spear, released in June 1952 as a 78-rpm record on the Oriole label, played by Frank Chacksfield's Tunesmiths. It was also a hit for American Jazz Guitarist Les Paul that same year on Capital Records. Another favourite venue was the *Hungaria* restaurant in lower Regent Street, next to the *Criterion*, offering dancing and cabaret every night.

Back in January 1952, *The Stage* newspaper had announced Bertie Meyer was celebrating half a century in theatrical management and that he had three new projects in the pipeline, including a new Peter Cheyney play *Dangerous Curves* as well as my father's version of *Towards Zero*. *Dangerous Curves* was my father's second Cheyney adaptation and a year later it was put on at the Garrick Theatre by Terence De Marney Productions Limited.

Slim Callaghan has left the drab, shabby office in Chancery Lane, which formed the background to Meet Mr. Callaghan, for the splendour of a luxurious penthouse apartment-cum-office overlooking Park Lane. Callaghan Investigations are doing well. Gone are the days of shoes that let in the rain, the empty packet of cigarettes, the few coppers which will not even buy a cup of coffee. But Slim is still hard up-for hundreds. He is the type who will always be hard up, no matter how much money he makes.

The play opened 14 April 1953. Terence De Marney directed the play and reprised his role as Slim Callaghan. He suffered from laryngitis on the opening night, received lukewarm applause and was booed. Some of the gallery shouted *disgraceful!* One angry woman shouted:

"You always spoil every first night you ever appear in!"

Terence de Marney stepped forward bravely and said in Bernard Shaw fashion:

"There is one thing to be pleased about tonight and that is the agreement of the people who don't agree with us."

Not an auspicious start!

The play ran for three and a half hours at the dress rehearsal and had to be cut by forty minutes for the opening performance. De Marney had spent most of the day at his Curzon-street flat spraying his throat, cutting the £6000 production, and going over new lines. De Marney admitted they cut the play in the wrong places and upset the continuity. It was not successful running for only 53 performances.

On a happier note, the acclaimed stage adaptation of *Meet Mr. Callaghan* was made into a film in 1954 by Eros Films Limited, produced by Derrick de Marney and Guido Coen, with a screenplay by Brock Williams. The film was directed by Charles Saunders. When it came to casting, they chose Derrick de Marney to play Slim Callaghan not his brother, as in the stage production. The film ran for 1 hour 28 minutes. It was made as a *pilot* for a proposed Callaghan movie series. Disreputable private detective Slim Callaghan is required to solve the death of a much-hated rich man. *Meet Mr. Callaghan* was filmed on a modest budget and made money for the producers, but no sequels resulted. In June 2009 the film became available on DVD through Renown Pictures and was also included in a Renown Pictures DVD collection of 6 British Films titled: *British Cinema Crime & Noir.*

# Chapter Eleven – Disaster

N ovels were not forgotten during the West End runs of the stage plays. In 1953 my father wrote *Mr. Midnight* for Wright & Brown. The sons Eric Wright and Alan Brown had taken over the reins of the company. This is the first Gerald Verner book issued from their new premises at 18, Stukeley Street, London WC2.

On 21 February 1955, a contract was issued to Gerald Verner for an original TV series of thirteen 13.5 min programmes to be called *Told by the Desk-Sergeant* at £60.00 a script. I have a file of synopses for some of them:

Number 02 *Lady Milstead's Indiscretion*
Number 03 *The Cleverness of Mr. Gaynor*
Number 04 *The Eccentric Lodger*
Number 05 *The Persecuted Poet*
Number 06 *The Love-Lorn Soldier*
Number 07 *The Undoing of Mr. Dawes*
Number 08 *The Count's Goodbye*
Number 09 *The Ugly Sisters*
Number 10 *The Teddy Boys Pic-Nic*
Number 11 *The Three Graces.*
No synopsis for 1,12, or 13.

I think at some point, the duration of each story was revised to 30mins. In any event the whole project was shelved. The programme was never broadcast. Three of the stories were published as short stories. *The Undoing of Mr. Dawes* was the fourth story making up book three of *The Cleverness of Mr. Budd* (1935) comprising 5 short stories. *The Extraordinary Problem of the Eccentric Lodger* was published in a Hutchinson Pocket Special, Summer PIE June 1947. *Lady Milstead's Indiscretion* turned up somewhere as *The Blackmailing of Lady Milstead.*

On 29 October 1955, TV Playhouse Season One, Episode Six, was

*French for Love,* adapted for television by Gerald Verner (an adaptation of the play by Derek Patmore and Marguerite Stein) and starring Zena Howard, George Curzon, Saun O'Riordan, Prunella Scales, Barbara Couper, Dennis Buckley and Rene Leplat. A Towers of London Production for the Incorporated Television Programme Co., the TV play was Produced and Directed by Hugh Rennie. My father's fee for this adaptation was £75.

"Victor's happy years of agreeable separation from an incompatible wife in the South of France and his tranquil life with his housekeeper (Hortense) is rudely chattered when his wife and daughter descend on him suddenly. The reason for this visit is to receive the male parent's blessing on the hoped-for engagement of Robin and Gabrielle. The French have a way with triangles, and the amusing denouement after several misunderstandings leaves us with the thought that at least two people learned something in the South of France."

The 3rd of July 1956 saw my father's television serial play in seven episodes *The Crimson Ramblers* begin on London (Channel 9). Directed by Robert Evans, it was a Television Serial Play in seven episodes on Tuesday evenings for Associated Rediffusion.

Episode One: *The Girl in Black.*
Episode Two: *Enter Mr. Hargreaves.*
Episode Three: *A Face in The Dark.*
Episode Four: *The Man in Tinted Glasses.*
Episode Five: *Nocturnal Adventure.*
Episode Six: *Death at The Dome.*
Episode Seven: *The Real McCoy.*

David Griffiths writes in *TV Times* 7 July 1956:

"The Crimson Ramblers concert party is on their way to appear at the Dome pier pavilion, Westpool, for the summer season. Into their railway carriage is thrown a package. Puzzled, they examine the wrapping. On it is the message:

122

## CHAPTER ELEVEN: DISASTER

*'Please keep this safely. Will call at Dome for it. Do not open.'* Soon the Ramblers are more than puzzled. They are fearful. Because of that package, murder has been committed. And further mayhem is clearly pending. That is the opening of The Crimson Ramblers, a serial in seven half-hour instalments. It starts on Tuesday and is the first thriller serial on ITV."

*The Crimson Ramblers* had the distinction of being the first serial to be televised by a commercial company and finished No.2 in the top 10. Above is a photograph of the cast with my father on the far right.

The year 1956 also heralded *Sorcerer's House* published by Hutchinson. It was the second book to feature amateur sleuth Simon Gale:

> "A legend surrounds Threshold House that the appearance of a light in the long room will be followed by a corpse."

One reviewer commented:

"Mr. Verner has supercharged his writing with eerie suspense and any sudden noise while one is reading the last few pages can affect the heart. Stampeding through this supernatural atmosphere comes Mr. Verner's Simon Gale, his roaring earthiness only serving to heighten the shivers. A good novel this, very good…but, oh, how I should love to see one of these tough American 'tecs tangle with Richmond's Simon Gale."

From *Sorcerer's House,* here is a description of the detective:

"The door was flung open violently – so violently that it crashed against a chair – and into the room marched an extraordinary figure. It was a huge man, dressed in very stained and very baggy corduroy trousers and an open-necked shirt of a vivid and startling shade of green. His shock of unruly hair was the colour of a freshly ripened horse-chestnut, and he had an aggressive beard of the same vivid hue which projected belligerently from an out-thrust chin. "Mornin'" boomed this apparition in a voice that set all the ornaments in the room rattling."

My father viewed Hutchinson as a more respectable publisher. There is no doubt they were a better *class* of publisher altogether than Wright & Brown. Taking on my father should have led to great new opportunities…

The 4th of March 1957 saw my father's play *Design For Murder* open for a short run at The Intimate Theatre, a modest repertory house of some 450 seats in Palmers Green, London N13. The theatre was originally built in 1931 as St. Monica's Church Hall, but four

INTIMATE THEATRE
PALMERS GREEN
LONDON, N.13

Week commencing Monday, March 4, 1957

INTIMATE PLAYERS
present
**DESIGN FOR MURDER**
By Gerald Verner
Characters (in order of appearance) :

| | |
|---|---|
| Marion | JILL GRIVER |
| Mrs. Kirby | MARGARET GIBSON |
| Doctor Dudley | MICHAEL BILTON |
| Joyce Ludlow | LYNNE FURLONG |
| James Kirby | HUGH CROSS |
| Philip Conway | AUBREY WOODS |
| Irene Jordan | PEARL CATLIN |
| Det.-Inspector Trimmer, C.I.D. | IAN AINSLEY |
| Det.-Sergant Gregg | DAVID RUSH |

Produced by FREDERICK TRIPP
Scenic Designer Edward Furby

BOX OFFICE OPEN 10 a.m. to 9 p.m. : : Phone PAL 3798

years later was converted into a theatre by the actor John Clements and became a well-respected full-time professional playhouse.

The entire action of the play passes in the living room of James Kirby's house in Hill Green, a suburb of London. This would have been a *try-out*, with the hope of attracting investment to present the play in the West End – which didn't happen.

Just over a year later, *Mr. and Mrs. Bluebeard* opened at The Intimate Theatre. This was the play gifted to my mother as a wedding present by my grandmother Geraldine.

\* \* \*

A contract to produce *Mr. and Mrs. Bluebeard* was issued on 19 December 1956 by my father's agents Hughes Massie & Co Ltd, to Anna Deere Wiman of 31, Dover Street, London W1 (the licensee). £150 was to be paid on signing with a further £100 payable if the license needed to be extended. I have no idea if the contract was ever signed. I am certain Anna Deere Wiman had been a difficult person to deal with.

Anna was the daughter of impresario Dwight Deere Wiman, who produced 56 plays and musicals in 26 years on Broadway and who died in New York an alcoholic aged fifty-five in 1951 leaving more than $5 million. He was a direct descendant of John Deere of *tractor* fame and fortune. Anna was born in 1920 and educated by private tutors. Anna studied ballet in Paris and danced in New York with the Ballet Russe and the American Ballet Company before becoming a TV Producer in Hollywood. Having inherited a fortune upon the death of her father Anna came to England in 1954 where she produced a series of plays in London. The plays included *The Reluctant Debutante,* in conjunction with E. P. Clift, May 1955, *The Iron Duchess, At the Drop of a Hat, The Grass is Greener* and *A Shred of Evidence* with Sam Wanamaker (father of Zoë).

During April 1957, only four months since the contract for *Mr. and Mrs. Bluebeard* was issued, Anna provided the money for Sam Wanamaker to acquire the lease of the beautiful Pigalle Theatre in Liverpool. Anna became chairman and Sam Wanamaker managing director. They renamed it *The New Shakespeare.* This new cultural centre which opened in October of that year with Arthur Miller's *A View From The Bridge* is likely to have claimed her undivided attention—sending her in a more classic direction. The venture began promisingly but did not progress smoothly and came to an end in 1959. Wanamaker blamed financial mismanagement for its demise, in particular Anna Deere Wiman, complaining he was constantly being harassed and thwarted by her *unpredictable and irresponsible behaviour.* Her erratic behaviour was most likely due to alcoholism, as was her premature death in 1963, following a fall on the stairs at *Landmark,* the twelve-acre waterfront estate at Southampton, Bermuda, she inherited from her father. She was only forty-three years old.

On 2 June 1958 *Mr. and Mrs. Bluebeard* opened at The Intimate Theatre, Palmers Green. The play was put on by former variety agent and manager of the theatre, Frederick Marlow for G. M. Productions. There was no mention of Anna Deere Wiman.

The entire action of the play passes in the living room at Oast Cottage, a lonely house near the Romney Marshes. *The Stage* newspaper wrote:

INTIMATE THEATRE
PALMERS GREEN
LONDON, N.13

Week commencing Monday, June 2, 1958

FREDERICK MARLOW
(for G.M. Productions Ltd.)
presents

**Mr. and Mrs. BLUEBEARD**
By GERALD VERNER

Characters (in order of appearance):

| | |
|---|---|
| Elsie | VALERIE KIRKBRIGHT |
| Mrs. Wellington-James | DAPHNE RIGGS |
| Doctor McRaith | JOHN MARQUAND |
| Roger Wentworth | GEORGE COOPER |
| Catherine Wentworth | MARGARET GIBSON |

Produced by FREDERICK TRIPP

Scenic Designer : Diana Rush

BOX OFFICE OPEN 10 a.m. to 9 p.m. : : Phone PAL 3798

"New plots are hard to come by and Gerald Verner is to be congratulated on finding one on which to develop his play, *Mr. and Mrs. Bluebeard* presented at the Intimate, Palmers Green. He does not, I think, use his idea as well or efficiently as he might, but there is certainly an intriguing touch of novelty in the notion of marrying together two professional mate-murderers, establishing them in a lonely country house and then obtaining much gentle fun from the double-meaning which their mutual efforts to exterminate each other gives to almost everything they say and do."

On 4 March 1958 Gerald Verner signed a contract with W. E. Johns to adapt a play from one of his *Biggles* books. As a young boy of eight years I remember a large parcel arriving at 15 Marlborough Road resulting in a pile of *Biggles* books stacked up in my father's study by the single bar electric fire. The play was never written. The varied and busy years 1956 to 1958, pregnant with so much opportunity, held great promise for many future projects. Alas they were not to blossom. Our lives were to be turned upside down.

# CHAPTER ELEVEN: DISASTER

\* \* \*

Searching through my mother's handbag for some missing keys, my father came across something as toxic as Paris Green and as dangerous as gunpowder—a letter.

He had unintentionally discovered a love letter to my mother from a Lt. Col William Swanson Whimster, a 1st Airborn Division officer, whom everyone called Wimpy. He owned the top flat in a house on Richmond Hill called *Ashburton,* with a million-dollar view looking out over the terrace gardens to the River Thames. He'd retired from the army on 2 September 1958.

I suspect my mother had met Wimpy at The Marlborough pub, which hosted my father's firework displays, a stone's throw from where we lived. On Sundays I played in the extensive pub gardens or on the allotments beyond where we had a vegetable patch while my parents joined friends in a boozy, smoky, drinking session in the lounge bar. When the bar closed, we often ate a late Sunday lunch in the pub dining room. My father, unaware of what was going on, had probably met Wimpy on several of these occasions.

The discovery of the letter caused a seismic rift in my parents' relationship. It understandably led to rows, heated arguments and further rows, and eventually the breakdown of their marriage. Divorce ensued. A bitter custody battle raged in court over me, which my father won. I knew nothing about any of this drama going on. Eventually the *Ashburton*

flat was sold and my mother and Wimpy moved to Gloucestershire where they married in the district of Thornbury in 1959. I remained in my father's care.

My mother told me years later, on several occasions, she was convinced that my father had carried on an affair with Anna Deere Wiman who, at that time, was indisputably an attractive woman of thirty-six as her photo testifies. This belief helped to assuage my mother's guilt and provided her with ammunition to fire during the inevitable arguments that ensued during the divorce and custody battle. Once mother had an idea in her head it was hard to eradicate. Mother's suspicions might also have been fuelled by the fact *Mr. & Mrs. Bluebeard* had been gifted to her as a wedding present by Geraldine Verner but had now been sold on to Anna Deere Wiman, presumably to pay household bills. Years later, when I mentioned this accusation of an affair with Anna to my father, he strongly denied it. He assured me he met with her purely for business reasons attempting to iron out problems to get his play produced. Anna had plenty of funds available to achieve that goal and I could see he might view her interest in his work as highly beneficial for future projects. He was doing all he could *to keep the show on the road.* However, my father was a true gentleman, extremely good-looking and charismatic. Who knows what *her* true motivations were?

This was a painful time for all concerned. The divorce and bitter custody battle in court (as to who would take custody of me) had a very bad effect upon my father's health preventing him from writing anything. Several projects he was working on at the time like *Biggles* had to be abandoned which understandably didn't go down too well with producers. Another of these projects was a second book, as part of the Hutchinson deal. It was a follow up to *Sorcerer's House.* The book was *The Snark Was A Boojum*, and its forthcoming publication was announced in the press. Unfortunately, this intriguing opus was never completed in his lifetime. It was to be the third book to feature his detective Simon Gale.

The book was divided into three parts commencing with *The Vanishing.* Part two was *The Hunting*, concluding with part three *The Snark!* The first two parts of this story, *The Vanishing* and *The Hunting*, were begun in 1957. Through all the upheavals, moving from place to place, I managed to hang on to the unfinished manuscript. In 2015 I resolved to finish the book (see Chapter Thirteen - Postmortem) beginning a process of completely revising the story from the beginning, major additions and rewrites for part two, and adding the final part, the solution: *The Snark!*

\* \* \*

Aunty Gerry kept herself to herself turning out lampshades for all she was worth as if the more she made the longer she might be able to stave off impending doom. She worked the treadmill of her *Singer* sewing machine like an all-in-one gym.

My father managed to secure a job four days a week as relief cinema

# CHAPTER ELEVEN: DISASTER

manager at the Essoldo Cinema, Hayes. It was the rock 'n' roll Tommy Steele era when *teddy boys* ripped up seats and anything they could find. He was forced to stop the film on several occasions because of this behaviour and to stand in front of the screen to bravely announce to a wild and hostile cinema audience in the front seats that if the disruption didn't stop immediately the film wouldn't continue. He used to commute from Richmond to Hayes arriving back late at night. He was attempting to get back into writing mode, but his heart wasn't in it. His imagination wouldn't flow. There were too many distractions.

My father told me he wasn't much good at acting. I would dispute this. When I was about seven years old, he began reading books to me. The first book he chose was Edgar Wallace's *The Fellowship of the Frog*. This was followed by another Wallace yarn, *Jack O'Judgement*. Two of his own books followed, *Terror Tower* and *The Angel*. By assuming a different voice for each character, he made the stories explode into life. I remember sitting enthralled, begging for him to read to me another chapter as the previous one ended with an irresistible cliff-hanger.

The effect of hearing these books read to me was to increase my determination to be able to read them myself. I was able to read at an early age devouring such stories as *The Circular Staircase* by Mary Roberts Rinehart, a turn-of-the-century American woman who later earned distinction as *the true mistress of mystery*. Her 1908 mystery enthralled and petrified in equal measure.

My first school was The Vicarage on Richmond Hill followed by Kings House Junior School in Kings Road followed by Kings House Senior. Form members at Kings House included Michael son of Richard Attenborough and Jonathan son of John Mills. With mother beginning a new life and both brothers living elsewhere pursuing their careers in the theatre, at eight years old I found weekends and holidays soulless. I rattled around the house at Marlborough Road, which felt empty and neglected despite Aunty Gerry holed up in her own apartments. Children live from day to day, so I found ways to keep myself amused. I read a lot of thrillers or played *Cowboys and Indians* with other children who lived nearby. For my birthday my father bought me a *Hopalong Cassidy* outfit from the manageress of the Essoldo box office whose son had grown out of it. Dressed up in this gear and no doubt looking ridiculous, brandishing a six-shooter cap pistol with several rolls of caps in my pocket, I proceeded to terrorise the street.

# PLOTS AND GUNPOWDER

I had been warned by my mother and father on various occasions not to associate with a boy who lived a few doors down whose name was Alan Hickey. I had no idea why at the time and I am still none the wiser beyond the fact he was considered a bit rough. He didn't attend private school and he and his family were considered not quite *Marlborough Road*. One afternoon, in my *Hopalong Cassidy* outfit, and armed with my six-shooter, I bumped into Alan Hickey. I was about to shoot him but remembered the warnings I had been given and thought better of it. We started chatting and he began talking about *Cheyenne* which I'd never heard of. As he was talking, I attempted to grasp what he was getting at. He could see I didn't understand because I didn't have a television, but his descriptions were so vivid he could see I was fired up by the thought of it.

*It's on tonight,* he exclaimed enthusiastically. *Would you like to see it?*

I nodded a firm *yes*. He invited me inside and for a moment I was worried I might be entering Dracula's castle, but as soon as I met his mother all concerns melted away. She brought us both beans on toast and a cup of tea which we ate at the table and then we sat on the sofa and watched *Cheyenne*. This was an American Western *television series* of 108 black-and-white one-hour episodes broadcast on ABC from 1955 to 1962 starring Clint Walker. As I left to go home Alan's father walked in returning from work. He looked quite stern until I was introduced when his face broke up into a welcoming smile and he bent down and shook my hand in a very grown-up manner.

When I told my father where I'd spent the evening, he was none too pleased until I tackled him about his prejudice describing what an amazing time I'd had and what nice people the Hickeys were. He relented. From that moment on *Cheyenne* was a weekly rendezvous where I was always welcome and given supper. These evenings once a week were very special to me and helped to momentarily dispel the anxiety I felt at home.

One Sunday, I can't remember what the occasion was, maybe a birthday, my brothers Tony and Jimmy came to lunch at Marlborough Road. I think my father cooked chicken, and as a rare treat a bottle of Sauterne appeared. All any of us can remember with clarity about the meal was the rice pudding for dessert. It came in a shallow dish, browned on top, looking inviting and delicious. We all tucked in appreciatively. Lifting the third or fourth spoonful towards my mouth I noticed something strange about the rice. I could see small brownish heads. I examined the rice closely and saw the heads belonged to small curved bodies. My father, who was by now short-sighted, and wore glasses for close work like typing, had managed to cook a little rice, but mainly maggots.

I leapt from the table and spat what remained in my mouth into the fireplace. There was a gas fire burning and my spit sizzled. I felt like retching.

*What's the matter?* They all yelled at me at once in alarm, as if I had gone completely mad.

When I yelled back at them the reason, they all stopped eating, staring at the contents of their spoons frozen in different positions in a ghastly tableau like the diners described in *They Walk in Darkness*. One by one they came back to life closely examining the rice pudding, first in disbelief, and then seeing the evidence for themselves. Tony liked fishing. Maybe the maggots were from some bait he had left behind in the same cupboard in which the unsealed bag of rice was kept, and they had migrated to it. Whatever the explanation, all agreed the rice pudding tasted uncommonly good! It certainly didn't lack protein. Tony and Jimmy congratulated my father on the best meal they'd had in weeks! Once recovered from the shock we all thought the incident was very funny. I never forgot it and dined out on the story for years.

The money eventually ran out again. From earnings averaging £2000 to £3000 a year, a considerable sum in those days, income dwindled to the extent my father could no longer pay the rent. He had lived an irregular life, a rollercoaster of flush one minute and in debt the next. He was a very generous person, no good at all at financial planning. When he had money, he spent it. When he ran out of money, he borrowed it, so that when some did arrive it was sucked backwards to settle debt. He was always waiting for a cheque to turn up to pay off current debts. To be fair, a cheque usually did in the nick of time. It never occurred to him to save anything for the future. What was really maddening was that at this time, as a sitting tenant, he could have bought the entire house in Richmond freehold for just over £3000.

It was great that the court awarded my father custody of me, but this only added to his responsibilities. His mother, Aunty Gerry, who should have helped look after me, had suffered a stroke which left her completely helpless. My mother leaving had left him psychologically wounded. I wasn't old enough to understand fully at the time but the stress of the divorce during 1957 had brought on a nervous breakdown.

PLOTS AND GUNPOWDER

My father was emotionally drained and unable to fulfil contracts. This was particularly unfortunate as television companies and others were demanding work that he was unable to supply. As a result, several potentially valuable contracts were lost. His post war career collapsed, and the rent didn't get paid. He held on as long as he could until the day eventually arrived when we were evicted. He describes the effects of this traumatic period in his own words, looking back on it, in a letter written to Noel Lee in 1961.

"A few years ago, I was forced to divorce my wife and the worry and trouble of that period brought on a nervous breakdown and I was completely unable to write a line. It was particularly unfortunate as the Television companies were demanding work which I was quite unable to supply. I lost several very valuable contracts. This situation continued for nearly three years and I was forced to give up writing completely. It was a very difficult time. The court had awarded me the custody of my son, Christopher, then aged eight, and I had him to look after. My sister, who was looking after us, had a stroke which left her completely helpless, as she still is, so I had two people in my care. However, I'm glad to say, that I have weathered the storm and my ability to write has returned. I believe you have copies of nearly all my early books. Mine were destroyed in a raid during the war, together with the original manuscripts. W & B's file copies were also destroyed when their offices in Farringdon Avenue were bombed. I think a number of these stories would adapt for television. I remember two in particular – *The Huntsman* and *Phantom Hollow*. Would you, if you have them, kindly lend them to me for say a couple of months? I would return them to you, of course. I have tried to get them by advertising but without success."

*Yours sincerely* had now become, *kindest regards*.

I still have no idea where my grandmother or the furniture went when we vacated 15 Marlborough Road. Having suffered a stroke most likely she was in hospital.

My father and I waited at a bus stop in Richmond one day with minimum luggage. At nine years old I didn't really know what was going on, mainly because my father kept all the bad things to himself. He just

132

# CHAPTER ELEVEN: DISASTER

kept assuring me everything would be alright. I did have enough sense to realise everything hadn't been alright and wasn't likely to be anytime soon. I didn't know what *anytime soon* meant, only that it looked bleak and far away. I had no answers. My imaginings were too frightening and too painful to contemplate so I shut them down.

We waited at that bus stop in Richmond for ages and ages… There was no sign of a bus. Looking along the empty road, waiting…around us people were going about their daily routine, but for us standing there waiting time stood still. Life had reached a full stop that punctuated the end of one sort of life and signalled the beginning of another waiting to be written.

It was the end of a chapter. The beginning of a journey in search of pastures new that would take me away from my roots, my school, and my friends. I knew we had to get to Victoria Bus Station and catch another bus from there, but our final destination meant nothing to me. It was a daunting experience that would lead us into circumstances that would stifle my father's imagination further and lead to a job taken out of necessity that would prove detrimental to his health.

We had no idea what the future held as we waited for that bus.

# Chapter Twelve – Fireworks!

A bus came along. My father and I clambered on board. We eventually arrived at Victoria Bus Terminal. After a long wait, which we filled by going to a station café and having a cup of tea and a cake, we boarded a coach to Hemel Hempstead. The journey took ages. We got off at a place called Cupid Green. The weather was cold and damp. After the sophistication of Richmond this was arriving in the sticks. As I looked at the few workman's cottages and open fields in bewilderment, I could see Cupid Green was the back of beyond - the complete opposite, in every respect, of my life so far.

We made our way to St. Agnells Lane, small workman's cottages on one side, open fields on the other. We arrived at number 22 and knocked on the door. There was a long delay but eventually the door was opened by a thin, angular, woman who looked as if she had walked straight out of a Dickens novel. Her name was Irene. She was eccentric, to say the least. Every cupboard, every nook and cranny, was stuffed with boxes of twigs. The shed in the unkempt garden was also packed to the roof with twigs. The place was overflowing with twigs. Twigs were everywhere! It was mouse heaven providing an irresistible breeding ground for them.

Irene had lived alone until we turned up. She rented us the front bedroom, which my father and I shared. We ate dinner early and I developed a habit of taking a pack of Crawford's Cream Crackers up to bed with me in case I felt peckish. One night, shortly after we'd arrived, I was woken up by a munching sound. At first, I didn't understand what it was. I turned on the light and immediately located the sound was coming from the Cream Crackers pack I had foolishly left open on the bedside table. I discovered a mouse buried deep in the packet busy munching through several layers of crackers. Its tail was sticking up in the air!

Like the weather, the house was cold and damp. The ceilings were low compared to what I was used to, and space was cramped. There was one open fire in the living room to heat the whole place, which was laid and lit every morning, hence the twigs. I'd been used to gas and electric fires in Richmond. This was the first time I experienced a living fire burning lumps of coal. Coming in out of the cold there is nothing to beat warming your hands in front of it. There was no instant hot water. If you wanted a bath the water had to be boiled in a *copper* in the kitchen and then poured into a tin bath.

One morning, after my father had left early for work, I didn't have to attend school and lay in bed. I felt a desperate need for motherly warmth and tiptoed along the hall to Irene's bedroom. I pushed open the door and crept into her bed. I remember she wore a long cotton nightgown. I snuggled up and luxuriated in the warmth from her body for about twenty minutes. I was like a cat curling up on a lap. I purred, I smiled, I felt happy. She didn't resist or say a word. I closed my eyes and felt things weren't so bad after all. The incident was never spoken of and never reoccurred. It healed something inside me I can't put into words—a kind of foreboding went away. Afterwards, I felt more content and positive about the future.

The house still exists, gutted and modernised, surrounded by many new properties. The fields have gone. The area is built up and unrecognisable compared to how it was then. Someone my father had met at the factory had suggested that we stay at these *digs* temporarily until more suitable accommodation could be found.

My father had secured a job as chief tester at Brock's Firework Factory, a leading firework manufacturer at that time with their famous *Crystal Palace* brand name. The 207-acre site of Brock's Firework Factory at *Woodhall Farm* was then the world's largest firework factory. It was a thriving concern, manufacturing fireworks for shops and providing displays for the British Empire around the world. The site is now built over, transformed into the *Woodhall Farm Housing Estate*. This job had obviously been my father's purpose behind our destination, though I didn't know that as I left Richmond.

As a young boy, I remember leafing through a wonderful book *A History of Fireworks* by Alan St. Hill Brock, paying attention to the full-page colour plates, particularly the rare and exotic *Liquid Fire Rockets* because of the danger involved in manufacture and transportation. The rocket head was filled with phosphorous in oil which upon the rocket bursting spontaneously burst into flame upon exposure to air. Obviously, these rockets were reserved for special display purposes and never sold to the public! I didn't realise at the time that Alan Brock specialised in real-life crime investigation until recently.

# PLOTS AND GUNPOWDER

Alan Brock was born in 1886 and died in 1956. He not only published books on pyrotechnics, but nine fictional crime novels under his own name, from 1934 to 1952, and two biographical books on police procedures. It is totally conceivable, though not confirmed, that my father met him on past occasions, probably in London, and they became friends with strong mutual interests being crime and pyrotechnics. This association with the Brock family would explain how he walked into Brocks Fireworks and secured a top job. He was putting his pyrotechnic knowledge to good use in a financial emergency.

My father's job as chief tester was to select fireworks at random from the small wooden buildings in which they were made. He then tested them at an isolated *firing ground* at specifically arranged times of the day so they couldn't be mistaken for an accidental explosion. He made out a performance report on each type of firework in a ledger, in his neat, microscopic, handwriting. He was out in all weathers and eventually contracted a form of bronchitis. This started out as a chest cough, but grew gradually worse into a hacking cough, not helped by smoking, until eventually, after about a year, he was forced to give the job up because of ill health.

His stories of witnessing the famous Crystal Palace displays as a boy together with his real passion for all thing's firework were infectious and he became very popular with the people he met at Brock's. He quickly made firm friends, among whom were pyrotechnicians Ralf Reading and Johnny Marshall. They were to remain friends long after he had left the factory. He became a good friend of Brock's chief chemist Mr. Hall, with whom he exchanged the elegant *A History of Fireworks* for the practical *Pyrotechnics* by George W. Weingart, which contained detailed products of manufacture. He had lengthy conversations with Mr. Hall about chemical formulae, particularly how to achieve deep strong colour in the stars put in aerial shells. Apart from the bronchitis and financial worries he was in his element getting paid for pursuing his hobby.

He used to bring back fireworks for me he had smuggled out of the factory. I couldn't wait for him to return to the cottage to see what was in his bag. The most magnificent of these fireworks were rockets. These rockets were wonderful to behold. A Ruby Plume rocket or an Empire rocket, both selling at 7/6d. They measured well over a foot in length. To a young boy, these were *huge* rockets, beyond pocket money and bigger and more expensive than any that could normally be bought in shops. I hid them at the bottom of the wardrobe in readiness for November 5th.

# CHAPTER TWELVE: FIREWORKS!

Unfortunately, these rockets had no sticks. On a Sunday, when the factory was closed, and there was supposed to be no one around, I would walk down St. Agnells Lane to where it cut through woodland. I entered Brock's through the woods that bordered the factory and scrambled up the steep slope that led to the firing ground. Here I foraged for used rocket sticks that had been attached to rockets for testing. Falling back to earth, the rocket sticks, about five feet long and a half-inch square, would stick out of the ground. I would yank them out and return home with as big a bundle as I could carry. This was very exciting and got my heart racing. There was always a fear of being caught. On one occasion I was almost nabbed when a figure appeared and yelled at me. I scarpered back into the surrounding woodland with an armful of rocket sticks as fast my legs would carry me. Guess who had the best fireworks when bonfire night came on November 5th?

While my father was at Brock's, earning just enough to pay Irene some rent and buy us food, Associated Rediffusion tracked him down. This proved to be a stroke of luck. Following the success of his 1956 television serial play *The Crimson Ramblers,* in November 1958, they asked him if he would edit the scripts of a six-part TV mystery called *Eight Wreaths Backstage.*

The serial had been written by Ken Wyatt and Joyce Chapman Kerr, who were not professional writers. Ken Wyatt visited the cottage a few times. He was a very enthusiastic, jovial person, and very kind, but he was an electrician, not a writer. The producers thought the serial had potential but realised in its present form it was a complete mess! My father was paid £25 per 30-minute episode to make something of it. I don't think the serial ever went into production.

Following a hard day on the firing ground, my father worked on the *Eight Wreaths Backstage* project in the evenings, sitting at the living room table typing busily by the light of a small Anglepoise lamp, while Irene sat on the left of the fire knitting. She knitted most of the time. I sat on a creaky wood chair on the right of the fire staring fascinated into crumbling and erupting blocks of coal, listening to the typewriter keys and the clickety-click of the knitting needles. There wasn't much else to do after dark. The room was lit by firelight except for the Anglepoise. The atmosphere was cosy compared to the cavernous high-ceilinged rooms at 15 Marlborough Road, but grew very hot if the fire wasn't damped down, like sitting inside a kiln. There was a radio, and *The Archers* provided a welcome continuity link with the past, a reassuring comfort before I went to bed.

# PLOTS AND GUNPOWDER

By my tenth birthday, December 1959, we had moved from Cupid Green and rented a detached house at 22, George Street, in the old town of Hemel Hempstead. The house was semi-detached, but quite spacious with a good-sized front living room and a kitchen that led out into the garden. Upstairs there were three bedrooms and a bathroom with running hot water. Bliss! After Cupid Green it was like arriving in paradise.

Outside was a part constructed garage, just four pillars and a concrete foundation as if the owner had lost interest or run out of money. The house was surrounded by a large garden, shielded from the road behind a protective row of Laburnum trees with lovely golden-rain blossoms.

The garden boasted several apple trees and plenty of room for growing vegetables and flowers. There were red currant bushes, black currants, gooseberries, and masses of rhubarb. My father planted several rows of Night Scented Stock which in a voice filled with nostalgia he told me would be wonderful and immediately caused me to wonder where he might have planted them before? Carisholme perhaps?

At the bottom of the garden, a low wall divided us from a large tract of waste ground where people would take their dogs for a walk. It was a great place to explore and play in. My grandmother suddenly appeared from exile and came to live with us. I have no idea where she had been staying while we had been living at Cupid Green, but it was clear she was still unwell and might never recover from her stroke.

I went for many walks with my father through the beautiful and tranquil Gadebridge Park. I also walked across the River Gade with its watercress beds, to Heath Lane, to a public preparatory school I attended called *Heath Brow*. My father struggled to manage the school fees—yes, bless him, he was still sending me to a private school. It never occurred to him he was already living beyond his means and should have sent me to a state-run school.

He set about writing a novel based on his television serial play *The Crimson Ramblers*, to be published by Wright & Brown early in 1960. It heralded a small recovery in his work output and paid the rent now that he wasn't fit enough to continue at Brock's.

Meanwhile, my mother and her new husband Wimpy had moved into a period cottage at Westbury on Trym, a suburb in the north of the City of Bristol. On 24 August 1959, my father wrote to me while I was staying there for a couple of weeks during the school holidays:

## CHAPTER TWELVE: FIREWORKS!

"I'm very busy working on two new books. I do a chapter of one and then a chapter of another, alternately, so that I shall have them both finished at the same time."

These books were *Grim Death*, a rewritten version of *Thirsty Evil* originally published in 1945 by John Westhouse, which went bankrupt shortly after a small print run, and an original story *The Nursery Rhyme Murders*. A total of three books published by Wright & Brown in 1960.

On 5 April 1960, there was a mammoth firework display above St. James Park to celebrate the state visit of President Charles de Gaulle. My father was determined we should see this. Friends at Brock's managed to obtain a duty pass for us and smuggled us in. We watched the display from an exclusive and unobstructed vantage point looking out over the firing ground. We had all to ourselves a wide strip of grass dividing the massed crowds behind railings and the park and firing ground. Behind the crowds was the palace balcony on which I could clearly see de Gaulle and the Royal family waiting for the fireworks to begin. The morning papers carried a front-page photo of the event that included two small figures, my father and I, one half the size of the other, who could clearly be seen standing watching the awesome spectacle. The display began with the Cross of Lorraine outlined in fire followed by a spectacular display of hundreds of roman candles and aerial shells. We travelled back to Hemel in a Brock's van with the men who had fired the display. It had been an exciting and unforgettable evening. The van smelled of gunpowder, charcoal, and sulphur, which reminded me of my bedroom at Richmond.

# Chapter Thirteen – Broadstairs

W e moved to Broadstairs, a coastal town on the Isle of Thanet, East Kent, about eighty miles south-east of London, in the summer of 1960. For a while, my father and I stayed for a month with some friends in the High Street, while he looked for somewhere to live and a school for me to attend. This turned out to be a private school called Haddon Dene and I was to start on 20 September 1960.

That autumn, he found a large, sprawling, flat at *The Dutch Tea House*, a distinctive blue and white gabled building situated at the North Foreland. This was a chalk headland, the eastern extremity of the Isle of Thanet, where the North Sea and English Channel  meet. The owner lived abroad. It was a spacious first-floor furnished flat. The rooms had glass doors opening onto a wide wrap-around balcony giving the place a cool, light, and airy feel with a wide sweep of unrestricted sea views.

Standing on the balcony looking out to sea was like being on the deck of a ship. Sunrise and sunset were beautiful to behold and the moon reflecting in the sea quite magical. Storms at sea were spectacular. Sheet lightning, like a silent artillery barrage, flashed right across the horizon. Forked lightning, not so silent, piercing through dark roiling clouds, was accompanied by deafening claps of thunder as nature unleashed its incredible power. Wind and rain would lash against the windows with great ferocity. The air was always fresh, filled with a salty sea tang. It started life as the *North Foreland Tea House* and was a stopping off point for visitors to the town. It was a unique and special place to live.

## CHAPTER THIRTEEN: BROADSTAIRS

On the landward side stood the imposing North Foreland Lighthouse, warning ships of the treacherous Goodwin Sands. The North Foreland Light would sweep my bedroom at night 5 times every 20 seconds. I found this dependable light reassuring, restoring order after all the upheaval.

The flat was above a general shop, post office, and café. The shop sold basic groceries, sweets, and postcards, including several postcards of The Dutch Tea House itself. The café area was beneath our balcony and served up tea and coffee and fresh chocolate éclairs to holiday makers throughout the summer, and to us when we could afford it. The business was run by Mrs. Sinclair, a kind, practical woman, whose husband drove off every day in a van to run a small electrical repair business rewinding the armatures of electric motors. They had a key to the gate at the top of the *39 steps* at North Foreland, of John Buchan fame, as did others who lived on the estate.

For a young boy growing up it seemed life was looking pretty good, because this location was new and exciting. Memories of Richmond were receding. I felt a great sense of freedom and adventure in this amazing location. It was a short walk down a steep hill to Joss Bay, with windswept fields to the cliff edge. While my father got back into writing, I would often go exploring on my own amongst the rock pools. When the tide was out a miniature marine world was revealed. Slippery with seaweed, the pools were filled with a fascinating variety of life; small crabs, starfish, limpets, mussels, whelks, sea snails and anemones waving their brightly coloured tentacles.

I cycled to school along my regular route, turning right off North Foreland Road onto Lanthorn Road passing the entrance to Stone House School where (my grandfather) John Charles had taught and who I never met. It was still a school back then and hadn't been converted to private housing.

At about this time, my father was asked to write for the American Hank Janson series, a pulp fiction character, and a pseudonym, created by the English author Stephen Daniel Frances. A parcel of paperbacks arrived one day with lurid covers of half-naked women with ripped blouses and hitched up skirts. There were titles like *When Dames Get Tough* or *Cutie on Call.* When my father caught me browsing one of these Hank Janson paperbacks, he was very annoyed and threw the whole lot in the dustbin. *I'd rather be dead than write that sort of trash,* he told me angrily.

During April 1961, my father had a meeting with Ian Hendry and Patrick Macnee to discuss scripts for a forthcoming TV series to be called *The Avengers.* Something did come of that! He wrote Episode 18 called *Double Danger,* Directed by Roger Jenkins and produced by Leonard White. The first actors' read through of *Double Danger* was held at The Tower, RCA Building, Brook Green Road, Hammersmith, from 10.30am on Monday 26 June 1961. Rehearsals began later the same day. *Double Danger* was transmitted on Southern Television, Saturday 8 July 1961.

My father wasn't happy with the final production, to say the least. He accused the script editor John Lucarotti of tampering with his script to a point where it no longer made any sense. On 13 July 1961, *The Stage and Television Today* reviewed the episode unfavourably:

**8.50 THE AVENGERS**
starring
IAN HENDRY
in
DOUBLE DANGER
Teleplay by Gerald Verner
Also starring
PATRICK MACNEE

*Cast in order of appearance:*

| | |
|---|---|
| Mark Crawford | Charles Hodgson |
| Harry Dew | Robert Mill |
| Al Brady | Peter Reynolds |
| Bert Mills | Ronald Pember |
| David Keel | Ian Hendry |
| Carol Wilson | Ingrid Hafner |
| Lola Carrington | Vanda Hudson |
| John Steed | Patrick Macnee |
| Bruton | Kevin Brennan |
| Bartholomew | Gordon Phillott |

*The Avengers theme composed and played by Johnny Dankworth*
*Designed by James Goddard*
*Producer LEONARD WHITE*
*Directed by ROGER JENKINS*

A few words spoken by a wounded man to Keel involve the doctor and Steed with a group of thieves who are fighting among themselves over a fortune in stolen diamonds

*An ABC Television Network Production*

"...the plot is reminiscent of a poor second feature with unrealistic gangster types, blonde hanger-on, and decent English chappie in hot pursuit of the criminals. Even the setting on the boat has been done before and the dialogue is like a primer for intending thriller-story writers. Only there were no thrills, and the clichés thrown up in the ambling wake of the story should make the presenting company blush. Ian Hendry, stern and resolute, aided by Patrick Macnee, whose style suggests he might be better doing something on his own instead of playing a rather peculiar undercover man. The plot

142

does not even seem to try for reasonable credibility, which is a pity when an hour has been allocated to the task. Rather than cutting the story down to the exciting bone, an attempt seems to be made to fill out the hour slot."

My father wrote a letter in reply to this scathing review, in hindsight a foolish thing to have done. It upset Iris Productions and marked the end of what might have been a successful career move. The opportunity was there to write many more *Avengers* scripts. There was to have been a contract for a further three. His letter went:

"I couldn't agree more with your critic's view of *Double Danger* in the *Avengers* series on Saturday, July 8th. Although I was credited with writing this dreadful hotchpotch, I must, in fairness to myself, refuse to take either credit or blame for the result. It bore not the slightest resemblance to the original script which I did write. The plot, the dialogue, settings, and characters were all completely altered. Apart from making the presenting company blush, it made me see red! I have written over 70 published novels, the first serial for commercial television, *The Crimson Ramblers* which was number two in the top ten – incidentally nothing in the original script of this was altered – the stage adaptation of Peter Cheyney's novel *The Urgent Hangman* which was a big success at the Garrick Theatre under the title of *Meet Mr. Callaghan*, a number of BBC sound serials, and a host of other material. I should, therefore, know something about plot construction, characterization, dialogue, and suspense. Certainly, enough not to have perpetrated the fiasco of *Double Danger* as finally presented."

One of the most annoying rewrites by Lucarotti was to change the original scripted way in which Steed covertly gains access to the houseboat and picks off members of the gang with his umbrella handle to a clichéd rewritten version, in which Steed calls out to a non-existent army and suggests they surround and then rush the boat.

The original script for *Double Danger*, and Lucarotti's rewrite, can be compared and examined on Alan Hayes *The Avengers Declassified* website, which focuses on the cultural phenomenon of *The Avengers*.

My thanks to Alan Hayes, for his comments:

"One of those instances where you wonder what might have been. The episode as transmitted varied greatly from the rehearsal script submitted by the credited writer, Gerald Verner. As originally written, *Double Danger* is full of invention and snappy dialogue. Sadly, much of this was eschewed by script editor John Lucarotti when he ghost-wrote the camera script. Reading this latter script, which is our closest record of what was transmitted, it is not difficult to see why the episode prompted poor notices in the press. There are some terrible adventure series clichés in this one, such as the sequence where Steed, alone in the night, scares off the crooks by pretending to shout to his 'team' of men. The equivalent scene in Verner's version is far more stylish and original. At the heart of the whole debacle, there is actually an involving plot to be found, in which plenty goes on and all three of our heroes get a decent slice of the action. However, it doesn't appear to have sparkled quite so much as it might have done had it been filmed as originally written."

The episode has been reconstructed as part of *The Avengers, The Lost Episodes volume 3*, produced for *Studio Canal,* and released by *Big Finish*. It includes where possible some of the original script.

\* \* \*

My father felt at home in Broadstairs and had recovered his health. The sea air had healed his bronchitis, as many years ago it may also have helped his ancestors John and Robert Pringle when leaving the smoke of London to spend their remaining days in Margate. The terrible hacking cough he suffered after working at Brock's was gone despite chain-smoking cigarettes.

Six copies of *The Third Key* arrived from Wright & Brown, one of three books he had published in 1961, the other two being *Ghost House*, and *The Shadow Men* (a rewritten version of *The Midnight Men* originally published in 1936 under his pseudonym Nigel Vane).

During 1961, my father had obtained an evening job at *Gourmet Club* in Broadstairs. This was a small members club with an upstairs bar near the seafront where he was paid to liven the place up by chatting to guests and entertaining them. The owner of the club was Mr. Chambers a wealthy American who drove around the town in a big black Ford

## CHAPTER THIRTEEN: BROADSTAIRS

Galaxy. He was quite a character, was a pilot, and I believe had once built his own plane back in the States. We didn't have a TV at home, so he allowed me to sit in the club foyer and watch *77 Sunset Strip*! He befriended my father and gave him the use of his enormous treble garage, complete with a fully equipped woodworking shop at the back, so he could indulge his love of making fireworks. I spent many a happy day there helping. We always stopped work for a lunch of fresh farmhouse bread, apples, and cheese.

On Wednesday 16 August 1961 I helped my father fire a fabulous display of fireworks at Victoria Gardens, Broadstairs Sea Front. I helped erect the various set-pieces that he had made in Mr. Chambers's garage. As it grew dark, we fired them. This occurred after the *Carnival* and *Miss Broadstairs* Competition. I proudly saw on the poster; *presented by Gourmet Club and Gerald Verner, Esq.*

I was recruited to sell brochures for the Carnival and tramped door to door for a week, flogging hundreds of them for pocket money. It was my first job. I was twelve years old. I saved my earnings as brand new ten-shilling notes which I kept in an envelope in a drawer of the dresser in the living room. I had twenty of them and felt worth something, reassured by this little nest egg. No doubt I was prompted to save in this way by the knowledge my father was one of those people who was never able to save money. As soon as money was earned it was dispersed to creditors, all used up, clearing the decks for debts to build up again. My little stack of ten-shilling notes was my back up so I wouldn't end up in debt!

The autumn of 1961 was the herald of a cascading run of misfortune.

My father had an appointment with Ray Dicks, the producer of *No Hiding Place* to discuss doing some scripts for a new series that would be broadcast after Christmas. He wrote a *No Hiding Place* script and completed a new book for Wright and Brown called *The Ghost Squad*.

He writes to his friend Noel Lee, 29 November 1961. The extracts I have chosen provide a first-hand diary of events:

"My first blow came when I took up the new book to Wright & Brown on Monday. As you know it has always been the custom with them to receive the MS with one hand and pay out the cheque with the other. This is really the only thing that makes working for them at all worthwhile. Having counted on this to feed the ravening wolves that are howling at the door, I got a severe shock when Alan Brown said that business had been so bad that they couldn't take any more books until next year. All he would do is take the manuscript and promise to try to let me have the money in March. Not very much use to me as I was counting on returning with the cash. This would never have happened in the days of old Mr. Brown. But the sons are different, and they have not, I'm afraid, improved the business. In these days of paperbacks, they should have started paperback editions at half-a-crown long ago. I think they would have made a lot of money.

When I did get back, having spent the last of my available cash on the fare, I found that Associated Rediffusion had returned a complete script for *No Hiding Place* the reason being that they had just bought one with a practically similar idea. They still want me to do some *No Hiding Place* scripts, which, of course, when I can get a little peace from these financial difficulties, if ever, I shall do.

The result of all this is that I am now facing a deluge of bills that all require immediate settlement and which I have kept at bay until I had completed this work. I have no time to write anything else because none of these people are prepared to wait any longer."

Four months later in March 1962, he writes again to Noel to inform him *Haddon Dene School*, run by a bad-tempered Mr. Boucher and draconian Miss Vyse, a vindictive couple putting it mildly, had issued a bankruptcy petition against him without hesitation for a total amount of £87.8s for unpaid school fees.

The agents for the flat at The Dutch Tea House have served him with a notice to vacate the premises unless he pays £109, two quarters rent outstanding. He writes:

## CHAPTER THIRTEEN: BROADSTAIRS

"I should have been hard put to it to find even the money for a stamp recently and we have been living on bread and butter and tea. I have had no cheque from Wright & Brown although proofs of another book arrived this morning. The ITV strike still goes on and shows no sign of breaking. However, when you get to the bottom there's only one way to go and that's up, which I am hoping is what will happen."

Mostly we lived on boiled Spanish Onions and Tomato Ketchup. On 18 March 1962, he writes again to Noel:

"I have had to disclose all my affairs to the Official Receiver and spent over eight hours on Tuesday. The Wright & Brown cheque will have to go to him now. I am not yet actually bankrupt but to avoid being so I shall have to pay all the debts I owe in a lump sum instead of being able to pay them gradually. I am worried to death about it. *The Daily Express* got wind of it somehow and rang me up the other night for a news column, but I managed to stop them printing anything yet. It could do me a great deal of harm if it became public. I am hoping that a miracle will happen to stop it."

Two days later the situation gets worse and the tension really starts to ratchet up.

"The amount of my liabilities comes to £600 with rent and other accounts. Everyone except the school has been very nice. There have been a couple of County Court writs, but they can be dealt with by instalments – a bankruptcy petition cannot. I am in the process of negotiating three TV film scripts at £500 per script which are not affected by the strike. My friend Leslie Charteris has just sold the rights of *The Saint* to Tempean Films for a TV series and suggested to them that I should do some of the scripts. The contracts, which are for each script, are being drawn up, but these things cannot be hurried. I might be doing more than three – there are 39 one hour plays altogether. This again cannot be hurried but would bring me in £5,250 if it came off. Also, Leslie Charteris has agreed to my writing a stage play featuring *The Saint* which I was working on – getting ideas for plot, settings, characters, etc – when the pot boiled over. This is going to be produced at the end of the year in the West-End of London and on Broadway and should be worth at least £70,000 to me in royalties and possibly an equal amount for my share of the film rights. Leslie has someone who is putting up the money for the production. Nearly every theatrical manager in London and America has been after the stage rights of *The Saint* and I am very lucky to have got them.

I also have a suggestion for a thirteen-episode serial for the BBC being considered by Brian Rix who is very keen on the idea. However, I am afraid that if the bankruptcy comes off all these things will become void. The natural reaction by these people is that if a man has to go bankrupt, he can't be much good, and they fade gracefully away."

My father is like a man dying of thirst who knows there is water nearby but can't reach it. We were both sure one of these prospects would materialise and we would get through this horrible situation. I say *we* because I was very much aware of how hard my father was struggling for survival. Most of the day and into the night the keys on his Remington portable were going clickety-clack. Little did I know how prophetic my father's last two lines in the above letter were to be.

On 27 March 1962, my father wrote to Noel:

"Thank you for your letter and the enclosed stamps. I could not have written to you without them because the small pension which my sister has, £2.18/6. is usually all gone by Monday. It doesn't go far at the moment to keep the three of us. I haven't any money coming in at all at the moment, you see. I can't describe to you how I feel - it seems as if all the life has gone out of me. I am not a young man anymore – I was sixty-five in January – so perhaps this is the reason, and the last three years have been very worrying and difficult. I feel that I can't face all this official business. My brain reels at the thought. But I am trying hard to keep up and praying for help and strength to carry on. If only I could get a little peace of mind to devote to my work, but I can't think clearly. I feel so frustrated. Time goes by and I am wasting it when I ought to be doing creative work, but my mind won't function at the moment."

## CHAPTER THIRTEEN: BROADSTAIRS

The following day he wrote again to Noel:

> "I am very worried concerning the effect this will have on the tenancy of my flat. Once they hear about the possible bankruptcy, I am afraid that they will insist that I vacate the flat at once. My sister is not in a fit state to be moved even if I had anywhere to move her to. She is unable to leave her bed now and I think that anything of the sort might kill her. And, of course, there is Christopher. I don't think, apart from yourself, that anyone can realise just how I feel. Every day is a nightmare. I am practically quite alone here. I cannot discuss the matter with my sister – her mind is not of the best these days – and although Christopher is a wonderful help he is, after all, only a little boy of twelve. How I wish that old Mr. Brown was alive or the people I knew in Fleet Street in the old days. They would have helped, I know. I've still got a week to find a solution."

These proceedings must have caused him to also relive those harrowing times after putting on his play *Sexton Blake* and ending up with debts he couldn't pay. It was all happening again. On 2 April he has an appointment with the solicitor who acts for the landlord of our flat. The landlord lives in Hong Kong. The solicitor is very sympathetic and is dead against bankruptcy at all cost. He has been in touch with the creditors and has got nearly all of them to vote against the bankruptcy at a meeting that will take place in two days' time, but not Haddon Dene Schools. Despite these efforts the Official Receiver insisted on the bankruptcy going through. A debt to the Inland Revenue comes to light, £1,523.7s.3d surtax and income tax on pre-1958 income. He said naively of the Inland Revenue:

> "They were awfully nice and wrote a letter from time to time asking if there was any chance of getting anything. I had paid them an awful lot in the past."

This new debt discovery adds to the total. It will now cost him over £2000 plus £250 costs to clear it. This and the first £400 on the Income Tax debt are taken from anything he pays in before creditors get a penny.

The public examination has been fixed for 22 May. Prior to this public examination we get an order from the landlord's agents to vacate the flat at once which means he must find somewhere else for us to live with no money for a rent deposit or to pay removal men. The stress makes him ill, as all these threats gang together like a darkening storm cloud prior to impending doom.

During all this negativity I go to check my ten-shilling notes for comfort one morning and find them gone. When I ask my father about this, he looks at me with a shameful expression as he admits he had to borrow them to pay for the laundry. I found it very hard to reconcile my hard work selling carnival programmes and cashing in birthday postal orders only amounted to enough funds to pay the laundry! I wasn't annoyed because I was glad to help but I was in shock. It was a salutary lesson I was never to forget.

The postman delivers six copies of *The Red Tape Murders*. My father's writes to Noel:

> "It is an entirely new one and I could have made it a great deal better if I hadn't written it in just over a week so as to collect the cheque!"

His public examination at Canterbury was less unpleasant than he expected. Both the Official Receiver and Mr. Registrar Booth were exceedingly nice and the whole thing took less than a quarter of an hour. He reports to Noel:

> "The press, however, were a great nuisance. They waited for me afterwards and hurtled questions like a barrage of machine guns. There have been a lot of garbled reports in the National Press as well as in the locals. I believe the *Daily Mail* published a photograph with their news item, though what interest it can be to the public at large I don't know. Fleet Street was ringing up here all the afternoon and evening. I believe all the papers carried an account. I doubt if this is going to do me much good professionally. However, the thing is over now, although I don't know how long I shall be able to stop here. I have been served a writ for possession, but nothing further has happened – yet."

I was able to check out these press accounts because downstairs Mrs. Sinclair had a rack of newspapers for sale. On June 20 we both went through them and she was very impressed that such a newsworthy celebrity was living in the flat above!

150

# CHAPTER THIRTEEN: BROADSTAIRS

He told reporters that he had received £224 for a 1960 TV script. This was for *The Avengers* episode, *Double Danger*. He attributed his failure to the actor's strike, to ill health, and to the folly in having a public row with ITV. In December 1961, he was negotiating to write three TV Scripts for the *Saint* TV series but because of the Equity actors strike this was postponed, contributing to a reduced income.

Following his Bankruptcy, he was very short of money and couldn't afford to buy any cigarettes. This was a very serious dilemma, the equivalent of a generator running out of petrol. Fortunately, I was now on my school holidays. I collected *dog-ends* for him, discarded by holiday makers at Joss Bay car park and local bus stops. Thankfully, there weren't many filters in those days. The *dog-ends* contained about an inch of tobacco. Using my thumbnail to split the dog-end open, I salvaged this tobacco and emptied it into jars with a slice of raw potato to keep it moist. Thus, he could indulge his habit with the help of Rizla cigarette papers and a rolling machine. I was pleased to be able to do something practical to help. It was branded into my brain that he couldn't work without a smoke. Growing up in rooms full of fug put me off the idea of smoking and, apart from trying a few as a teenager, I never took up the habit.

We still had an active account with the Sinclair's general shop below us. When my father sent down for a tin of baked beans, or a packet of cigarettes, I asked for two. I gave one to my father and hid the other under some loose floorboards in the hall, until over several weeks I had built up quite a general store of canned food and cigarettes. Eventually the day came when my father looked at me despairingly, telling me he'd completely run out of money and didn't know how he was going to feed me that evening. I had sensed this day was coming and been patiently waiting for it. With a dramatic flourish, I lifted aside the hall carpet and the loose floorboards like a magician, proudly revealing my secret stash of supplies. The effect of this revelation had exactly the effect I had hoped. He couldn't quite believe his eyes at this miracle. He was amazed, greatly relieved, and I could see much moved. We sat down and had a good meal that night as he puffed away contentedly. On 8 July he wrote to Noel:

> "I am trying to plan out a programme of work so far without success. It is very difficult in this unsettled state when any day or hour they may put us all on the street. So much money is being wasted every day by the various countries on things that really

don't matter – millions and millions of pounds - and yet it seems impossible to get hold of even a small amount that would give one peace of mind. I wish I had my life over again. I was never very interested in the money side of my work but only in the work itself, which was a mistake. Unfortunately, I was born without a business instinct and it's too late now to acquire one."

Regardless of paying the rent arrears, a new threat emerges. The Dutch Tea House has been put up for sale, the freehold, the contents, the business, the lot. The owners want £8500 for it. So, if we *had* managed to stump up the rent it would still have proved a fruitless effort because we would have had to leave regardless. Due to his bankruptcy, Brian Rix, Leslie Charteris, and the producers of *No Hiding Place*, stayed clear. Nothing further came of any of that potential, as my father had prophesised.

* * *

In September 1962 we sadly departed from The Dutch Tea House. Leaving was easier said than done. My father had to sell all our furniture, such as it was, to accumulate enough money to pay for the move and the advance rent on our new home. Luckily, the woman who bought the furniture agreed to move us across town later that week in her van for £3.

We moved to a semi-detached house in 15, Brassey Avenue, on the South Foreland. We had plenty of room. There were four bedrooms, two reception rooms, a dining room off the kitchen, and a large brick workshop. Doors opened onto a walled garden with plum trees. There was a large shed at the bottom of the garden with a rotten, leaky, roof. Once the shed roof was newly felted this garden shed was ideal for storing his firework frames.

Due to all the upheavals, the 1962 annual fireworks display had to be cancelled. The council stored the firework frames and other paraphernalia until such time as my father could accommodate them. We quickly settled into our new home. All the bankruptcy had succeeded in achieving was to force us to seek National Assistance. For a long time, my father had some peace of mind receiving £7.3s. per week from the N.A.B. My grandmother received £3.7s. Once the rent had been paid, that left us with £1.14s.

# CHAPTER THIRTEEN: BROADSTAIRS

Somehow, during the turbulent year of 1962, my father managed to write *The Red Tape Murders* and *The Last Warning* (a rewritten version of *The Crooked Circle* first published in 1935). These novels were swiftly followed in 1963, by *I Am Death* (a rewritten version of *The White Friar*, originally published in 1934, under his pseudonym Donald Stuart), *The Ghost Squad*, and *Murder in Manuscript*, all for Wright & Brown.

Meanwhile, I was no longer going to Haddon Dene School but had joined a state school in Broadstairs Road called Charles Dickens. This was a bit of a culture shock as I was mixing with a rough lot compared to what I was used to and exchanged brogues for winklepickers. However, when it came to teachers and facilities the school was way ahead of any private schools I had been to. There was a fully equipped woodwork and metalwork shop, a well-stocked library, a science laboratory, and an assembly hall with a raised stage, sound, and lighting, all of which I was destined to make good use of.

Possessing a clear speaking voice and a natural feel for drama, it was suggested I join *The Dickens Players* because they were looking for someone to play a young David Copperfield. I went to meet Miss Gladys Waterer at Dickens House, the cottage that was Charles Dickens' inspiration for the home of Betsey Trotwood in *David Copperfield*. She adapted Dickens novels for the stage. I got the part and joined The Broadstairs Dickens Players.

David Copperfield was performed at The Charles Dickens School for six nights during June 1963. It was exciting to see photographs and write-ups in all the local newspapers. The following year June 1964 I played Peter Cratchit in *A Christmas Carol* at the Community Hall, St. Peters Road, in which I found myself in the company of Bruce Robinson who played Ebenezer Scrooge as a youth. Bruce was to achieve fame as the writer of the cult classic *Withnail and I*, a biographical film with comic and tragic elements set in London in the late 1960s, which drew on his experiences as a struggling actor living in poverty in Camden Town. The following year I appeared as Blight in *Our Mutual Friend*. I could have been an actor but, like my father, didn't consider myself very good at acting and I hated learning lines.

During the beginning of 1964, my father began making fireworks again filling the house with them in preparation for a firework display at St. Lawrence Summer Fayre to raise money for St Laurence Church. The display took place in a field in which my father and I set up the fireworks at one end to a live performance of Adam Faith and his band who squeezed onto a temporary stage erected in the middle singing *Message to Martha* and other hits. The firework display was very successful, admired by all, and helped raise a record-breaking amount of money for the church. My father never personally accepted money towards the cost of any of his firework displays.

On Wednesday 26 August 1964 his radio play *There's No Escape* was broadcast by the BBC Radio Light Programme. It was a one-hour play produced by Audrey Cameron and based on his *No Hiding Place* script that was returned. It was written under the pseudonym of Gerard Stuart.

During this year my father also wrote three novels for Wright & Brown, an original story *The Faceless Ones,* and two rewritten stories. These were *Six Men Died* (a rewritten version of *The Glass Arrow* by Gerald Verner from 1937, and *The Three Who Paid* under his pseudonym Donald Stuart for the Sexton Blake Library 612 February 1938), and *The Moor House Murders* (a rewritten version of *The Man Outside* under his pseudonym Donald Stuart, originally published in 1934).

These thrillers were followed in 1965 by *Death Set in Diamonds.* In 1966, by *Mister Big* (a rewritten version of *Green Mask* from 1934 by Gerald Verner), and *The Tudor Garden Mystery* (a rewritten version of *The Riddle of the Sunken Garden,* under his pseudonym Donald Stuart, for the Sexton Blake Library 581 July 1937, and *The Three Gnomes,* 1937).

This new batch were all for publication by a declining Wright & Brown who went into voluntary liquidation at the close of 1969 leaving no debt. Wright & Brown had lost money for several years. Legally all contracts became null and void. The elder Mr. Wright & Mr. Brown were very shrewd, but the sons weren't motivated in the same way. If they had gone into the paperback field and found new outlets they might have kept the business going. Eric Wright died at the end of 1971. He was well over 90.

These sixties books, most of them rewritten earlier works, typed in a state of stress and desperation, are not his best work. This was the sixties! There was little modernisation in the stories. They remained rooted in a bygone age as if my father was caught up in a 1930's time loop, which of course he was, repetitively reliving the same experience over and over, being totally of the Edwardian period and reluctant to leave it. Life had moved on and our culture was changing forever.

\* \* \*

# CHAPTER THIRTEEN: BROADSTAIRS

Brock's carried out a regular firework display for Dreamland Amusement Park at Margate. Here my father met up with his friend Johnny Marshall and others from Brock's. He assisted them by firing the shells during the summer every Friday at dusk. The firework displays would be made up in two sheds around the back of the large coach park. The coach park would be cleared on the day of the display so the firework set-pieces would be erected.

Once all was ready, we would join the firework men taking a break before the show at the Jolly Dog Bar—the lit sign was a dog wagging his tail and smoking a cigarette. Inside the walls were painted with dogs in various poses by artist Vic McCoy. It was a packed *singalong* piano bar where we would find a table and sink a couple of pints of beer while joining in with the crowd singing good old-fashioned musical hall favourites mixed with the Beatles and other tunes everyone knew. There was a fantastic high spirited holiday atmosphere in the bar, such a contrast from the Dreamland Ballroom in the same building where on a Saturday night I would dance to the psychedelic music of *Pink Floyd (long before the mainstream Dark Side of the Moon), Geno Washington and the Ram Jam Band, Chris Farlowe and the Thunderbirds,* and other new arrivals contributing to a fast-changing culture, performing live in close proximity to a teenage audience. Many years later I was to carry out special effects for Pink Floyd's concert *The Wall* at Earl's Court in London, a slightly larger venue!

There was a fantastic atmosphere of anticipation and expectation from the Dreamland crowd as they filled the rows of raked seats below The Queen Mary façade facing the car park and the fireworks, waiting expectantly for the evening firework display to begin.

Eventually the lights in the amusement park were turned off. This was a signal for the first portfire to be lit - a sign the display was about to commence. Professional portfires are used for the safe and easy lighting of fireworks. Once lit they burn for about 5 minutes with a very hot pale green flame which is resilient to wind and rain. The noise of the crowd died down to a hush. You could feel the excitement and expectation like an electric charge in the night air.

As soon as we saw that pale green flame, we lit our portfire and waited… Johnny Marshall rotated his portfire. This was the signal for the first five-inch shell to be ignited to kick off the display. My father would bend forward to ignite the quick match before turning away as a *thumping thwack* shook the ground two seconds later as the lifting charge ignited, shooting the shell high into the night air where it burst with a pop and a bloom of coloured stars—one of the most satisfying experiences anyone could ever wish for.

In the background, the screams and cheers from the scenic railway echoed across the car park... The scent of hotdogs assaulted our nostrils from the food stalls... Squeaky pop music blared from the tannoy speakers...

As a teenager I accompanied my father and acted as his assistant. We were both unpaid. We were positioned in front of the crowd and the firework set-pieces. We always had a perfect unobscured view of the display. The shells were kept in a wooden box with a hinged lid. There were four steel mortars sunk into the ground close by—one five inch and a trio of three inch. I would load them up, in full view of the crowd. I stood back, making sure the lid of the box was closed. My dad fired the shells and I would re-load. It was a bit like artillery except no one fired back! If one shell didn't go off, I would wait to make sure it wasn't fizzing before hauling it out—that was a bit tricky! There was always a fear moment. At the time it didn't worry me, but later in life I used to have nightmares that the shell went off while my arm was plunged down the mortar tube. No more arm!

I loaded up the mortars with shells weekly for several summers and felt privileged to be given such an exciting task. When you're standing next to a five-inch shell when it goes off it can be scary but thrilling! You get used to it and later in life explosions and bangs never made me jump. There is a smell from a firework display. It is the scent of gunpowder: sulphur and charcoal mixed with burned cardboard. It is intoxicating to a true pyrotechnician.

Fireworks left over plus other bits and pieces were given to my father by the Brock's crew as a reward for our help. They were a vital contribution towards my father's own firework displays. I have plunged my hands into a stone jar of grain gunpowder and felt the polished granules trickle through my fingers like silk. Gunpowder burns with a ferocious flame in the open creating a lot of smoke. It is not explosive unless confined. My father used gunpowder for the lifting and bursting charges in his aerial shells which contribute the wow factor to any firework display, as we all know from watching the amazing firework displays from around the world that we see today.

My father would never have been able to get some of the materials he took back on the Margate to Broadstairs bus any other way than through his friends at Brocks and the Dreamland firework displays. He would have been forced to give up his own firework displays and unlike financial ruin that really would have broken his heart.

My father's mother, Ellen Emma Stuart Pringle, Nellie, Geraldine Verner, Aunty Gerry, born in Swansea in 1877, died on 2 December 1966, at Hill House hospital, at Minster, Kent. On the death certificate it states she was 92, widow of John Charles Stuart-Pringle, a schoolmaster. A mistake was made on the certificate as to her age. Born in 1877, she would have been 89.

\* \* \*

My father's eccentric agent Philip Ridgeway operated from a narrow four-story house in Endell Street, Covent Garden, London WC2. It was a chaotic place stuffed from floor to ceiling with books and papers. The house belonged to his mother. It must have been worth quite a lot in

1967 but a fortune now. He lived and operated there rent free. He was always coming up with wild ideas of one sort of another which he would try to action with a flurry of telephone calls. Most of these ideas led nowhere, sadly out of date. Times were a changing. Our culture changing through the sixties out of all recognition left many behind in a bygone era.

In 1967, Ridgeway asked my father to write a novel to lock up the copyright of a story in preparation for a possible film deal he was wildly enthusiastic about. The result was *Yu-Malu The Dragon Princess* published by Wright & Brown. My father wrote it under the pseudonym Thane Leslie as he felt it was too great a departure from his own *Gerald Verner* style. Once he'd got into it, he thoroughly enjoyed writing it! Ridgeway was ecstatic with the result, but nothing further ever came of any film. Here is the description from the front jacket flap:

"Princess Yu-Malu (The Dragon Princess), most beautiful, vastly wealthy, hates Western Civilisation and vows its downfall. She is assisted by a Corps of Dragonflies, members of the Hung, powerful Secret Society. As part of her campaign the Princess desires to obtain the formula of a cold rocket fuel invented by the West and gain China's admittance to the United Nations. Her price for her demands being ignored? She will destroy the entire gold stock of the West. Already gold planes have been disappearing, but Yu-Malu's patience is exhausted. She issues her final ultimatum utilising the General Assembly of the United Nations to add to her point. Anthony Race of the British Treasury and his Assistant, Katrina Evans, attempt to foil Yu-Malu's plots in this fast-moving international thriller which takes us through and under the Mediterranean, into international Casinos, on top of London's Post Office Tower and into, of all places, Buckingham Palace before the final (?) curtain is rung down."

August – December 1967 came a *curve ball* return to the world of Sexton Blake. BBC Radio 4 aired *Sexton Blake*. The entire series of 17 x 30 min case histories was scripted by my father writing as Donald Stuart, devised for radio by Philip Ridgeway and produced by veteran BBC radio producer Alastair Scott-Johnston. My father wrote an episode every two weeks, which at the age of 70 was a remarkable achievement. He declared to me he never liked writing as a speculation but could write quickly if commissioned. This radio series was proof of that.

The series starred William Franklyn who gave his suave approach to the title role. Franklyn was perhaps best remembered as the voice of the *Schhh... You Know Who*, Schweppes advertisements and the TV series *Top Secret*. David Gregory played Tinker and Heather Chasen was Blake's secretary, Paula Dane.

I met William Franklyn and Alastair Scott-Johnston when I accompanied my father to the BBC to hear the first Blake recording. After listening to Episode One *Lilies for the Ladies*, we all adjourned for drinks at The Westbury Hotel. I was 17 years old and an avid radio fan.

Lilies for the Ladies
The Sin-Eater
Hags Acre
The Fifth Dimension
The Black Widow
First Class Ticket to – Nowhere
Double or Quits

## CHAPTER THIRTEEN: BROADSTAIRS

You Must be Joking
Conjuror's Coffin
The Blood of Rameses
No Trees for the Peke
Bluebeards Keys
The Vampire Moon
The Beard of the Prophet
The Enchanted Editor
The Eight of Swords
A Murder of Crows

These stories reflect the modernisation of Blake's world placing emphasis on his female assistant Paula Dane alongside Tinker. The episodes went on air Thursday nights at 7.00 pm. At almost the same time as the radio version a Blake Television series appeared which shared the same theme music as the Radio series, continuing its run into 1971. Many of the radio stories were original, but some like *The Beard of the Prophet* or *You must be Joking* were extrapolated from past works.

On 14 December 1967 W. Howard Baker threw a party to celebrate Blake's 74th birthday and the launch of his TV tie-in strip in *VALIANT* comic. The Party was held by Fleetway Publications Limited. My father was on the guest list and attended. Eric Parker the prolific Blake illustrator was present with other personalities including W.O.G. Lofts, co-author with D.J. Adley of *The Men Behind Boys Fiction*, Howard Baker 1970.

Lofts, considered by many as an authority on authors of vintage crime fiction, stated in *The Collector's Digest* Vol 13, No 149, May 1959, that when the story of Gerald Verner offering up his first story on scraps of paper while down and out on the Embankment was brought up in a recent conversation with Harold Twyman, that *Twyman could not recollect his first tale coming to him in that manner.* Bill Lofts then states that *in his opinion* the story is not true. I have a letter from Bill Lofts to my father dated 5 February 1955, wherein he says:

> "I have always been amused to know that once you were 'down and out' on the Embankment when you submitted your first Sexton Blake Yarn to the Editor on scraps of paper written in pencil! I remember reading this somewhere and cannot think that it could be true. If it is so, please forgive me. Sometimes these

stories get around, and they are often highly exaggerated. I meant amused at the 'News Story'. I have nothing but admiration for a man who fights his way from the bottom until he reaches the top."

My father substantiated the story was a true one in his reply. In another letter 17 July 1974, Lofts refers to an idea of my fathers to have his stage plays published in one volume and doubts if one could find a publisher to take on the task:

"I mentioned this to an editor friend of mine at A.P., Chris Lowder – who is a great Blake fan, and he said he would be writing to you shortly with perhaps some suggestions."

Christopher Adrian Jervais Lowder (legal name) or pseudonyms Jack Adrian, Jack Hamilton Teed, Bill Henry, James R. Montague, and T. G. Cribbling, is a prolific writer of genre fiction and an editor, born in 1945. Moving forward to 1986, I find Christopher Lowder as Jack Adrian (being a friend of Lofts and probably having read Lofts account) saying the same thing but in a more emphatic manner in his introduction to *The Green Jester* by Donald Stuart, in a selection of Sexton Blake stories under the collective title of *Sexton Blake Wins* published by Dent 1986:

"It is said Donald Stuart wrote his first Sexton Blake novel on scraps of paper while roughing it on the Embankment. This, like a good many stories about Stuart (mostly emanating from the man himself) is wholly untrue, although his early life did have a certain nomadic twinge to it and his subsequent writing career was far from sedentary."

Note, Lowder makes the statement *is wholly untrue,* the implication being that this untruth came from Donald Stuart himself, together with several other stories that are also likely not to be true. Lowder has no proof of this statement. This was my first encounter with Adrian's caustic, putdown style.

My father told me of his *down-and-out period* on The Embankment on several occasions when reminiscing and how tough it was getting work. We are not talking of a smelly bundle of rags, a tramp begging for money, but someone down on their luck, homeless without money, writing a story on various sheets of paper in longhand that would need typing up—and I never suspected he was telling me anything other than the truth. This period *was* during the Great Depression. Years later, I came across a letter my father had written 21 June 1963 to his friend and fellow crime writer Noel Lee, in which he states:

> "It was with a sad heart that I looked at the last of the *SBL*. The first thing, as you know, that I ever wrote in my life was a Sexton Blake story *The Clue of the Second Tooth*. It was dear old Hamilton Teed who took it to the editor, Leonard Pratt, who bought it straight away and gave me a special cheque on account for £20, worth quite a bit in those days."

Harold Twyman wouldn't necessarily recollect this *true* account of what happened as the story was given to Leonard Pratt! The manuscript was given to Leonard Pratt not by Donald Stuart/Gerald Verner but by Blake author George Hamilton Teed. The absence of fact creates surmise and allows people to gain capital out of carelessly dipping into other people's lives.

* * *

That same year 1967, the last of my father's Wright & Brown books, *Dead Secret* was published (a rewritten version of the 1936 novel *The Watcher*). Following that publication he began writing a long fantasy novel called *Mr. Willows* which reached 204 pages but was never finished. The novel opens intriguingly.

> "From the front of his small cottage, Mr. Willows could see over a wide vista of open country to where the Great Forest covered the gently rising slopes of the low, undulating hillside, like a giant, mottled green, ragged-edged cloak, stretching away along the horizon. The Great Forest was a place of vast proportions, full of strange and wonderful things, if you knew where to look and what to look for; a place of sun-dappled glades and twisting paths that appeared inviting, but frayed out disappointingly into a tangle of impenetrable undergrowth, barring further progress; a place of dark and secret recesses, hidden in remote depths, where the light of the sun never shed even a glimmer, and known only

to the birds and the wild creatures and the ancient trees that guarded them. Even Mr. Willows, who had spent so many hours of his life in the Forest, and knew a great many of its secrets, did not know about these."

In 1970, at 73 years of age, my father was still going strong making fireworks in preparation for a display at the St. Laurence Fayre. The fireworks would be stored all over the house at 15, Brassey Avenue, in various stages of completion. Looking back, it was a miracle our open coke boiler didn't set them all off, and we weren't burned to death! When the day arrived to fire them at St. Laurence events didn't go quite as planned. He popped a shell into a heavy-duty cardboard mortar tube buried in the ground as he had done many times before. But on this occasion instead of shooting high in the air and exploding into stars the shell detonated as soon as it hit the bottom of the mortar tube shattering the cardboard like shrapnel, which tore chunks out of my father's right leg. It had been raining all afternoon and it was generally assumed that the cardboard mortar tube had got damp. Burning residue from a previous shell must have been smouldering inside the tube sufficiently to burn through the thin brown paper holding the lifting charge and igniting the shell before my father lit the fuse. My father explained:

"When it detonated, I didn't really know what had happened. Then I felt something warm running down my leg. It was blood."

I was working in London at the time as Deputy Stage Manager of the rock musical *Hair* at the Shaftesbury Theatre, produced by my brother James Verner, when I got a call from the hospital telling me what had happened. I had no idea how serious the accident was. The injuries to his leg were very bad. Much of the flesh had been blown away to the bone.

After attending hospital, he spent weeks in bed convalescing, growing increasingly irritable while his leg healed. Constant irritation from the slowly healing wounds and not being able to scratch them didn't help his mood. The whole healing process nearly drove him mad. With the utmost reluctance, he promised he wouldn't attempt any more firework displays. It was time to call it a day.

The year 1972 saw a short spate of writing short stories for *Argosy* Magazine. Three stories were written under his pseudonym Donald Stuart: *The Portable Typewriter* June Argosy 1972, followed by *The Able Mr.*

## CHAPTER THIRTEEN: BROADSTAIRS

*Kane* July Argosy 1972 and *The Will and the Way* January Argosy 1973. Another story written by Gerald Verner was called *Mr. Gilmot Goes Home* November 1972.

I began working for The National Theatre at The Old Vic in May 1971 and remained for five years. I commuted part of the time from Broadstairs to Waterloo. In 1974 I bought 15, Brassey Avenue for £6000 from the owners who lived at Taronga Park, Sydney, Australia. I visited them personally while I was staying in Sydney touring with the National Theatre production of *Front Page* and completed the deal.

\* \* \*

I arrived home from London early one evening to find a tall willowy woman in her seventies in a pale blue dress sitting in the back room chatting to my father. She had a pleasant countenance with neat silvery hair and grey eyes and was wearing a summer frock. She seemed happy and full of fun.

*This is Pat*, he introduced casually, looking at me with a nervous smile.

He turned to the woman:

*This is my son, Chris.*

I still didn't get it until he dropped his bombshell: *This is my first wife Patricia!*

I was instantly in shock. You really could have knocked me down with a feather! It took a few moments to register who this woman before me really was.

A ghost from the past.

This was my father's first wife whom he married in 1923, and whom I never dreamed I would ever meet. Was she really sitting in front of me? I must have looked half-witted as all this went through my head.

When I try to recollect the occasion, my mind is mostly blank. Infuriating. I remember she had brought with her a bottle of Gordon's Gin, some tonic water, and a brown paper bag of fresh prawns which she'd purchased from the fishmonger in Albion Street. When I arrived they were both drinking gin and tonic while working their way through the prawns building a pile of discarded shells. They were obviously enjoying a good chat until my arrival interrupted them. They looked at me like a pair of guilty teenagers.

A good chat!

Heavens! They certainly had enough to talk about. How many years to fill in?

Now, writing this biography, I am desperate to recollect this encounter.

I have wondered countless times how Pat had tracked my father down and if she was seeking some sort of reconciliation... Perhaps that's the wrong word. Companionship perhaps. How romantic to think that in the last years of their lives they might have been reunited.

Why she had visited and what she was looking for in the long term I never found out. I got the impression my father was pleased to see her but that was as far as it went. He was used to his routine and didn't relish it disrupted. Maybe he was terrified a hoard of skeletons would come bursting out of a cupboard that he didn't want anyone to know about!

I should have asked her a million questions but, to my *eternal regret,* I didn't. Not even a photograph. How many gaps in this biography could she have filled? I have kicked myself many times since meeting her that day that I didn't sit down with her and find out more about my father's past but at the time I felt I had intruded and kept discreetly out of the way. I caught an early train to London the following morning.

The truth is, when you are young, you are just not interested in your parents' lives and don't have the questions to hand. That thirst for knowledge comes later, often after they are dead and buried, sad to say. The following day my father told me how pleased she was to meet me and that she wanted to leave me her furniture when she died—she had no one else. She was living in a flat in Battersea, London. I have no idea what happened to her furniture because I never saw her, or heard from her, again.

\* \* \*

On 22 September 1979, I married Jenny Oliver at Chelsea register office. I am happy to say we are still together after over forty years. We have two grown-up children, Mark born in 1981, and Zoe in 1985. In 2014 Zoe married Andy Pitt and in 2018 their son Zac was born. My father would have been thrilled to see his grandchildren and great-grandson. Our wedding day was a lovely sunny day and I

am so pleased to report my father was a witness to our marriage, put his signature to that effect, and was in very jovial form. The polaroid is of my father signing the register.

Unfortunately, his health wasn't destined to last. I was staying in London when several months later I got a call to tell me our next-door neighbours had noticed the bedroom light had been on all night. Concerned something might have happened they let themselves in and found him lying prone on the bedroom floor. He had suffered a stroke. He was taken to *Hill House,* a private Nursing Home in Broadstairs where he was given professional care. The stroke had left him unable to look after himself. With several professional commitments, neither Jenny nor myself could devote the necessary time required to look after him. Once at the nursing home his health deteriorated rapidly. When I visited him, he didn't really know where he was. He spoke in a way that didn't make any sense and it was clear the stroke had affected his brain. He rambled on about Fleet Street and mentioned far ago names I didn't know. Maybe now, after researching his life, I might recognise some of them if I'd kept a recording. Six weeks later he died there, on 16 September 1980, aged 83, almost one year since I was married.

Both his wives survived him.

Here is a soul-searching extract from a letter to Noel written in 1971 which illuminates his relationship with his Grandfather, Robert Wallace, Professor of Music who died at the age of 75 in 1915 and other matters:

"Since the breakup of my marriage with Carol, and I took over the care of Christopher at an early age, I have always tried to give him as much love and understanding as I could. I am well aware that you and a number of other people believe that I erred on the side of kindness and leniency, but I never wanted to play the part of the *heavy father.* What I tried to establish was a relationship of friendship and camaraderie, such as existed in my own early childhood between myself and my Grandfather. I have never for a moment forgotten him during my life and although I have never been able to live up to his gentleness, kindness, and overall, his supreme *goodness,* my love for him had remained with me. I was very like Chris when I was young – excitable, enthusiastic, and quick-tempered. I was, and still am, rather weak-willed. By all kinds of devious means, I would put off as long as possible dealing with anything that was unpleasant and, believe me, Noel,

# PLOTS AND GUNPOWDER

I came up against so many unpleasant things that had to be dealt with in my life that I became an expert in postponing the crunch!

My Grandfather was a deeply religious man and I was brought up to believe firmly in God and Jesus Christ and Father Christmas. Looking back, I believe that my discovery that Father Christmas was a myth and that the presents he was supposed to bring really came from my Grandparents was the first thing that shook my faith in the existence of God. If one thing was an illusion why not all? I always believed that there existed a supreme governing factor responsible for the running of the Universe and all the infinite loveliness of nature. But as I grew older and saw the haphazard way things happened to people – that there was no kind of plan or planning in life, nothing but a pure element of chance, I was forced to the conclusion that this governing factor was an entirely impersonal one – that it was not concerned with individual people or with people in the mass. The idea of a *God of Love* which the church believed in was so ridiculous, in view of what happened to the nicest people, that it was quite impossible to accept. This God was a being full of vanity who wanted to be continuously praised and exalted and to whom one was expected to crawl abjectly on one's belly, like Uriah Heap, in order to placate him. It did not, and does not, conform with an *Ever-Loving God* or even with the teachings of Christ.

It is impossible for man, I include women, of course, to visualise God, if he exists. So, man has created a God in his own image and given him all the worst attributes of human nature. Since man cannot possibly *know* he has to fall back on invention – an invention bounded by his own finite mind. He declares God to be supreme and omnipotent and in the same breath destroys the image of omnipotence by stating that God, having given man free will cannot do anything unless man is willing that he should. In other words, God is powerless to interfere. Again, man states that God will do nothing unless man gives himself entirely to God. This, again, is making nonsense of God being a God of Love. Even a human being, with all his faults and sins, will not, usually, insist on complete subjugation before making the slightest move to help.

# CHAPTER THIRTEEN: BROADSTAIRS

So, where are we? A lot of ant-like creatures running around desperately in circles, trying to help each other, and praying for guidance. Some people may delude themselves that they get an answer. But ask all the starving children – and the poor, unhappy, people who have killed themselves because they have found they were carrying a burden too heavy to carry any longer – ask the child who is raped and dies in agony and fear, and the parents of that child – ask any of the unfortunate who are dying in their thousands, lonely, in misery and despair. What will they say? A loving God? A God of mercy and compassion? I doubt it. What evidence have they that such a God exists?"

It may seem to some that my father was wrong to take my ten-shilling notes, but I knew him well, and he would never have taken them if he hadn't been driven by circumstance and necessity. He was a very kind, generous, man. A good listener. At all times he behaved like the gentleman he was. I have never seen my father drunk, heard him swear, or lose his temper. Constant relapses into debt may brand him a loser in the eyes of those whose benchmark is capital. In his own words, he wasn't equipped to handle money. It trickled through his fingers. He was no accountant but entertained millions with his stories and his firework displays. He was no loser.

My wife Jenny and I travelled to Kenya for two weeks at the beginning of September 1980 to work on the mini-series *Flame Trees of Thika*. This was Elspeth Huxley's memories of an African childhood, adapted for a British television serial of seven 50-minute episodes made by Euston Films for Thames Television starring Hayley Mills, daughter of John Mills and sister of my old school chum Jonathan.

Sadly, on the day we returned my father died before we could get to see him.

I very much regret not being there at the end, but his great friend Noel Lee was on hand, as always in times of crisis.

When Jenny and I got to the nursing home that same day and saw him stretched out on the bed, I knew I was looking at an empty shell.

John Robert Stuart Pringle, Donald Stuart, Gerald Verner, the storyteller, and firework maker, had gone somewhere else.

# Chapter Fourteen – Postmortem

My father once said to me:

*"Don't worry about my body when I die, I've left it for anatomical research."*

When they realised his age and how many cigarettes he'd smoked each day nobody wanted it!

His cremation in Thanet echoed back to John and Robert Pringle who, you may remember, also died in Thanet in 1842. The cremation was a subdued affair at which only a few close friends and relations attended. They included my producer brother James and his wife Theo. The chap who did the reading performed a perfectly reasonable job attempting to summon up my father's life seeing he hadn't a clue about it. Afterwards James went over and shook hands with him. I asked him:

*What was that all about?*

James then confided to me he knew the chap, a jobbing actor he'd once met at an audition!

A perfect coda to an extraordinary life!

\* \* \*

What happened to both his wives who survived him?

Did Patricia read my father's obituary?

I was still living at my house in Broadstairs up to a year after my father died. To my regret Pat never got in touch. Newly married, with a blossoming career in movies to pursue, I was forging ahead and never went looking for her. I now realise with hindsight and endless regret there was so much she could have told me, so many discussions we could have had, filling in the gaps of my father's early life as first Donald Stuart and then as Gerald Verner. Born 28 February 1900, she died in Surrey, January 1988, aged 87. The name on the death certificate was Patricia Verner. Much of her life remains a complete mystery.

## CHAPTER FOURTEEN: POSTMORTEM

My mother, born 29 November 1916, now Isobel Whimster, died peacefully in her sleep on 17 July 1996, in Hove, Sussex, aged 80.

\* \* \*

Any artist, writer, actor, sculptor, painter, who has permeated popular culture lives on after death… Their legacy of innovation contributes to society's culture as a whole and becomes a matter of public record. My father's body of work is extensive and lives on… His books which used to change hands at £1 or less now sell on eBay and elsewhere for around £350 if in first-class condition with a dust jacket. They are collected worldwide as part of what has become known as *The Golden Age of Detective Fiction* – the *whodunits,* a type of fiction which was predominant in the 1920s and 1930s which has influenced every crime story, or thriller, we read and watch on TV today. However successful modern detective fiction might be it has never approached the popularity of Golden Age writing simply because our entertainment is now so diverse - multiple choices provided by many different types of media. At one time one in four books sold in England had been written by Edgar Wallace who sold over 50 million copies!

Originally my father's books were sold just for the stories—for good escapist entertainment. Today, the high prices they fetch are no longer just for the stories but also for the cover art, the nostalgic value, the romance of the age in which they were written, even the smell of the book that no *eBook* can replace.

To the modern reader the stories themselves will appear dated. I can't see any point in comparing them to modern crime stories. They are nostalgic, even quaint, and that is their value. To read them is to enjoy a style of writing from a bygone age. The stories have a certain charm, an English civility, an innocence, that in the main died out with the horrors of WW2. These essentially English stories were replaced by American influenced *hardboiled* pulps. A growing obsession with realism has led to the procedural stories we enjoy today obsessed with detailing forensic science. But on occasion, going back to one of these golden age detective stories is like putting on an old jacket—it's a bit worn but very comfortable.

\* \* \*

# PLOTS AND GUNPOWDER

Is my father correct in thinking there is *no kind of plan or planning in life?* Nothing but an element of chance? I have experienced throughout my life rather strange coincidences or what you might prefer to call *accidental connections*. For example, it has always seemed strange to me that most days on my way to school I cycled past Stone House School, Lanthorne Road, Broadstairs, unaware that was where my grandfather taught.

On 17 June 1967 I was at Margate's Dreamland Ballroom watching Pink Floyd perform *See Emily Play* for two shillings and sixpence. It was the first time I had seen coloured ink projectors mounted on a gantry to project psychedelic images onto a group. Years later I find myself carrying out pyrotechnic effects for their spectacular concert *The Wall* at Earl's Court, London, over five nights in July 1980, followed by performances in February 1981 in Dortmund, Germany.

I used to watch *The Avengers* on television. I adored the tongue-in-cheek performances of Diana Rigg and Patrick Macnee. How strange it was then, when years later at The National Theatre, I worked with Diana Rigg on *Jumpers* and *Macbeth*.

In January 1971, I travelled up to the Belgrade Theatre, Coventry, to see a friend perform in the pantomime Dick Whittington. While travelling back on the train to London, idly turning over the pages of the programme, I found the next presentation on 19 January was *Towards Zero* and when I looked up, I realised I was sitting opposite the actor Alan Bates, who looked particularly gloomy for the entire journey. The next time I saw Alan Bates he was sitting on a horse about to fire a pistol I had provided and loaded. I was working on the ill-fated film *The Wicked Lady,* directed by Michael Winner, in which Alan Bates was starring with Faye Dunaway and others.

I met in real life many of those stars I first watched on TV or Film as a teenager. If you snip out the time intervals you end up with a spooky multi-dimensional sphere of events, within which everything is nodal, with you at the centre, *your life*, as if someone else had worked out the plot to prove life is *not* totally random.

In 1984, I was fortunate to be carrying out special effects on the film of the same name, starring John Hurt and Richard Burton, for Umbrella-Rosenblum Films Production. The producer was Simon Perry. How surreal then to receive a call in October 1984 from Brian Stone, of Hughes Massie Limited, regarding the adaptation agreement between my father and Agatha Christie for *Towards Zero*. The original contractual

170

details at the time the play had been produced had been handled by Edmund Cork, (of the Hughes Massie agency)—Agatha Christie's friend and literary agent and the successor of Hughes Massey, who had died.

Brian Stone informed me that on 19 April 1954, Copyright Trading, a company owned by the Cork family who formally owned Hughes Massey, made a further agreement with my father to buy out the rights mentioned in the original 1951 agreement. He explained all the non-American rights bought by Copyright Trading from Gerald Verner remained with them. However, a share of the royalties coming in from America from the play itself, the published version of the plays script, and from the sale of rights in the film, will now be sent to me. As money started to roll in, I couldn't help thinking how unfortunate it was that my father had sold the non-American (i.e. United Kingdom) rights for urgently needed cash.

Zoom forward to July 1988. A letter from Brian Stone tells me he is presently negotiating a deal for Leasing of the film rights in *Towards Zero* to Simon Perry of Umbrella Films. Claude Chabrol was to direct. Having carried out special effects on Simon Perry's Orwell film *1984* and as an admirer of Claude Chabrol you can imagine how exciting this all sounded. By 31 December 1988 it was agreed that upon execution of the license the producer would pay £150,000 from which my share was 12.5%. It was paid to me on 3 November 1992.

Roll on to December 1993, when a further letter from Hughes Massey tells me that Agatha Christie Limited has turned down the script (they had approval) for various reasons. Many of the original characters had been left out. *Towards Zero* is set in an English seaside resort which had now been moved to the South of France. The final straw was the script altered the original story, in what was envisaged as a sexy new twist, but which horrified The Christies, daughter Rosalind Hicks and grandson Mathew Prichard. *Audrey and Neville Strange turned out in this last script to be brother and sister and there were heavy injections of incest!*

By February 1994 the name of the film has been changed to *Bloodlines* and any mention of the title of the book, Agatha Christie, and the names of all the original characters are excluded from the script – a real blow to box office potential.

When the film appeared in June 1995, the title had been changed yet again to *Halcyon Days*. Brian Stone commented:

"The Christies are very particular about the way their properties are adapted and were utterly decisive. Halcyon Days sounds like a shop."

The film ended up directed by Patrick Dewolf and re-titled yet again to *Innocent Lies*. The film was not well received and criticised on almost every level. The whole debacle seemed to me inexplicable. Why pay a lot of money for the rights to an original Christie in the first place if you intend to alter it drastically out of all recognition? Why not write a totally original script with as much incest, drugs, and infidelity as you can imagine? If my father had been alive to witness this mess, he would have been furious.

Two other adaptations of *Towards Zero* were produced in 2007 also altered, thus losing fidelity. The first, as part of *Agatha Christie's Marple* series for British television, is a screenplay by Kevin Elyot. Superintendent Battle never appears. He has been substituted by Miss Marple! The role of Macwhirter in the book has been replaced by a girl with a dog! The second is a French production, the screenplay adapted by no less than four people, Clémence de Biéville, François Caviglioli, Roland Duval, and Nathalie Lafaurie. This time Le commissaire Martin Bataille *is* on hand to work out the mystery set-in present-day Bretagne. The movie is faithful to the plot, but the general view was that the acting was hammy and the adaptation bad.

* * *

While looking up the facts concerning *Towards Zero*, I discovered a letter from a Gerald Verner fan from Kentish Town written in 1997, forwarded to me by Hughes Massey. The fan wrote:

"As a young man, I read several of your late father's novels, and was much entertained by them. Such titles as *The Huntsman*, *The Grim Joker*, and those featuring the Budd character are recalled. Other vintage crime novelists have survived in print with their stories being widely available. I pose the question, therefore, why not Verner? Apart from one Kent public library, which still holds a copy of *Mr. Big* among its stock of lending material, I have not perceived recognition of the huge output comprising of your father's novels, or of his reputation as a popular writer of crime fiction, circa 1932 – 1965, by any major publisher or bookseller. Would modern readers not similarly enjoy the books"

In May 2010 the situation posed in the above letter was resolved by an email I received from a Mr. Philip Harbottle, an author in his own right but also a literary agent specialising in finding niche markets for the reprinting of popular genre fiction. He was looking for mystery stories by well-known authors who were out of print for submission to F. A. Thorpe, for their *Linford Mystery Library*. The books are published under the auspices of *The Ulverscroft Foundation*, established in 1972 to provide funds for research, diagnosis, and treatment of eye diseases. The contract for each book was for the *Large Print* paperback format only, limited to a maximum sale of 1,000 copies of each title. The first book *The Nursery Rhyme Murders* by Gerald Verner was contracted on 11 June 2010. It was published in the spring of 2011.

The mammoth task began of reprinting my father's stories at F. A. Thorpe's request at the rate of about one per month – Donald Stuart, Nigel Vane, Derwent Steele, and Gerald Verner. At first it was straightforward until we discovered some stories were rehashes of others but with different titles and lead characters. These we had to reject. It became quite a detective operation to spot which were original and which rewritten. Some originals were very rare and near impossible to obtain.

I began to compile a bibliography, not just the titles and publishing dates of all his books under the various pseudonyms, but cross-referencing which titles were rewritten from others. I have listed this complex bibliography as an appendix to this book, together with all the *Linford Mystery* titles in order of publication, including those stories not covered by the Thorpe catalogue because they are duplicates.

In January 2015, Philip Harbottle sent me news that a publishing outfit in Vancleave, Mississipi, called *Ramble House* had built up their imprint by finding *out of print* rare books as collectors. They were looking to publish a special omnibus volume, bringing back into print, my father's Li-Sin books: *The Menace of Li-Sin* (1934) and *The Vengeance of Li-Sin* (1935), written by him under the pseudonym Nigel Vane. The omnibus would be print-on-demand. It would be available in paperback and hardback from 3 February 2015, as a John Pelan *Dancing Tuatara Press* edition, with a cover design by Gavin L. O'Keefe. I was asked to provide an in-depth afterword (which I extracted from this biography—a work in progress at that time) also a comprehensive bibliography of Gerald

Verner's writings, including the many originally published under
pseudonyms.

On 10 March 2015, I was discussing my father's unfinished opus *The
Snark Was A Boojum* with Gavin O'Keefe (mentioned in my *Afterword* to
*The Menace of Li-Sin*). I explained there were two versions of Part One of
the book, a third-person account and a revised version in the first person,
describing events seen through the eyes of Jeff Trueman a guest at
Hunter's Meadow. I pointed out there was a lot of work to revise Part
Two of the book which I thought started to fall apart about halfway
through. I told him there was no Part Three! I emphasised the whole
piece needed reworking and tightening, concluding with:

> "Writing the end is also tricky to keep it in the style and
> personality of the existing material. Coming up with a solution is
> quite another matter... I'll have a look at it!"

Gavin O'Keefe emailed back:

> "I really appreciate your giving the details of what exists in the
> manuscript of *The Snark Was A Boojum*. The second part could be
> rewritten in the first person - but the third part, unwritten, is the
> real challenge. Of course, you'd be the best person to tackle that,
> but I understand that you have other projects and the time just
> isn't there."

His words *Of course, you'd be the best person to tackle that* buzzed around
in my head until I finally began to believe it! Two days later on 12 March
I picked up the manuscript and read through it beginning with the two
drafts of the first part; *The Vanishing*.

The original in the third person begins:

> "Simon Gale realized afterwards, when all the facts were known,
> that murder must have been in the mind of the murderer long
> before the dinner-party at Hunter's Meadow. It probably existed
> then, only as a vague and formless shape, half-seen, like
> something emerging from a mist, but the desire to kill must have
> been there, needing just that chance remark of his to bring it into
> sharp and hideous focus."

# CHAPTER FOURTEEN: POSTMORTEM

Then I read the revised version in the first person and immediately understood why my father had made the changes—the story works much more intimately. The events are seen through the eyes of Jeff Trueman, a guest at Hunter's Meadow. The story now opens:

> "I realised, afterwards, that murder must have been in the mind of the murderer long before the dinner-party at Hunter's Meadow. There is no doubt that murder would have been committed in any event, but it is almost equally certain that it would not have taken the grotesque and horrible form it did, if Simon Gale, in that joking reference concerning the people at the dinner-table, had not supplied the murderer with a plan."

I began typing Chapter One in digital format noting the story is set during autumn with no year specified. I have chosen approximately 1935 when villages were still small villages, country houses still had butlers, cooks, and other servants, and guests dressed for dinner. The rural police were not particularly bright and did not have the backup they do now to solve crime. It is a period prior to a World War that would change life in England forever. As I have mentioned, it was an era beloved by my father who despite writing well into the sixties kept stories firmly entrenched in the Edwardian period.

As I typed up Part One, I jotted down Gale's character traits by looking up passages in *Noose for a Lady* and *Sorcerer's House*. This also helped me to avoid inconsistency in the writing style and enabled me to adapt or borrow elements of the two books when my father's pages ran out... Of course, eventually they did run out. It was like travelling along on a train and suddenly noticing there were no more rails ahead. I was suddenly on my own! In moving forward, I also had to go backwards and rewrote most of Part Two cutting quite a lot out and replacing it with different scenes to make my plot work. The story wouldn't let me go and I couldn't let it go, because I realised, I would never be able to pick it up again once it had gone out of my head. Bit by bit I laid down new track and inched along it giving chapters to my wife Jenny to read to get the point of view of someone not down in the cake mix. If it didn't feel right, I worked it again until it did. It was an intense process and I thoroughly enjoyed it. Suddenly, the book was finished, and in the surprisingly short time of 35 days. I sent the completed manuscript to Philip Harbottle, with some trepidation, on 16 April. He emailed back:

"I was thrilled to receive your latest enclosure! Your completing the novel to an ideal length of 55,000 words is a wonderful thing to have done. And your introduction sets it up beautifully."

On 17 April, Philip Harbottle sent an email to Gavin O'Keefe:

"I have some exciting news for you! Following your earlier expression of interest in Gerald Verner's unfinished "lost" novel, *The Snark Was A Boojum*, Chris Verner accepted the challenge of trying to complete it, by writing the final third part. I've just today finished reading the completed mss, which he e-mailed me last night, together with his fine introduction. You'll find the latter attached herewith. Let me say at once that I think Chris has done a brilliant job—quite uncanny! The novel is a good length—56,000 words and I would defy anyone (who didn't read the intro!) to realise that it had not been written by Gerald Verner himself. I think it's a real tour de force."

Then all hell broke loose! Four days later Ramble House issued a contract, a proof of the book and a draft of the cover design by Gavin L. O'Keefe! By 24 April, the paperback was on sale at Amazon! That must be a record. The contract with Ramble House runs for five years.

Thorpe published a *Large Print* paperback format, for their *Linford Mystery Library*, in September 2017, and Endeavour Media Limited a Kindle edition in June 2018:

*"What incredible fate had overtaken William Baker? The man had vanished — literally into thin air! He had walked out of his house at a quarter past nine and disappeared . . . but leaving behind his clothes, lying in a heap on the pavement . . ."*

I would like to thank my wife, Jenny for putting up with, and contributing to endless conversations as to how the story would progress and reach a conclusion. I would like to thank Gavin O'Keefe from Ramble House for suggesting I'd be the best person to tackle it. I would particularly like to thank Philip Harbottle for his help and advice and all his hard work to ensure this story is finally published 58 years after it was started. I hope I have done it justice. Some have mentioned the third part feels rushed and finishes quite abruptly. It could have been longer but wouldn't have fitted in with the publisher's requirements.

In Mystery Scene 146, 2016, in an article called *The Authorship Whodunit, Determining a Work's True Creator*, Jon L. Breen writes:

> "The ambitious plot of *The Snark Was a Boojum* might also have appealed to Agatha Christie or S.S. Van Dine in its use of familiar verse, not a nursery rhyme in this case but Lewis Carroll's nonsense poem *The Hunting of the Snark*, which provides epigraphs to the novels three sections. The murderer appears to be basing his series of crimes on elements of the poem, apparently as a result of a remark made by sleuth Gale at a country-house dinner party. Because Chris Verner edited and reworked the whole manuscript, there is no marked inconsistency in the writing style, and he's done a good job of bringing the story to a satisfactory climax. True, the killers use of the poem is very hard to make believable and the solution falls short of the problem, but it's a commendable effort and could lead readers to seek out the elder Verner's other novels."

Having completed *The Snark Was A Boojum*, I found myself at a bit of a loose end. I thought I might try and revitalise another part finished Gerald Verner story. All I could find was a few chapters of one begun at 15, Marlborough Road, and abandoned. It was titled *The Case of the Waxen Dolls*. It had *Length 75,000 words approx.* typed on the title sheet and was obviously intended to be a full-length novel.

The story opens with a scene in the railway buffet where Mr. Budd is waiting to board his train having been told by his doctor to take a holiday. He meets a crook called Snoopy Soames:

> "Cor luverduck, if it ain't Sup'ntendent Budd," said the newcomer in a nasal voice. "Wotcher doin' 'ere, eh? Tailin' some poor devil, I'll bet."
>
> Mr. Budd looked up into the thin face of the little man standing beside him.
>
> "You'd lose, Snoopy," he said.
>
> 'Snoopy' Soames, so called for obvious reasons, uttered a rude and derisive sound.

"That's what you say," he declared. "What's the game, eh? Usin' this place as an office now?"

"One of these fine days your curiosity's goin' to get you in trouble," said Mr. Budd. "If you want to know, I'm on leave. I'm waitin' to catch a train for Westpool."

Budd catches a train to the coast, and on the train a murder is committed.

I thought about this unfinished story for a while and perused the original pages a few times. I didn't like the character 'Snoopy' Soames and the direction which the story was taking. I could understand why my father had abandoned it. At various moments, I kept thinking about it, intrigued by the idea of Mr. Budd taking a train to Westpool and encountering a murder on the train journey. I love mysteries that take place on a moving train, particularly a British murder mystery set in the golden age of steam. The enclosed environment, bounded but moving, makes a wonderful location to set a crime. I woke up the following morning with most of the story mapped out in my head.

Michael Dene of *Dene of the Secret Service etc.* would bookend the story, and a character of my own invention called Tania Watts would take the place of Snoopy Soames.

> "A girl in her early thirties walked in. She was smartly dressed in a tweed suit and matching brown high heels and carried an expensive handbag. Her long blonde hair fell about her shoulders in curls. She paused and looked round, aware that every eye in the room was watching her.

> Mr. Budd recognised her immediately. He recalled that back at Scotland Yard there was a file full of facts on Tania Watts. He recalled she came from an old Deptford family, all of them crooks. Her upbringing hadn't encouraged her to aspire to much, other than continue in the family trade. He also remembered she had three brothers, one of them he knew, if not two, were residing at His Majesty's pleasure in Pentonville. Unlike the rest of her family Tania was smart. She concealed her roots carefully. She'd taken elocution lessons and sought work in several good hotels in order to observe and learn social skills. It hadn't taken her long to move into the West End of London and then a few years later graduate to a flat in Knightsbridge.

As she caught sight of him, she gave him a mocking smile.

"Good morning, Superintendent," she greeted.

Mr. Budd sighed.

Tania Watts was a vision of loveliness there could be no denying that fact.

"Good morning to you, Miss Watts," he answered, "and what brings yer to this wondrous place at this particular hour?"

"Call me Tania," answered the girl sweetly, avoiding answering the question. "I could ask you the same thing?"

Mr. Budd grunted. "If yer want to know, I'm on leave. I'm waiting to catch a train for Westpool."

I finished the story – a novella, by 29 April 2015. I called it *The Man on the Train* and sent it to Philip Harbottle. He replied:

"I just finished your story and am delighted to confirm that I found it another first-class piece of work. I can't tell where you take over from your father—very smoothly done."

The story was published in December 2016, as the second story in *Sinister House* by Gerald Verner as part of Linford Mystery Library.

In September 2016, Philip Harbottle began selling titles of my father's books to Endeavour Press (now called Lume) for publication as eBooks. The first of these *Noose for a Lady* appeared on 2 February 2017.

That same month September 2016, author Jared Cade got in touch regarding my father's adaptation of Agatha Christie's book *Towards Zero* as a play, looking to write a couple of pages about it in a biography of Christie he was working on. He had previously written a book *Agatha Christie and the Eleven Missing Days*, lifting the lid on her real-life disappearance when she mysteriously vanished from Styles, her Berkshire home, on 3 December 1926. He was very helpful in obtaining through the British Library several missing *Sexton Blake Library* stories I required in order to reference their corresponding *de-blaked* titles, as part of my task to complete the cross-referenced bibliography of my father's works.

In October 2016, Ramble House chose to publish two more of my father's books. The third in their series, originally published as a Donald Stuart novel by Wright & Brown in 1935, was to be *Midnight Murder*, for which I was asked to supply a foreword. This was the book you may remember he gave to Rex Harding, who was in a hurry for a story for use in *Detective Weekly*. The fourth in the Ramble series was *They Walk In Darkness*.

On 6 January 2017 I purchased a 1st edition copy of *The Menace of Li -Sin* written by my father under the pseudonym of Nigel Vane from a bookseller. He emailed me back saying that he'd mentioned our correspondence to Martin Edwards, a British crime novelist, critic, and solicitor, who was keen to get in touch with me. Thus, began a series of emails between myself and Martin Edwards culminating in an invitation for me to write four paragraphs on completing *The Snark was a Boojum*, which he published on his blog on 6 February 2017.

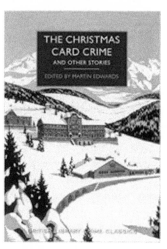

A further series of communications led to my father's short story *The Undoing of Mr. Dawes*, to be included in *The Long Arm of the Law* a collection of classic police stories edited by Martin Edwards, published in August 2017, as part of the popular *British Library Crime Classics* series. The story was originally published in *The Cleverness of Mr. Budd* 1935 by my father writing as Gerald Verner. Following on from this in October 2018, the *British Library Crime Classics* series published *The Christmas Card Crime* featuring the story originally published in 1934, by my father writing as Donald Stuart and in March 2020 in their anthology *Settling Scores* a Trevor Lowe short story by Gerald Verner originally published in 1939 *The Red Golf Ball*.

During the Spring of 2017, I came across a radio script in my father's archives for a proposed thirty-minute series based upon the Thames River Police called *The Wet Beat*. The first episode had been written titled *The Seventh Virgin*. I read through the story and thought the first third of it would make a good opening for a Mr. Budd yarn. Having cut my teeth on *The Snark was a Boojum* and the Mr. Budd novella *The Man on the Train*, I thought plotting a full-length book based on an original scenario and characters created by Gerald Verner would be fun to attempt. The first two chapters rely on the radio transcript to a degree, the rest of the plot doesn't, and Mr. Budd wasn't in the original at all. I finished the book by September. I sent the story off to Phil Harbottle, who liked it and submitted it to F. A. Thorpe who accepted the book for their large print

## CHAPTER FOURTEEN: POSTMORTEM

*Linford Mystery Library* for publication in April 2019.

When Constable Joe Bentley rescues what he thinks is a nude woman from the freezing waters of the River Thames, his catch turns out to be an exquisitely modelled tailor's dummy stuffed with thousands of pounds' worth of banknotes. Later that same morning, the dead body of a man is found further downriver. Superintendent Budd of Scotland Yard, under pressure to prevent millions of counterfeit notes from entering general circulation, must discover the connection between the incidents, and stop a cold-blooded murderer on a killing spree.

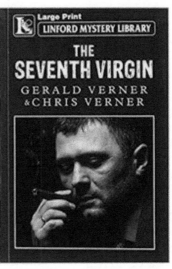

The manuscript was also sent to Jasmin Kirkbride, the editor at Endeavour Media Limited. Jasmin read the story and suggested some changes which I implemented. The revised manuscript was then sent to proof-reader and copy-editor Miranda Summers-Pritchard, and several further suggestions were made, all of which greatly improved my manuscript. Jasmin finally accepted the final revision submitted by Phil Harbottle on 21 November 2017, replying:

*"Many thanks, Phil, this is fab. We'd like to schedule it in for 11th May."*

Phil Harbottle began selling novels to Thorpe Publishing in 2004 through his Cosmos Literary Agency, so it was with profound sadness that on 11 July 2019, fifteen years later, he received an email from Thorpe Publishing stating that they were to cease publishing any further Linford Mystery titles beyond April 2020. The 86th book (which completes the Gerald Verner collection) *The Ghost Man*, first written by Gerald Verner in 1936, had already been contracted and had just scraped through to be published in April 2020 as the final Linford Mystery, ending a ten-year project itemised in Appendix 2.

Noel Lee died 28 February 2002 in Minsterworth near Gloucester. I believe there is a near satisfactory conclusion to the *Poisoner* saga. In 2018, I mentioned his name to Philip Harbottle who immediately got in touch with Noel's daughter Janice and offered to read, digitise, and then send her father's thrillers to Thorpe for their consideration with a view to including them in their Linford Mystery Library. *The Poisoner* was given a second life now properly retitled *The Manuscript Killer* by Noel Lee and published by Thorpe June 2019. It was followed by *Village of Fear* August 2019 (a collection of unpublished manuscripts edited by Phil Harbottle), and *Danger In Numbers* February 2020.

\* \* \*

I was born Christopher Stuart Verner and have remained so never addressed by anyone by another name. But what must it feel like to have been born John Robert and constantly be referred to as Donald Stuart? Not *Hi John* but *Hi Don*? And later as *Gerald*—knowing in the back of your mind that you weren't really Don or Gerald. These were not aliases or pseudonyms like Nigel Vane, Derwent Steele, or Thane Leslie, they were replacement identities, names used to sign documents. It is not uncommon for an author to hide behind a pseudonym to protect a government or academic position while carrying on their day job under their orthonym. Women wrote under men's names and vice versa if men wrote romantic fiction. But my father lived under different names in real life. He was constantly blocking out his past—even from his son and second wife.

Fans picked up on this subterfuge and invented mysterious pasts, invariably getting his name and birth date wrong. He became a man of mystery like a suspicious character in one of his own stories. I'm sure covering his tracks became a necessity, avoiding debt collectors and the Inland Revenue attempting a fresh start.

Brought up to refer to his own mother as his sister and never referring to his errant father no doubt sowed the seed of identity concealment until it became quite normal to him. Who was the man behind these veils?

There was a man of extraordinary good looks and charm—a showman. How could he not have been a showman, born into a family of music and drama, with a pedigree of music halls and theatre plus the larger-than-life cultural first-hand experience of The Crystal Palace in all its glory with its breath-taking firework displays. Music, plays, charcoal and sulphur flowed in his blood. He was weak when it came to handling money but strong as a Dad. I found him a good listener and dispenser of advice, when he could get a word in. Above all he was kind—a gentleman.

# Acknowledgments

To Verena Rose at Level Best Books for editing and steering the manuscript through to publication, to Shawn Reilly Simmons, for her awesome book cover, and not forgetting Rita Owen for sorting out the layout.

To the late Bob Adey for loaning me several of my father's stories and for getting in touch with Philip Harbottle regarding my father's work.

To Philip Harbottle for his Ernest Dudley contribution and for getting the ball rolling to enable Thorpe to publish my father's complete works in one complete edition over ten years, a truly incredible achievement. I must thank Phil for so many other additional endeavours, it would take another book to mention them all!

To Norman Wright for helping me acquire some hard to get titles and who published a bibliography of my father's works compiled by Bill Bradford.

To my brothers Jimmy and Tony Verner for their memories of growing up in Richmond.

To my wife Jenny for being patient and allowing me to read passages to her in order to help calibrate my writing.

To Noel Lee's daughter Janice Layton-Smith, for passing on to me her father's collection of my father's books, particularly my father's letters to Noel written across many years extracts from which have been invaluable.

To Fender and Gavin O'Keef at Ramble House in Vancleeve for being so enthusiastic about my Forewords and Afterwords, extracted from early drafts of this biography, and publishing them in my father's books.

To Alan Hayes for *The Avengers Declassified*.

To Jared Cade for finding the Sexton Blake Libraries I was missing which enabled me to complete my correlation between those and Wright & Brown hardbacks, digging out *The Silver Horseshoe* illustration in The Australian Woman's Weekly, and his immense help with information regarding the stage adaptation of Agatha Christie's *Towards Zero*, reading through my manuscript and suggesting helpful alterations.

To Martin Edwards for his enthusiasm in printing three of my father's short stories in the *British Library Crime Classics* series, for inviting me to write a blog (6 February 2017) on completing *The Snark Was A Boojum* and for bringing to my attention the important fact that Alan Brock was a crime writer as well as a pyrotechnician.

To Jasmin Kirkbride at Endeavour (now Lume) for her hard work in preparing the Gerald Verner Kindle books and for her advice regarding the manuscript of *The Seventh Virgin* and her acceptance of it after many of the excellent suggestions by Miranda Summers-Pritchard had been applied.

Apologies to anyone I may have inadvertently left out.


Chris Verner
Berkhamsted
February 2021.

# Appendix 1: Bibliograhy

<u>(All Published by Wright & Brown except where stated)</u>

<u>Wright & Brown 12-14 Red Lion Court, Fleet Street, London E.C.4</u>

The Embankment Murder (1933)
> Originally *The Clue of the Second Tooth* anonymous Sexton Blake Library (105 August 1927)
> Rewritten as *The Embankment Crime* by Donald Stuart Sexton Blake Library (341 July 1932)

The Black Hunchback (1933)
> Originally *The Mystery of Sherwood Towers* anonymous Sexton Blake Library (152 July 1928)
> Rewritten as *The Mystery of Sherwood Towers* by Donald Stuart Sexton Blake Library 714 April 1940.

Alias the Ghost (1933)
> Originally *The Mystery of the Phantom Blackmailer* anonymous Sexton Blake Library (157 September 1928) Serialised as *The Shadow over Iris* by Gerald Verner The Evening Telegraph, Angus, Scotland (February 25)

Phantom Hollow (1933)
> Originally *The Case of the Missing Estate Agent* by Donald Stuart Sexton Blake Library (350 September 1932)

Black Skull (1933)
> Originally *The Black Skull* anonymous Sexton Blake Library (217 December 1929)
> Rewritten as *The Hooded Terror* by Donald Stuart Bulls Eye Library (243 June 1930)
> Rewritten as *The Hooded Stranger* by Gerald Verner Bulls Eye Library (702 Jan 1940)

The Death Play (1933)
> Originally *The Fatal Manuscript* anonymous Sexton Blake Library (No 198 July 1929) anon.
> Rewritten as *Murder in Manuscript* by Gerald Verner 1963

The Next to Die (1934)
> Originally *The Next Victim* by Donald Stuart Sexton Blake Library (286 May 1931)
> Rewritten as *The Third Victim* by Donald Stuart Sexton Blake Library (653 January 1939)

# APPENDIX 1: BIBLIOGRAPHY

## Wright & Brown 4 Farringdon Avenue, London EC4

The Squealer (1934) First Edition possibly Red Lion Court
> Originally *The Squealer's Secret* by Donald Stuart Sexton Blake Library (334 May 1932)

Sinister House (1934)
> Book One: Sinister House
> Originally *Sinister House* by Donald Stuart The Thriller (64 April 1930)
> Rewritten as *The Terror of Grey Towers* Detective Weekly (176 July 1936)
> Book Two: Mr. K
> Originally *The Sinister Quest* by Donald Stuart The Thriller (245 October 1933)
> Book Three: The Big Fellow
> Rewritten as *The Fatal Hour* by Donald Stuart Detective Weekly 188 (26 September 1936)

Green Mask (1934)
> Originally *The Fence's Victim* Sexton Blake Library (266 Dec 1930)
> Rewritten as *Mr. Big* by Gerald Verner 1966

The Hangman (1934)
> Originally *Guilty But Insane* by Donald Stuart Sexton Blake Library (385 June 1933)

The Con Man (1934)
> Originally *The £1,000,000 Film Murder* Donald Stuart Sexton Blake Library (401 October 1933)

The Lady of Doom (1934)

White Wig (1935)
> Originally *The Motor Bus Murder*, by Donald Stuart Sexton Blake Library (422 March 1934)

Terror Tower (1935)
> Originally *The Village of Fear*, by Donald Stuart Sexton Blake Library (430 May 1934)

Queer Face (1935)
> Originally *Queer Face* Thriller Library (No 21 May 1935)

The Crooked Circle (1935)
> Originally *The Secret of the Sealed Room*, by Donald Stuart, Sexton Blake Library (470 March 1935)
> Rewritten as *The Last Warning* by Gerald Verner 1962

The Q Squad (1935)
> Rewritten as *The Hidden Menace* Sexton Blake Library (690 Oct 1939)

The Cleverness of Mr. Budd (1935)
> Book One: The Ghost of Rufus Manners
> Originally *The Ghost of Rufus Manners* by Gerald Verner The Thriller (December 1934)

Book Two: The Whispering Man
Originally *The Whispering Man* by Gerald Verner The Thriller (March 1935)
Book Three: The Cleverness of Mr. Budd comprising 5 Short Stories:
The Man Who Vanished
The Grey Monk (*The Grey Monk* first appeared 17 Dec 1934 The Leader).
The Clue
The Undoing of Mr. Dawes
The Clever Crook

*The Grim Joker (1936)*
Originally *The Green Jester* Union Jack (1379 March 1930)
Rewritten as The Grim Joker The Boys' Friend – Bulls Eye Library (721 June 1940)

The Hand of Fear (1936)
Originally *The Garden City Crime* by Donald Stuart Sexton Blake Library (314 December 1931)

The Seven Clues (1936)
Originally *Blake of The Secret Service* Detective Weekly (176 July 6 1936)

The Watcher (1936)
Originally *The Truth about Lord Trench* Sexton Blake Library (503 November1935)
Rewritten as *Dead Secret* by Gerald Verner1967

The Ghost Man (1936)
Originally *The Cottage of Terror* by Donald Stuart Sexton Blake Library (481 June 1935)

The River Men (1936)
Originally *River Rats* The Thriller Library (September 1936)
Rewritten as *The River Men* The Boys' Friend - Bulls Eye Library (718 May 1940)

Mr. Whipple Explains (1936)
Book One: Mr. Whipple Explains
Originally *The Riddle of the Red Queen* by Gerald Verner Detective Weekly (133 September 1935)
Book Two: Red Snow
Originally *The Clue of the Crimson Snow* by Donald Stuart Detective Weekly (44 December 1933)
Book Three: Death at the Microphone
Originally *Murder at the Microphone* by Donald Stuart Detective Weekly (111 April 1935)

The Glass Arrow (1937)
Revised as *The Three Who Paid* by Donald Stuart Sexton Blake Library (612 February 1938)
Rewritten as *Six Men Died* by Gerald Verner 1964

## APPENDIX 1: BIBLIOGRAPHY

The Frightened Man (1937)
>Originally *The Unknown Menace* Donald Stuart Sexton Blake Library (561 February 1937)

The Token (1937)
>Originally *The Bells of Doom*, as by Donald Stuart Sexton Blake Library (545 October 1936)

The Jockey (1937)
>Originally *The Sign of the Jockey* Detective Weekly (203 September 1936)

The Three Gnomes (1937)
>Originally *The Riddle of the Sunken Garden* by Donald Stuart Sexton Blake Library (581 July 1937)
>
>Rewritten as *The Tudor Garden Mystery* by Gerald Verner 1966

The Return of Mr. Budd (1938) (published as *Case Book of Mr. Budd* Macaulay Company New York 1938)
>Book One: The Clue of the Whispering Pines
>Originally *The Clue of the Whispering Pines* by Gerald Verner Detective Weekly (234 August 1937)
>Book Two: The Black Widow
>Originally *The Black Widow* by Gerald Verner Detective Weekly (206 January 1937)
>Book Three: The Devil's Footprint
>Originally *The Terror of Lonely Tor* by Donald Stuart Sexton Blake Library (302 September 1931)
>Rewritten as *The Valley of Terror* by Donald Stuart (W&B 1935)
>Rewritten as *The Devil's Footprint* by Gerald Verner Detective Weekly (May 1937)

The Silver Horseshoe (1938)
>Originally *The Sign of the Silver Horseshoe* by Gerald Verner Detective Weekly (231 July 1937)

The River House Mystery (1938)
>Originally *The Time of the Crime*, as by Donald Stuart Sexton Blake Library (605 January 1938)

The Clue of the Green Candle (1938)

The Witches Moon (1938)
>Originally *The Witches Moon* by Donald Stuart Union Jack (1488 April 1932)

The Angel (1939)
>Originally *Alias – The Angel* by Gerald Verner Detective Weekly (No 255 January 1938)

Mr. Budd Again (1939)
>Book One: The Beard of the Prophet
>Originally *The Beard of the Prophet* by Gerald Verner Detective Weekly (No 246 November 1937)

Book Two: The Vanishing Men
Originally *The Devil's Brood* by Gerald Verner Detective Weekly (No 285 August 1938)
Book Three: The Leering Lady
Originally *Crimson Smile* Union Jack (1523 December 1932)
Rewritten as *The Clue of the Painted Smile* Detective Weekly (304 December 1938)

The Football Pool Murders (1939) aka *The Coupon Crimes* USA.
Originally *The Football Pool Murders* by Gerald Verner Detective Weekly (318 March 1939)

The Huntsman (1940)
Originally *The Huntsman* by Gerald Verner Detective Weekly (No 288 Aug 1938)

Mr. Budd Investigates (1940)
Book One: The House of the Goat
Originally *The House of the Goat* by Gerald Verner Thriller Library (December 1939)
Book Two: The Seven Sleeping Men
Originally *The Seven Sleeping Men* by Gerald Verner Thriller Lib (January 1940)
Book Three: The Seal of Solomon
Originally *The Seal of Solomon* by Gerald Verner Thriller Lib (February 1940)

The Poisoner (1940)
Recently established as written by Noel Lee and published by Thorpe June 2019 under his name as *The Manuscript Killer*

The Vampire Man (1940)

The Secret Weapon (1940)
Listed/advertised by W&B in *The Nightmare Murders* as being published in Autumn 1940 but never published under that title, originating from *Secret Weapon* Detective Weekly No 377 May 1940. Published as *The Heel of Achilles* (1945)

Dene of The Secret Service (1941)
Rewritten version of *The Man From Tokio* by Warwick Jardine (F.Warwick) Sexton Blake Library (409 Dec 1933)

<u>Wright & Brown 1 Crane Court, Fleet Street, London EC4</u>

The Heel of Achilles (1945)
Listed in *The Nightmare Murders* forthcoming books as: *The Secret Weapon* but never published in novel form under that title. Originally *The Secret Weapon* Detective Weekly (No 377 May 1940)

# APPENDIX 1: BIBLIOGRAPHY

Come not, Lucifer (1945) Anthology Pub: John Westhouse 49 Chancery
Lane London WC2.
> Collects 12 stories by Edgar Allan Poe (3), Herman Melville, Charles
> Dickens, J. Sheridan Le Fanu, Honore de Balzac, Villiers de l'Isle Adam,
> Alexander S. Pushkin (2), and Robert Louis Stevenson (2). Suite of
> illustrations by R.A. Brandt

Thirsty Evil (1945) Pub: John Westhouse 49 Chancery Lane London
W.C.2.
> Rewritten as *Grim Death* by Gerald Verner 1960

Prince of Darkness (1946) Anthology Pub: John Westhouse 49 Chancery
Lane London WC2.
> Numerous authors: Gerald Verner, Dorothy L. Sayers, Montague
> Summers, Sax Rohmer, Saki, Algernon Blackwood, F. S. Loring, John
> Buchan and Margaret Irwin

The Seven Lamps (1947)

The Twelve Apostles (1946)

They Walk In Darkness (1947)

The Royal Flush Murders (1948)

The Tipster (1949)
> The Novel of the April 1948 BBC Radio Serial Play

The Whispering Woman (1949)

The Show Must Go On (1950)
> The Novel of the August 1948 BBC Radio Serial Play

Noose For A Lady (1952)
> The Novel of the July 1950 BBC Radio Serial Play


Wright & Brown 18 Stukeley Street London W.C.2


Mr. Midnight (1953)

Sorcerer's House (1956) Pub: Hutchinson

The Crimson Ramblers (1960)
> The Novel of the 1956 Television Serial Play

Grim Death (1960)
> Originally *Thirsty Evil* 1945 John Westhouse

The Nursery Rhyme Murders (1960)

Ghost House (1961)

The Shadow Men (1961)
> Originally *Mr. Midnight* The Union Jack (1422 January 1931). Based on the
> Donald Stuart play *Sexton Blake* (September 1930 Prince Edward Theatre)
> Rewritten as *The Midnight Men* by Nigel Vane 1936

The Third Key (1961)

The Red Tape Murders (1962)
The Last Warning (1962)
> Originally *The Secret of the Sealed Room*, by Donald Stuart, Sexton Blake Library (470 March 1935)
> Rewritten as The Crooked Circle by Gerald Verner (W&B 1935)

I Am Death (1963)
> Originally *The Death Card* by Donald Stuart Sexton Blake Library (255 September 1930)
> Rewritten as *The White Friar* by Donald Stuart (W&B 1934)

The Ghost Squad (1963)
Murder in Manuscript (1963)
> Originally *The Fatal Manuscript* anonymous Sexton Blake Library (198 July 1929)
> Rewritten version of *The Death Play* by Gerald Verner 1933

The Faceless Ones (1964)
The Moor House Murders (1964)
> Originally *The Man Outside* by Donald Stuart 1934 from the 1933 film by Donald Stuart
> Rewritten as *The Secret of Moor House* Sexton Blake Library (634 August 1938)

Six Men Died (1964)
> Originally *The Glass Arrow* by Gerald Verner 1937
> Rewritten as *The Three Who Paid* by Donald Stuart Sexton Blake Library (612 February 1938)

Death Set in Diamonds (1965)
> Originally *The Secret of the Vault* by Donald Stuart Sexton Blake Library (227 February1930)

The Tudor Garden Mystery (1966)
> Originally *The Riddle of the Sunken Garden* by Donald Stuart Sexton Blake Library (581 July 1937)
> Rewritten as *The Three Gnomes* (W&B 1937)

Mister Big (1966)
> Originally The Fence's Victim Sexton Blake Library (266 Dec 1930)
> Rewritten as *Green Mask* 1934 by Gerald Verner

Dead Secret (1967)
> Originally *The Truth about Lord Trench* Sexton Blake Library (503 November 1935)
> Rewritten as *The Watcher* (W&B 1936)

---

# APPENDIX 1: BIBLIOGRAPHY

**Mr. Budd Steps In (2011) Pub: Thorpe**
> Reprint large format from *The Cleverness of Mr. Budd* (W&B1935)
> but excluding *The Whispering Man*. Comprising the stories:
> Ghost of Rufus Manners
> The Man Who Vanished
> The Grey Monk (*The Grey Monk* first appeared 17 Dec 1934 Leader
> Magazine).
> The Clue
> The Undoing of Mr. Dawes
> The Clever Crook

**The Dragon Princess (2012) Pub: Borgo Books**
> Reprint of *Yu-Malu, The Dragon Princess*, Gerald Verner as Thane Leslie
> (W&B 1967)

**The Chained Man (2014) Pub: Thorpe**
> Originally The Christmas Card Crime by Donald Stuart Detective Weekly
> (96 December 1934)
> Rewritten and edited as The Chained Man in *My Most Exciting Story*
> Anthology Faber and Faber 1936
> +The Mystery of the Unfortunate Undertaker Christmas PIE (Dec 1946)
> +The Strange Affair of the Dancing Parson Spring PIE (Feb 1947)
> +The Extraordinary Problem of the Eccentric Lodger Summer PIE (June
> 1947)
> + Death at the Microphone Originally *Murder at the Microphone* by Donald
> Stuart Detective Weekly (111 April 1935)
> Rewritten from Book Three: *Mr. Whipple explains*

**The House of the Goat (2014) Pub: Thorpe**
> Book One: The House of the Goat Book 1 from Mr. Budd Investigates
> (W&B 1940)
> Book Three: The Seal of Solomon Book 3 from Mr. Budd Investigates
> (W&B 1940)

**Sinister House (2015) Pub: Thorpe**
> Sinister House (1934) Book One: *Sinister House* Rewritten from *The Secret
> of the Whispering Beeches* by Donald Stuart Union Jack and *Sinister House* by
> Donald Stuart The Thriller (No 64 April 1930)
> Plus, short stories: Flowers for the Dead, (originally published as *Murder
> Flowers in the Spring* Leader Magazine 1944)
> Design for Libel, (first publication)
> The Weir (*The Morning Story* on BBC radio Tuesday 31 July 1951)

**The Evil of Li-Sin (2015) Pub: DTP Ramble House Omnibus Edition**
> The Menace of Li-Sin (Modern Publishing Company1934)
> The Vengeance of Li-Sin (Modern Publishing Company 1935)
> Afterword and Bibliography by Chris Verner

PLOTS AND GUNPOWDER

The Snark Was A Boojum (2015) Pub: Ramble House
>First Publication Edited, Completed, and with an Introduction by Chris Verner

### *Short Stories:*

The Adventures of Lattimer Shrive:
The Mystery of the Unfortunate Undertaker
>Christmas PIE Dec 1946 reprinted in *The Chained Man* Thorpe (2014)

The Strange Affair of the Dancing Parson
>Spring PIE Feb 1947 reprinted in *The Chained Man* Thorpe (2014)

The Extraordinary Problem of the Eccentric Lodger
>Summer PIE June 1947 reprinted in *The Chained Man* Thorpe (2014)

---

The Chained Man
>My Most Exciting Story Anthology Faber and Faber (1936)
>Cut down from *The Christmas Card Crime* by Donald Stuart Detective Weekly (96 December 1934) reprinted in *The Chained Man* (2014) Thorpe

The Man Who Vanished
>Book Three: *The Cleverness of Mr. Budd* comprising 5 Short Stories (of which this is the first)
>Reprinted in *Mr. Budd Steps In* (2011) Thorpe

The Grey Monk
>Leader Magazine 17 Dec 1934 - a weekly pictorial magazine published in the United Kingdom by the Hulton Press. It was disestablished in Spring 1950
>Book Three: *The Cleverness of Mr. Budd* comprising 5 Short Stories of which this is the second
>Reprinted in *Mr. Budd Steps In* Thorpe (2011)

The Clue
>Book Three: *The Cleverness of Mr. Budd* comprising 5 Short Stories (of which this is the third)
>Reprinted in *Mr. Budd Steps In* Thorpe (2011)

The Undoing of Mr. Dawes
>Book Three: *The Cleverness of Mr. Budd* comprising 5 Short Stories (of which this is the fourth)
>Reprinted in *Mr. Budd Steps In* Thorpe (2011) and the British Library Crime Classics Anthology *The Wrong Arm of the Law* (2017)

The Clever Crook
>Book Three: *The Cleverness of Mr. Budd* comprising 5 Short Stories (of which this is the fifth)
>Reprinted in *Mr. Budd Steps In* Thorpe (2011)

# APPENDIX 1: BIBLIOGRAPHY

The Riddle of the Red Queen
> Book 1 of *Mr. Whipple Explains* from The Riddle of the Red Queen
> Detective Weekly (No 133 September 1935) Reprinted in *Mr. Whipple
> Explains* Thorpe (2014)

Sinister House
> Book One: *Sinister House*) Rewritten from *The Secret of the Whispering Beeches*
> by Donald Stuart Union Jack and *Sinister House* by Donald Stuart The
> Thriller (No 64 April 1930)
> Reprinted Thorpe (2015)

Mr. K
> Book Two: *Sinister House*) (Rewritten from *The Sinister Quest* by Donald
> Stuart The Thriller (No 245 October 1933)
> Republished as *The Green Pen Mystery* Thorpe (2016)

The Big Fellow
> Book Three: *Sinister House*) (Rewritten from *The Fatal Hour* by Donald
> Stuart Detective Weekly 188 26 September 1935)
> Reprinted Thorpe (2015)

The Man on The Train
> Unfinished work completed by Chris Verner. First published in *The Big
> Fellow* Thorpe (2016)

Flowers for the Dead
> Originally published as *Murder Flowers in the Spring* Leader Magazine 1944
> Republished in *The Green Pen Mystery* Thorpe (2016)

Design for Libel
> First published in *The Green Pen Mystery* Thorpe (2016)

Sheer Luck (c1959)

Poor Percy! (Star, London)
> Also titled The Spirit of Adventure

Mr. Gilmot Goes Home
> Argosy (November 1972)

The Night in the Charge Room
> Ideas London (Sept 1935)

The Red Golf Ball also known as *The Fatal 13th* The Sexton Blake Annual 1938
reprinted SBL (672 May 1939)
> Rewritten as *The Red Golfball* by Gerald Verner, reprinted in the British
> Library Crime Classics Anthology *Settling Scores* (2020)

Anomalies untraced:
> The Tenth Time
> A Matter of Detail
> The Mistake
> The Vengeance of the Trees
> The Eye of God

A Lady of Quality
The Ears of Mr. Neap
The Blackmailing of Lady Milstead
Death in the Charge Room

## *Detective Weekly:*

The Riddle of the Red Queen (No 133 September 1935)
    Rewritten as Book 1 of *Mr. Whipple Explains* 1936)
Blake of the Secret Service (No 176 July 1936)
    Rewritten as *The Seven Clues* (1936)
The Sign of the Jockey (No 203 September 1936)
    Rewritten as *The Jockey* (1937)
The Black Widow (No 206 January 1937)
    Rewritten as Book 2 of *The Return of Mr. Budd* (1938)
The Devil's Footprint (No 221 May 1937)
    Originally written as *The Terror of Lonely Tor* by Donald Stuart Sexton
    Blake Lib 302 Sept 1931
    Rewritten as *The Valley of Terror* by Donald Stuart (W&B 1935) and Book
    3 of *The Return of Mr. Budd* (1938)
The Sign of the Silver Horseshoe (No 231 July 1937)
    Rewritten as *The Silver Horseshoe* (1938)
The Clue of the Whispering Pines (No 234 August 1937)
    Rewritten as Book 1 of *The Return of Mr. Budd* (1938)
The Beard of the Prophet (No 246 November 1937)
    Rewritten as *Book 1 of Mr. Budd Again* (1939)
Alias - The Angel (No 255 January 1938)
    Rewritten as *The Angel* (1939)
The Devil's Brood (No 285 August 1938)
    Rewritten as *The Vanishing Men Book 2 of Mr. Budd Again* (1939)
The Huntsman (No 288 Aug 1938)
    Rewritten as *The Huntsman* (1940)
The Football Pool Murders (No 318 March 1939)
    Rewritten as *The Football Pool Murders* (1939)
Secret Weapon (No 377 May 1940)
    Rewritten as *The Heel of Achilles* (1945)

## *The Thriller:*

The Ghost of Rufus Manners (Dec 1934)
    Rewritten as *Book One of The Cleverness of Mr. Budd* (1935)

# APPENDIX 1: BIBLIOGRAPHY

The Whispering Man (March 1935)
> Book Two of The Cleverness of Mr. Budd (1935)

River Rats (September 1936)
> Rewritten as *The River Men* (1936)

The House of the Goat (December 1939)
> Rewritten as *Book One: Mr. Budd Investigates* (1940)

The Seven Sleeping Men (January 1940)
> Rewritten as *Book Two: Mr. Budd Investigates* (1940)

The Seal of Solomon (February 1940)
> Rewritten as Book Three: Mr. Budd Investigates (1940)

## *Thriller Library:*

Queer Face (No 21 May 1935)
> Rewritten as Queer Face (1935)

## *Thrilling Detective (USA 10c):*

Haunted House Murders (Aug 1935)

## *The Boy's Friend – Bulls Eye Library*

The Hooded Stranger (No 702 Jan 1940)
> Rewritten and abridged version of The Hooded Terror by Donald Stuart (Bulls Eye Library No 243 June 1930) and Black Skull (Wright & Brown 1933

The River Men (No 718 May 1940)
> Originally published as River Rats (The Thriller September 1936) and The River Men (Wright & Brown 1936)

The Grim Joker (No 721 June 1940)
> Originally published as The Green Jester (Union Jack 1379 March 1930) and The Grim Joker (Wright & Brown 1936)

## *Plays:*

Meet Mr. Callaghan
> Adapted from the Book The Urgent Hangman by Peter Cheyney (May 1952 Garrick Theatre London)

Dangerous Curves
> Adapted from the Book Dangerous Curves by Peter Cheyney (April 1953 Garrick Theatre, London)

Towards Zero Adapted from the book Towards Zero by Agatha Christie
(1956 St James's Theatre, London)
Design for Murder
(March 1957 Intimate Theatre, Palmers Green)
Mr. & Mrs. Bluebeard
(June 1958 Intimate Theatre, Palmers Green)

## BBC Radio:

The Tipster
April 1948 BBC Radio Serial Play rewritten as a novel W&B 1949
Answer Next Week
(1948-49) Radio series including posers on crime and law by Gerald
Verner and a lawyer. 7th 14th 21st 28th November 1948 5th 12th 19th
26th December 1948 2nd 9th 16th 23rd 30th January 1949 6th 13th 20th
27th February 1949 6th 13th 20th 27th March 1949 3rd April 1949
The Show Must Go On
August 1948 BBC Radio Serial Play rehashed as a novel in 1950 and
filmed as *Tread Softly* in 1952
The Weir
*The Morning Story* on BBC radio in Tuesday 31 July 1951 and in *Sinister
House* (2015) Pub: Thorpe. Audio Reading 1972
Meet Mr. Callaghan
Excerpt from Act 1 of (Oct 1952) from the Garrick Theatre, London
Noose for A Lady
July 1950 BBC Radio Serial Play rehashed as a novel in 1952 and filmed
in 1953

## Films:

Tread Softly (1952)
Directed by David Macdonald from the BBC radio serial *The Show Must
Go On*
Noose For A Lady (1952)
Insignia Films Directed by Wolf Rilla from the BBC radio serial *Noose For
A Lady*
Meet Mr. Callaghan (1954)
Eros Films Ltd Directed by Charles Saunders from the Stage Play *Meet
Mr. Callaghan* (May 1952 Garrick Theatre, London) Adapted from the
Book *The Urgent Hangman* by Peter Cheyney

# APPENDIX 1: BIBLIOGRAPHY

*Television:*

French for Love
> (October 1955) ITV Television Playhouse: (adaptation of the play by Derek Patmore and Marguerite Stein) Directed by Hugh Rennie

The Crimson Ramblers
> (July 1956) Television Serial Play Directed by Robert Evans

Double Danger
> 8 July 1961 (Season 1, Episode 18) *The Avengers* Directed by Roger Jenkins

*Novels:* Donald Stuart (All Published by Wright & Brown except where stated)

The White Friar (1934)
> Originally *The Death Card* by Donald Stuart Sexton Blake Library (255 September 1930)
> Rewritten as *I Am Death* (1963) Gerald Verner

The Man Outside (1934)
> Originally from the 1933 film *The Man Outside* by Donald Stuart
> Rewritten as *The Secret of Moor House* Sexton Blake Library (634 August 1938)
> Rewritten as *The Moor House Murders* (1964) Gerald Verner

The Shadow (1934)
> Originally from the play *The Shadow* (1928 Embassy Theatre)
> Rewritten as the film *The Shadow* (1933)
> Rewritten as *Danger at Westways* by Donald Stuart Sexton Blake Library (645 November 1938)

The Man in the Dark (1935)
> Originally *The Case of the Burmese Dagger* by Andrew Murray Sexton Blake Library (102 November 1919) Rewritten as *The Burmese Dagger* by Donald Stuart Sexton Blake Library (675 June 1939)

Midnight Murder (1935)
> Rewritten as *The Phantom Pearler* by Rex Harding Detective Weekly (May 5 1939)

The Valley of Terror (1935)
> Originally written as *The Terror of Lonely Tor* by Donald Stuart Sexton Blake Library (302 September 1931) Rewritten as *The Devil's Footprint* by Gerald Verner Detective Weekly (May 1937)
> Rewritten as *The Devil's Footprint*, Book 3 of *The Return of Mr. Budd* by Gerald Verner (W&B 1938)

The Green Pen Mystery (1933) Pub: Thorpe

> *Sinister House* by Gerald Verner Book Two: Mr. K Rewritten from *The Sinister Quest* by Donald Stuart, The Thriller (245 October 1933) + short stories:
>
> The Able Mr. Kane Argosy (July 1972)
> The Will and the Way Argosy (January 1973)
> A Flush in Diamonds (c1973)
> Ransom for a Wife (c1973)

The Hooded Terror (1930) Pub: Thorpe

> *The Hooded Terror* by Donald Stuart The Boys' Friend – Bulls Eye Library (No 243 June 1930)
> Rewritten as Black Skull by Gerald Verner (W&B 1933) Abridged (most likely by the editor) as The Hooded Stranger by Gerald Verner The Boys' Friend – Bulls Eye Library (702 Jan 1940)

## *The Sexton Blake Library—In date order with Gerald Verner equivalents:*

The Clue of the Second Tooth (105 August 1927) anon.

> Rewritten as *The Embankment Crime* Sexton Blake (341 July 1932) and *The Embankment Murder* by Gerald Verner 1933

The Box of Doom (125 January 1928) anon.

> Rewritten as *The Devil's Dozen* by Nigel Vane (1935)

The Riddle of the Phantom Plague (143 May 1928) anon.

> Rewritten as *The Purple Plague* by Derwent Steele 1935

The Mystery of Sherwood Towers (152 July 1928) anon.

> Rewritten as *The Black Hunchback* by Gerald Verner 1933 and reprinted *The Mystery of Sherwood Towers* in Sexton Blake Library (714 April 1940)

The Mystery of the Phantom Blackmailer (157 September 1928) anon.

> Rewritten as *Alias the Ghost* by Gerald Verner (1933) Serialised as *The Shadow over Iris* by Gerald Verner 25th Feb 1935 The Evening Telegraph, Angus, Scotland

The Silent Slayer (195 June 1929) anon.

> Rewritten as *The Phantom Slayer* by Derwent Steele 1935

The Fatal Manuscript (198 July 1929) anon.

> Rewritten as *The Death Play* by Gerald Verner 1933 and *Murder in Manuscript* by Gerald Verner 1963

The Black Skull (217 December 1929) anon.

> Reprinted as *The Hooded Terror* Bulls Eye Library No 243 June 1930 by Donald Stuart and reprinted as *The Hooded Stranger* by Gerald Verner Bulls Eye Library (No 702 Jan 1940) rehashed as *Black Skull* by Gerald Verner 1933

# APPENDIX 1: BIBLIOGRAPHY

The Secret of the Vault (227 February 1930) anon.
> Rewritten as *Death Set In Diamonds* by Gerald Verner 1965

The Crime of Four (237 May 1930) anon.

The Death Card (255 September 1930)
> Rewritten as *The White Friar* by Donald Stuart (1934) and Revised as *I Am Death* (1963) Gerald Verner

The Fence's Victim (266 Dec 1930)
> Rewritten as *Green Mask* 1934 by Gerald Verner and *Mr. Big* by Gerald Verner 1966

The Hooded Raider (278 March 1931)
> Rewritten as *The Menace of Li-Sin* (1934) by Nigel Vane

The Next Victim (286 May 1931)
> Rewritten as *The Third Victim* by Donald Stuart Sexton Blake Library (653 January 1939) rehashed as the novel *The Next to Die* by Gerald Verner 1934

The Terror of Lonely Tor (302 September 1931)
> Rewritten as *The Valley of Terror* (W&B 1935) and *The Devil's Footprint* Detective Weekly May 1937) Pub as *The Devil's Footprint*, Book 3 of *The Return of Mr. Budd* (W&B 1938)

The Garden City Crime (314 December 1931)
> Rewritten as *The Hand of Fear* by Gerald Verner (1936)

Dead Man's Secret (322 February 1932)
> Rewritten as *The Avenger* by Derwent Steele 1935

The Squealer's Secret (334 May 1932)
> Rewritten as *The Squealer* by Gerald Verner 1934

The Embankment Crime (341 July 1932)
> Originally written as *The Clue of the Second Tooth* (Sexton Blake 105 August 1927) anon. and Rewritten as *The Embankment Murder* by Gerald Verner (W&B 1933)

The Case of the Missing Estate Agent (350 September 1932)
> Rewritten as *Phantom Hollow* by Gerald Verner (1933)

The Secret of Seven (363 December 1932)

The Empty House Murder (373 March 1933)
> Rewritten as *The Veils of Death* by Nigel Vane (1935)

Guilty, But Insane (385 June 1933)
> Rewritten as *The Hangman* by Gerald Verner 1934

The £1,000,000 Film Murder (401 October 1933)
> Rewritten as *The Con Man* by Gerald Verner 1934

The Motor Bus Murder (422 March 1934)
> Rewritten as *White Wig* by Gerald Verner 1935

The Village of Fear (430 May 1934)
> Rewritten as *Terror Tower* by Gerald Verner 1935

# PLOTS AND GUNPOWDER

The Secret of the Sealed Room (470 March 1935)
> Rewritten as *The Crooked Circle* by Gerald Verner1935 and *The Last Warning* by Gerald Verner 1962

The Cottage of Terror (481 June 1935)
> Rewritten as *The Ghost Man* by Gerald Verner 1936

The Truth about Lord Trench (503 November 1935)
> Rewritten as *The Watcher* by Gerald Verner 1936 and *Dead Secret* by Gerald Verner 1967

The Bells of Doom (545 October 1936)
> Rewritten as *The Token* by Gerald Verner 1937

The Unknown Menace (561 February 1937)
> Rewritten as *The Frightened Man* by Gerald Verner 1937

The Riddle of the Sunken Garden (581 July 1937)
> Rewritten as *The Three Gnomes* by Gerald Verner 1937 and *The Tudor Garden Mystery* by Gerald Verner 1966

The Time of the Crime (605 January 1938)
> Rewritten as *The River House Mystery* by Gerald Verner 1938

The Three Who Paid (612 February 1938)
> Rewritten as *The Glass Arrow* by Gerald Verner 1937 and *Six Men Died* by Gerald Verner 1964

The Secret of Moor House (634 August 1938)
> From the 1933 film The Man Outside by Donald Stuart and rewritten from the novel The Man Outside by Donald Stuart 1934 and rewritten as The Moor House Murders by Gerald Verner 1964

Danger at Westways (645 November 1938)
> Rewritten from the novel *The Shadow* by Donald Stuart 1934 from his play *The Shadow* (1928 Embassy Theatre) which became the film *The Shadow* in 1933

The Third Victim (653 January 1939)
> Originally The Next Victim by Donald Stuart Sexton Blake Library (286 May 1931) Rewritten as the novel *The Next to Die* by Gerald Verner 1934

The Fatal 13th (Sexton Blake Annual 1938)
> Reprinted SBL No 672 May 1939. Rewritten as *The Red Golfball* by Gerald Verner published in British Library Crime Classics *Settling Scores* 2020

The Burmese Dagger (675 June 1939)
> Revised and abridged version of 1st series No 102 November 1919 *The Case of the Burmese Dagger* by anon. (Andrew Murray)

The Hidden Menace (690 Oct 1939)
> Rewritten from *The Q Squad* by Gerald Verner 1935

The Secret of the Hulk (708 Febuary1940)
> Revised and abridged version of *The Secret of the Hulk; or, The Stricken Town* 1st series No 63 1918 by anon. (Andrew Murray). Republished 1940 under the name Donald Stuart

# APPENDIX 1: BIBLIOGRAPHY

The Mystery of Sherwood Towers (714 April 1940)
> Reprint of 2nd series No 152 1928 reprinted as *The Black Hunchback* by Gerald Verner 1933

Twenty Years of Hate (732 August 1940)

## *Union Jack:*

The Green Jester (1379 March 1930)
> Rewritten as *The Grim Joker* by Gerald Verner 1936

Mr. Midnight (1422 January 1931)
> Based on the Donald Stuart play *Sexton Blake* (September 1930 Prince Edward Theatre) Rewritten as *The Midnight Men* by Nigel Vane 1936 and *The Shadow Men* by Gerald Verner 1961. NB: No relation to the 1953 *Mr. Midnight* by Gerald Verner

The Witches Moon (1488 April 1932)
> Rewritten as *The Witches Moon* by Gerald Verner 1938

The Crimson Smile (1523 December 1932)
> Rewritten as *The Clue of the Painted Smile* (Detective Weekly 304 December 1938) and Book Three: *The Leering Lady* from *Mr. Budd Again* 1939 by Gerald Verner

## *The Thriller:*

The Midnight Gang (No 26 August 1929)

Sinister House (No 64 April 1930)
> Rewritten as *Sinister House* 1934 by Gerald Verner Book One: *Sinister House*
> Rehashed as The Terror of Grey Towers Detective Weekly (No 176 July 1936)

The Sinister Quest (No 245 October 1933)
> Rewritten as *Sinister House* 1934 by Gerald Verner Book Two: *Mr. K)*

## *Detective Weekly:*

The Clue of the Crimson Snow (44 December 1933)
> An abridged reprint appears in Sexton Blake Annual 1942. Rewritten as *Mr. Whipple Explains* 1936 by Gerald Verner Book Two: *Red Snow*

The Christmas Card Crime (96 December 1934)
> Original full-length version was abridged as *The Chained Man* for *My Most Exciting Story* Anthology Faber and Faber 1936 and published full-length

for the British Library Anthology *The Christmas Card Crime* 2018
Rewritten as *The Chained Man* in *My Most Exciting Story* Faber and Faber
Anthology 1936

Murder at the Microphone (111 April 1935)
Rewritten as *Mr. Whipple Explains* 1936 by Gerald Verner Book Three:
*Death at the Microphone*

The Riddle of the Red Queen (No 133 September 1935)

The Terror of Grey Towers (No 176 July 1936)
Rewritten from *Sinister House* 1934 by Gerald Verner Book One: Sinister
House originally Sinister House (The Thriller No 64 April 1930)
Rewritten from *The Secret of the Whispering Beeches* Union Jack

The Fatal Hour (No 188 September 1936)
Rewritten from *The Big Man* Book 3 of *Sinister House* 1934 by Gerald
Verner

The Clue of the Painted Smile (304 December 1938)
Rewritten from *Crimson Smile* Union Jack 1523 December 1932 and as
Book Three: *The Leering Lady* from *Mr. Budd Again* 1939 by Gerald Verner

### *The Boys' Friend—Bulls Eye Library:*

The Hooded Terror
(No 243 June 1930) rewritten as Black Skull 1933 by Gerald Verner and
abridged as The Hooded Stranger by Gerald Verner Bulls Eye Library No
702 (Jan 1940)

### *Short Stories:*

4 Adam Kane stories:
The Able Mr. Kane
Argosy (July 1972) republished in *Sinister House* Thorpe Large Print
paperback 2015

The Will and the Way –
Argosy (January 1973) republished in *Sinister House* Thorpe Large Print
paperback 2015

A Flush in Diamonds
(c1973) first published in *Sinister House* Thorpe Large Print paperback
2015

Ransom for a Wife
(c1973) first published in *Sinister House* Thorpe Large Print paperback
2015

Other:
The Portable Typewriter
Argosy 1972 (June) & Audio Reading 1972

# APPENDIX 1: BIBLIOGRAPHY

## *Plays:*

Sexton Blake (September 1930 Prince Edward Theatre)
> Became *Mr. Midnight* the story of the play Union Jack 1422, Rewritten as *The Midnight Men* by Nigel Vane 1936, and *The Shadow Men* 1961 by Gerald Verner

The Shadow (1928 Embassy Theatre)
> Became the film *The Shadow* (1933) and the book *The Shadow* (1934)
> Rewritten as *Danger at Westways* (Sexton Blake Lib 645 November 1938)

## *BBC Radio:*

Sexton Blake (August – December 1967) 17 x 30 min Case Histories by Donald Stuart
> 1. Lilies for the Ladies
> 2. The Sin-Eater
> 3. Hags Acre
> 4. The Fifth Dimension
> 5. The Black Widow
> 6. First Class Ticket to – Nowhere
> 7. Double or Quits
> 8. You Must be Joking
> 9. Conjuror's Coffin
> 10. The Blood of Rameses
> 11. No Trees for the Peke
> 12. Bluebeards Keys
> 13. The Vampire Moon
> 14. The Beard of the Prophet
> 15. The Enchanted Editor
> 16. The Eight of Swords
> 17. A Murder of Crows

## *Films:*

The Man Outside (1933)
> Real Art Productions Directed by George A Cooper

The Shadow (1933)
> Real Art Productions Directed by George A Cooper

# PLOTS AND GUNPOWDER

**As *Derwent Steele*** (The Modern Publishing Company:

The Black Gangster (1934)
> No 640 Rewritten version of *The Secret of the Vault* by Donald Stuart,
> Sexton Blake Lib 227 February. 1930 and Revised as *Death Set in Diamonds*
> by Gerald Verner 1965 & Large Print paperback 2012

The Phantom Slayer (1935)
> No 655 Rewritten version of *The Silent Slayer* by Donald Stuart, Sexton
> Blake Library195 June 1929 Large Print paperback 2011

The Purple Plague (1935)
> No 664 Rewritten version of *The Riddle of the Phantom Plague* by Donald
> Stuart, Sexton Blake Library143 May 1928 Large Print paperback 2013

The Avengers (1935)
> No 684 Large Print paperback 2011 Rewritten version of *Dead Man's
> Secret* by Donald Stuart, Sexton Blake Lib 322 February 1932

The Poison Gang (1937)
> No 716 Large Print paperback 2011

**As *Nigel Vane*** (The Modern Publishing Company except *The Midnight
Men*):

The Menace of Li-Sin (1934)
> No 629 originally The Hooded Raider by Donald Stuart Sexton Blake
> Library (278 March 1931) Large Print paperback 2011, Ramble House;
> First omnibus edition (18 Jan. 2015)

The Vengeance of Li-Sin (1935)
> No 654 Large Print paperback 2013, Ramble House; First omnibus
> edition (18 Jan. 2015)

The Devil's Dozen (1935)
> No 665 Large Print paperback 2011 (DJ Not MW) Originally *The Box of
> Doom* Sexton Blake Library (125 January 1928)

The Veils of Death (1935)
> No 681 Large Print paperback 2011 (DJ MW) Originally *The Empty House
> Murder* by Donald Stuart *Sexton Blake Library* (373 March 1933)

The Midnight Men (1936) Pub: by Stanley Smith 59 New Oxford Street
London WC1.
> Based on the Donald Stuart play *Sexton Blake* (September 1930 Prince
> Edward Theatre) and *Mr. Midnight* the story of the play published in The
> Union Jack 1422 January 1931, Rewritten as *The Shadow Men* by Gerald
> Verner (1961) Large Print paperback 2011

## APPENDIX 1: BIBLIOGRAPHY

The Vanishing Death (1937)
> No 722 Large Print paperback 2011

**As Gerard Stuart:**

There's No Escape
> (60 min play for BBC Radio 26 August 1964)

**As Thane Leslie:**

Yu-Malu, The Dragon Princess (1967)
> Wright & Brown novel reprinted as *The Dragon Princess* by Gerald Verner 2011

# Appendix 2: Linford Mystery Series

F. A. Thorpe publishers *Linford Mystery Series*: Large type reprints of selected originals from the above books in paperback format. In order of publication:

01. The Veils of Death (1935) Vane (2011)
02. The Last Warning (1962) Verner (2011)
03. The Avengers (1935) Steele (2011)
04. The Menace of Li-Sin (1934) Vane (2011)
05. Dene of The Secret Service (1941) Verner (2011)
06. The Nursery Rhyme Murders (1960) Verner (2011)
07. The Phantom Slayer (1935) Steele (2011)
08. The Midnight Men (1936) Vane (2011)
09. Terror Tower (1935) Verner (2011)
10. The Vanishing Death (1937) Vane (2011)
11. The Cleverness of Mr. Budd Verner (2011)
> The Whispering Man Originally Book 2 The Cleverness of Mr. Budd (1935)
> The Black Widow Originally Book 2 The Return of Mr. Budd (1938)
12. The Seven Lamps (1947) Verner (2011)
13. They Walk in Darkness (1947) Verner (2011)
14. The Poison Gang (1937) Steele (2011)
15. The Devil's Dozen (1935) Vane (2011)
16. The Heel of Achilles (1945) Verner (2011)
17. Dead Secret (1967) Verner (2011)
18. Mr. Budd Steps In Verner (2011)
> Originally The Cleverness of Mr. Budd (1935) but excluding The Whispering Man. Comprising the stories:
> Ghost of Rufus Manners
> The Man Who Vanished
> The Grey Monk (The Grey Monk first appeared 17 Dec 1934 The Leader).
> The Clue
> The Undoing of Mr. Dawes
> The Clever Crook
19. The Return of Mr. Budd (1938) Verner (2012)
> Book One: *The Clue of the Whispering Pines* (Detective Weekly No 234 August 1937)
> Book Three: *The Devil's Footprint* originally written as *The Terror of Lonely*

*Tor* by Donald Stuart (Sexton Blake Lib 302 Sept 1931) Rewritten as *The Devil's Footprint* by Gerald Verner (Detective Weekly May 1937) also Pub as *The Valley of Terror* by Donald Stuart (W&B 1935)

20. Midnight Murder (1935) Stuart (2012)
21. Mr. Budd Again (1939) Verner (2012)
    Book One: The Beard of the Prophet (Detective Weekly No 246 November 1937)
    Book Two: The Vanishing Men
22. Queer Face (1935) Verner (2012)
23. The White Friar (1934) Stuart (2012)
24. The Crimson Ramblers (1960) Verner (2012)
25. Ghost House (1961) Verner (2012)
26. The Angel (1939) Verner (2012)
27. Death Set in Diamonds (1965) Verner (2012)
28. The Clue of the Green Candle (1938) Verner (2012)
29. The "Q" Squad (1935) Verner (2012)
30. Mr. Budd Investigates (1940) Verner (2013)
    Book One:   The Leering Lady Book 3 taken from Mr. Budd again (1939)
    Book Two:   The Seven Sleeping Men Book 2
31. The Man in the Dark (1935) Stuart (2013)
32. The River House Mystery (1938) Verner (2013)
33. Noose for a Lady (1952) Verner (2013)
34. The Faceless Ones (1964) Verner (2013)
35. The Purple Plague (1935) Steele (2013)
36. The Man Outside (1934) Stuart (2013)
37. The Vengeance of Li-Sin (1935) Vane (2013)
38. Grim Death (1960) Verner (2013)
39. Murder In Manuscript (1963) Verner (2014)
40. The Glass Arrow (1937) Verner (2014)
41. The Third Key (1961) Verner (2014)
42. The Royal Flush Murders (1948) Verner (2014)
43. The Squealer (1934) Verner (2014)
44. Mr. Whipple Explains (1936) Verner (2014)
    Book One: Mr. Whipple Explains (Gerald Verner The Riddle of the Red Queen Detective Weekly No 133 September 1935)
    Book Two: Red Snow (Donald Stuart The Clue of the Crimson Snow Detective Weekly 44 December 1933)
45. The Seven Clues (1936) Verner (2014)

46. The Chained Man (1936) Verner (2014)
    The Chained Man in My Most Exciting Story Anthology Faber and Faber
    1936 (Trevor Lowe story)
    +The Mystery of the Unfortunate Undertaker Christmas PIE Dec 1946
    (Lattimer Shrive story)
    +The Strange Affair of the Dancing Parson Spring PIE Feb 1947
    (Lattimer Shrive story)
    +The Extraordinary Problem of the Eccentric Lodger Summer PIE June
    1947 (Lattimer Shrive story)
    + 1 Book Three: Death at the Microphone (Donald Stuart Murder at the
    Microphone Detective Weekly 111 April 1935) From Mr. Whipple
    explains. (Augustus Whipple story)
47. The House of the Goat (1940) Verner (2014)
    Book One:    The House of the Goat Book 1 from Mr. Budd Investigates
    (1940)
    Book Two: The Seal of Solomon Book 3 from Mr. Budd Investigates
    (1940)
48. The Football Pool Murders (1939) Verner (2015)
49. The Hand of Fear (1936) Verner (2015)
50. Sorcerer's House (1956) Verner (2015)
51. The Hangman (1934) Verner (2015)
52. Mr. Big (1966) Verner (2015)
53. The Con Man Verner (2015)
54. The Jockey (1937) Verner (2015)
55. The Silver Horseshoe (1938) Verner (2015)
56. The Tudor Garden Mystery (1966) Verner (2015)
57. The Show Must Go On (1950) Verner (2015)
58. Sinister House (1934) Verner (2015)
    Sinister House (1934) Book One: *Sinister House* Rewritten from *The Secret
    of the Whispering Beeches* by Donald Stuart Union Jack and *Sinister House* by
    Donald Stuart The Thriller (No 64 April 1930)
    Plus, short stories: Flowers for the Dead, (originally published as *Murder
    Flowers in the Spring* Leader Magazine 1944)
    Design for Libel, (first publication)
    The Weir (*The Morning Story* on BBC radio Tuesday 31st July 1951)
59. The Witches Moon (1938) Verner (2016)
60. The Green Pen Mystery (1933) Stuart (2016)
    Sinister House Book Two: Mr. K (Rewritten from Donald Stuart The
    Thriller (No 245 October 1933)
    Plus, short stories: The Able Mr. Kane, Argosy (July 1972)
    The Will and the Way, Argosy (January 1973)
    A Flush in Diamonds, (c1973)
    Ransom for a Wife, (c1973)

61. Alias the Ghost (1933) Verner (2016)
62. The Hooded Terror (1930) Stuart (2016)
63. The Shadow (1934) Stuart (2016)
64. The Big Fellow (1936) Gerald Verner, Chris Verner (2016)
    Sinister House Book Three: Rewritten from The Fatal Hour by Donald
    Stuart Detective Weekly 188 26 September 1936 Plus: The Man on The
    Train (c1956) Verner (first publication)
65. The Lady of Doom (1934) Verner (2017)
66. The Black Hunchback (1933) Verner (2017)
67. Phantom Hollow (1933) Verner (2017)
68. White Wig (1935) Verner (2017)
69. The Ghost Squad (1963) Verner (2017)
70. The Next to Die (1934) Verner (2017)
71. The Twelve Apostles (1946) Verner (2017)
72. The Whispering Woman (1949) Verner (2017)
73. The Snark Was a Boojum (c1957) Gerald Verner, Chris Verner (2017)
74. The Grim Joker (1936) Verner (Abridged) (2017)
75. The Huntsman (1940) Verner (Abridged) (2017)
76. The Nightmare Murders (1940) Verner (Abridged) (2018)
77. The Tipster (1949) Verner (2018)
78. The Vampire Man (1938) Verner (2018)
79. The Red Tape Murders (1962) Verner (2018)
80. The Frightened Man (1937) Verner (2018)
81. The Token (1937) Verner (2019)
82. Mr. Midnight (1953) Verner (2019)
83. The Seventh Virgin (1957) Gerald Verner, Chris Verner (2019)
84. The Embankment Murder (1933) Verner (2019)
85. The River Men (1936) Verner (2019)
86. The Ghost Man (1936) Verner (2020)

# About the Author

Christopher Verner was born on 13th December 1949 and brought up in Richmond, Surrey, England. His father was thriller writer Gerald Verner, born John Robert Stuart Pringle on 31 January 1897. He lived a colourful life while producing an extraordinary output of novels and plays. Chris began writing a biography of his father in 2010, Plots and Gunpowder, completing it this year. He was delighted to have the biography accepted by Level Best Books for publication in 2021.

Like his father, he began his working life in Stage Management. He began as a student at the original Mermaid Theatre in Blackfriars, London, in 1967; spent five years at The National Theatre at the Old Vic in Waterloo until 1974; then Company Manager for The Black Mikado musical until 1976—after which he left the theatre world to form his own company to design and carry out special effects, principally for film and television, including Danger UXB, Time Bandits, and 1984, plus over four hundred television commercials.

Apart from a posthumous collaboration completing his father's unfin -ished manuscript, The Snark Was A Boojum, he has completed a novelette The Man On The Train and a full-length novel The Seventh Virgin, both featuring his father's detective 'Mr. Budd'.

He lives in Berkhamsted, Hertfordshire, England with his wife Jenny.